DYNAMICS OF NEW PANCHAYATI RAJ SYSTEM IN INDIA

Volume III : SELECT STATES

Dynamics of New Panchayati Raj in India Series.

Vol. I	:	Select States
Vol. II	:	Select States
Vol. III	:	Select States
Vol. IV	:	Panchayati Raj and Empowerment of Women
Vol. V	:	Panchayati Raj and Multi-level Planning
Vol. VI	:	Panchayati Raj and Empowerment of Dalits
Vol. VII	:	Finance in Panchayati Raj System
Vol. VIII	:	Panchayati Raj and Common Property Resource Management
Vol. IX	:	Participatory and Direct Democracy : Gram Sabha
Vol. X	:	Capacity Building for Panchayati Raj Leaders and Functionaries
Vol. XI	:	State-Local Body Relationship
Vol. XII	:	Panchayati Raj and Socio-Political and Economic Transformation
Vol. XIII	:	Leadership in Panchayati Raj Institution
Vol. XIV	:	Thinkers Framework on Panchayati Raj
Vol. XV	:	Theoretical Nuances of Local Bodies

About the Editor

Prof. Ganapathi Palanithurai, Coordinator in Rajiv Gandhi Chair, Gandhigram Rural Institute is an academic activist working with the people in rural areas for building the capacity of the leaders and people to reinvent sustainable grassroots democracy. He is heading the Department of Political Science and Development Administration, in Gandhigram Rural University, Tamil Nadu. His policy advocacy role at the governmental level is increasingly felt at present in all the three levels, namely sub-regional, regional and national as he does more field work than theorisation. He has been associating himself with Centre Planning Commission, State Planning Commission of Tamil Nadu, Population Foundation of India, Ford Foundation, UNICEF, Rajiv Gandhi Foundation, CAPART, Ministry of Rural Areas and Employment and DANIDA (Danish-Indo Development Agency) in specific areas of activities in connection with empowerment of people. He is in the network of the Non-Governmental Organisations for Panchayat activities. He involves himself in capacity building exercise for local body leaders. He has to his credit twenty-nine books, seventy-five articles on three major areas, namely, Legislative Behaviour, Ethnicity and Panchayati Raj System. He was a recipient of Fellowship from Sastri Indo-Canadian Institute, New Delhi and World Academy of Art and Science, USA. He is the Chairman of the Tamil Nadu Council for Sustainable Livelihoods. He has visited the US and Canada, on academic assignments. He was a visiting fellow in the MiGill University, Canada in 1989. He is a life member of Indian Institute of Public Administration, Indian Association of Public Administration, Indian Association of Political Science, Indian Association of American Studies and Indian Association of Canadian Studies. He is a member of the expert committee constituted by the Government of Tamil Nadu to monitor the training programme for local body leaders.

DYNAMICS OF NEW PANCHAYATI RAJ SYSTEM IN INDIA

Volume III
SELECT STATES

Edited by
G. PALANITHURAI

CONCEPT PUBLISHING COMPANY, NEW DELHI-110059

Cataloging in Publication Data—DK
Courtesy: D.K. Agencies (P) Ltd. <docinfo@dkagencies.com>

Dynamics of new panchayati raj system in India /
edited by G. Palanithurai.
v. cm.
Includes bibliographical references.
Includes index.
ISBN 81-7022-910-3 (set)

1. Panchayat—India. 2. Local government—India. I. Palanithurai, G. (Ganapathy), 1953-

DDC 320.840 954 21

ISBN 81-8069-129-2 (Vol. III)
ISBN 81-7022-910-3 (Series)

First Published 2004

Published and Printed by
Ashok Kumar Mittal
Concept Publishing Company
A/15-16, Commercial Block, Mohan Garden
New Delhi-110059 (India)

Phones: 25351460, 25351794
Fax: 091-11-25357103
E-mail: publishing@conceptpub.com

TO

THE DIVINE MOTHER

We trust the people

We have faith in the people

It is the people who must

determine their own destinies

and the destiny of the Nation

To the people of India, let us

ensure maximum democracy and

maximum devolution. Let the

people be empowered.

– *Rajiv Gandhi*

PREFACE

The village Republic will be managed by a panchayat which will be living political force and entity. Panchayats will be united in a free and voluntary association by "ever widening circle of village republics". It will not be an "apex sustained by the bottom" but an oceanic circle where centre will be the individual always ready to perish for the village, the latter ready to perish for the circle of villages and so on, sharing the majesty of the oceanic circle which they are parts.

– Mahatma Gandhi

Dynamics of New Panchayati Raj System in India volume three comprises articles drawn from experts covering a few other states apart from an overall picture that is emerging out of experience. Experience sharing about Panchayati Raj requires good amount of field work and view. For studying Central and State governments one can rely on the available records of the governments. But to study the Panchayati Institutions one has to have a grip over the field apart from the documents. Micro politics and micro economics both tend to change frequently commensurate with the changes take place in the community. A constant touch with the field would bring the reality to the world. Normally scholarse specially from the academic institutions are interested in writing articles on federal and state polity and not down below the district. Panchayati Raj needs thousands of scholars for intensive research activities as three millions representatives are managing. Panchayat institutions. Interaction between the communities and the governing institutions are very intensive. Politics, election, governance at grass roots provide new dimensions which require proper analysis and explanation. Thus this emerging field needs more researchers.

We rely at present more on the academics who work in Development organizations to study Panchayati Raj. Since they have established their grip over the field, their articles provide new insights and new analysis. Most of the times, their contributions are valid for policy advocacy but not for knowledge building.

For Panchayati Raj evaluation and analysis, 73rd Amendment to the Constitution of India is the basic framework. Panchayati Raj Institutions have been evaluated from political, sociological, legal, anthropological and economic perspective. Most of the occasions the activists look at the institutions from the perspective of community and the people. Further the perspective varies from one another. In this context, the whole contribution in this work has to be seen.

For successful completion of any work one needs the cooperation of many. For my activities in Panchayati Raj, our team in our Department both academic and project staff, in my home my family unit, in my institute, our authorities are responsible and I register my thanks to all for their valuable contributions and support.

I record my thanks profusely to our contributors for their painstaking efforts in preparing papers for this volume. Finally a word of thanks to the publisher Ashok Mittal who in fact taken pain to remind many scholars to contribute papers. His interest and commitment in Panchayati Raj is always appreciable.

G. PALANITHURAI

CONTENTS

(In India) one should begin with the old panchayat system in the villages and the work upto the top. The panchayat system and the guilds are more representative and they have a living contact with people, they are the parts of the people's ideas.

– *Sri Aurobindo*

LIST OF CONTRIBUTORS

B.S. Bhargava
Senior Fellow, Institute of Social Sciences,
No. 25, Chamundi 4th Main, 9th Cross, Malleswaram,
Bangalore – 560 003.

Chandan Datta
PRIA, 42, Tuglakabad Institutional Area
New Delhi – 110 062

C.S. Singhal
Faculty, National Institute of Rural Development,
Rajendranagar, Hyderabad – 500 030

George Mathew
Director, Institute of Social Sciences,
5, Nelson Mandela Road, New Delhi – 110 070

V. Venkatakrishnan
NABARD CHAIR, Institute of Rural Management,
Anand 388001, Gujarat

S.S. Meenakshisundaram, *IAS*
Secretary to Government of India,
Department of Rural Development,
New Delhi

P.R. Sharma
Senior Research Associate
Institute of Development Studies,
Jaipur

R.P. Joshi
Prof & Head
Department of Political Science, MDS University,
Ajmer

G. Palanithurai
Prof & Head
Department of Political Science
and Development Administration
Gandhigram Rural Institute – Deemed University,
Gandhigram – 624 302

V.A. Vasudevaraju
Executive Director
IICD
5, 6th Cross, Brindavan,
Pondicherry – 608 013.

INTRODUCTION

The first volume has introduced the major subject *Decentralization of Powers* and brought out the experience of decentralization of powers in some of the leading States in India. The second volume has highlighted the experience of decentralization in another category of States in India. The experience of these States in decentralization indicates the direction in which it moves and what will be the consequences and implications of decentralization of powers.

The present volume provides insights into the process of decentralization of powers in some more States. B.S. Bhargava's "Lakshadweep: Evolving Dimensions of Decentralized Governance" is an excellent piece of research portraying the evolutionary process of decentralization despite the centralized move towards it. Bhargava has traced the socio-economic profile of the land and analyzed the social system that works in the Lakshadweep islands. He has touched upon the economic life of the people also. While explaining the backdrop he has furnished a brief administrative history of the place. Against the backdrop of the above said factors, he has explained the composition and functions of the Island Councils and their representation in the Pradesh Councils. Following the 73rd Amendment to the Constitution of India, the Lakshadweep islands passed a conformity legislation which he has explained in detail. Further he has evaluated the structures created and the powers, functions, functionaries and finances conferred upon the Panchayat Raj System in the Lakshadweep Islands. He has also assessed the functioning of the system in the islands. He provides a complete history of the Panchayati Raj System in the Lakshadweep Islands.

Chandan Datta's article "New Panchayat Raj System in Bihar" is another interesting article which provides the status of the State in terms of the conditions in social development and the process of decentralized governance in Bihar. He has briefly touched upon the historical background of the Panchayati Raj System in Bihar. He has brought to light the tactics adopted by the Bihar State Government in not conducting the Panchayati elections by using a lacuna in the 73rd Amendment to the Constitution of India. He has explained the basic structure of the Panchayati Raj System in Bihar, and the powers conferred upon the Panchayats. In the context of the poor attention paid to the Panchayats, the efforts taken by various developmental agencies to strengthen the Panchayats have been explained. The interface between the Panchayats and the development agencies has been succinctly portrayed. It is almost a status report of decentralization of powers in Bihar.

Though an article has been included in the previous volume on Maharashtra, the present article on Maharashtra by C.S. Singhal is different as all the three components of decentralization, namely, powers, functions and finances in the Maharashtra Panchayati Raj System have been explained. It provides a textbook overview of the Maharashtra Panchayati Raj System in the light of the 73rd Amendment to the Constitution of India. It will be very useful to students to get a cursory glance at the decentralized experience in Maharashtra.

George Mathew's "Panchayati Raj: Challenges Ahead" is a rendering of a lecture delivered in Gandhigram. He highlighted the scenario in India in terms of devolution of powers. He has made an evaluation of the Panchayat System against the backdrop of the observations made by Dharampal and Saraswathi in their works on the Tamil Nadu Panchayat Raj System. He has touched upon the emerging institutions and organizations proliferated by the State Government to counter the Panchayati Raj System. He had drawn many lessons from the studies conducted on various aspects of decentralization of powers in India. He has brought to light the trends that are emerging all over the country. He has also cautioned the State Government and appealed to the development organizations to create a congenial atmosphere for devolution of powers.

S.S. Meenakshisundaram's article "Rural Development as a Mechanism to Strengthen Panchayati Raj" has introduced a new perspective in the present context. His argument stems from the fact that the institutional mechanism which has been evolved over a period of time is intended to sharpen the process of delivery of services to the people. In the new context it has been emphasized that the system should have a permanent footing and should be under the control of the stakeholders. The new mechanism should bring the people and the government close. He has explained the decentralization process against the backdrop of history. He has highlighted the linkages between the implementation of the programmes and strengthening of the Panchayati Raj Institutions. He has drawn examples from Karnataka. For effective delivery of services he has suggested the strengthening of the Gram Sabha by which people's participation can be ensured. He has concluded the article by saying that the successful implementation of rural development programmes will add strength to the Panchayati Raj System.

P.R. Sharma and R.P. Joshi, in their article "Dimensions of Decentralization" have tried to project the emerging dimensions at the grass roots as a result of devolution of powers. They have taken twenty-four States for their analysis. The structure and the functions have been taken as unit of analysis. In their evaluation they have fixed the basic objectives and principles of the 73rd Amendment to the Constitution of India as a base. How these states have conceived and perceived these objectives and how these states have taken efforts to realize the objectives of the amendments have been seriously viewed. For those who are interested in evolving a framework for evaluation of Panchayats in the States, this article serves as a useful base material. It provides a comparative picture of the devolution process in the States in India.

"E-governance Strategy in India: An Urgent Need for Re-orientation towards Local E-Governance" by V. Venkatakrishnan provides a new dimension in governance at the grass roots. The fast changes in the domain of governance will make other allied institutions change themselves to the new mode. E-Governance is an imperative of the time. In accordance with the changing circumstances, it is necessary to revitalize the grass roots institutions by building up their capacity. The author has taken instances from other countries to substantiate his argument. He has explained his arguments with the support of the experiments conducted in Karnataka and Andhra Pradesh.

G. Palanithurai's article entitled "Towards Participatory Governance at Grass Roots: Synergization of Rural Communities and Rural Institutions" introduces a new dimension in the decentralization process. It analyses the importance and the implications of the new approach, participatory governance in achieving sustainable development and social justice at the grass roots, through the newly created institution—Panchayati Raj. It further analyses the linkages between the associations, organizations and the institutions formed and organized by the communities themselves and the institutions created by the Government.

The last article, "Panchayati Raj in Pondicherry: A Non-Starter" by V.A. Vasudevaraju highlights how the Pondicherry Government, led by an ethnic political party and a national political party successfully put off elections and gave reason for not conducting the elections. The author has explained the Local Body traditions maintained by the people following the French procedures.

Thus this volume carries some of the important articles dealing with the experience of the States individually and collectively. New insights have been offered. New dimensions have emerged.

1

LAKSHADWEEP

Evolving Dimensions of Decentralized Governance

B.S. BHARGAVA

Lakshadweep, formerly known as *Laccadive, Minicoy and Adindivi* Islands in the Arabian Sea, is an uni-district Union Territory. In fact, it is the smallest Union Territory of India consisting of 36 islands of which only 11 are inhabited (including Bangaram) and 25 uninhabited (including attached islets and submerged reefs). There are no streams, rivers and mountains in these islands. Many of the floras and fauna of the mainland are not found here. There is no train. Motor car, bus or lorry in this territory. The people have always in isolation in the islands encircled by the mighty sea.

Lying between 8° and 12° 13″ North Latitude and 71° and 74° East Longitude, these Islands are situated about 200 to 400 kilometres off the Kerala cost and at distances varying from 11 to 378 kilometres from one another. Though the land area of this typical coral paradise is only 32 sq. kms., the inclusion of about 4,200 sq. kms. of its lagoon area, 20,000 sq. kms, of its territorial waters and almost 4,00,000 sq. kms, of economic zone makes it one of the largest territories of the country. The lagoons and the economic zone teeming with marine life and mineral resources enhance the economic importance of Lakshadweep.

As regards the nomenclature, various explanations are given about the origin of the name 'Laccadives' or 'Lakshadweep'. These terms mean one lakh islands. The existence of a large number of islands clustered together might have prompted people to call them so in a rather exaggerated manner. The word 'laksha' in Sanskrit also means 'aim' or 'direction' etc. The Arabic word 'lac' too has the same meaning. Since Lakshadweep is situated directly on the trade between Africa, Arabia and Kerala coast, these islands might have served as landmark for the navigators during the early days of navigation. Some people hold that to be the reason for calling the island 'Lakshadweep' or "Laccadives' or the islands of direction.

Though the entire group of islands was generally known as 'Laccadives', these Islands were interpreted as 'Laccadive, Minicoy and Amindivi' Islands in the old official records, and this name persisted even after it became a Union Territory under the Government of India Act, in 1956. On 1st November 1973, the territory was officially named as 'Lakshadweep'.

Socio-Economic Profile of Lakshadweep

The islands from north to south are Chetlat, Bitra, Kiltan, Kadmat, Amini, Bangaram, Andrott, Agatti, Kavaratti, Kalpeni and Minicoy. Administratively, these Islands have been placed under three different groups. Culturally too, there are some differences between these three groups of islands. The first one is known as Amindivi group of islands. It consists of five islands, i.e., Cherlat, Bitra, Kiltan, Kadmat and Amini. The second is called as Laccadive group of islands, which consists of four islands, namely Andrott, Agatti, Kavaratti and Kalpeni. The latest inhabited island Bangaram could be categorised under this group. The third group has only one island called Minicoy.

Of all islands, Andrott has the largest land area (4.8 sq. kms.). Bitra is the smallest of all inhabited islands. With an area of just 0.1 sq. km., Bitra has a population of only 225 persons (Census 1991). Most of the Lakshadweep islands are long and narrow.

Minicoy has the maximum length (11 kms.). Minicoy, the southern most island, is the farthest from the mainland (444 kms. from Calicut).

Each island is a geological wonder and known for its speciality. For instances, the people of Chetlat are known as good sailors, fishermen and are the second best boat makers after the Minicoyans. The Chetlat boat makers receive orders for making boats from foreign countries also. Kadmat is a club shaped island. It has rich deposit of limestone, which is used for construction works in the Union Territory. Amini, the last one in Aminidivi group of islands, has the most beautiful coconut plantations. This was the island which was twice visited by Vasco da Gama. It is the place where he wrote his diary. Andrott, which is in Laccadive group of islands, is the biggest island. The people of this island are richer as compared to the people in rest of the islands. In Kavaratti, good examples of wood carving and mason work can be seen. Kalpeni has a conspicuous lead over other islands in the field of higher education. For this reason, the number of people belonging to this island having government jobs is the highest. Bangaram is the tourist spot of Lakshadweep. The last is Minicoy. Minicoy is different from other islands. The culture and language of the people of this island and their physical features resemble the Maldivian people.

Population and Language

According to the 1991 Census, Lakshadweep has a population of 51,707 persons. Table 1.1 and Table 1.2 given below show the area wise population of the sub-divisions with rural urban break-up and islandwise area and population respectively. It is found that more than 93 per cent of the population, who are indigenous Muslims and belong to the Shafi school of the Sunni sect. Due to their social and economic backwardness, they have been classified as Scheduled Tribes and Scheduled Castes do not exist in this Union Territory.

Table 1.1 : Rural-urban Break-u
Various Sub-Divisior

Union Territory/ Sub-Divisions	Total	Rural
Laksha-dweep	51707 (100)	22593 (43.69)
Chetlat	277.6	227.6
Kiltan	3065	3065
Kadamat	3985	3985
Amini	6447	—
Andrott	9122	9122
Agatti	5731	61
Kavaratti	8677	—
Kalpeni	4084	4084
Minicoy	8320	—

Note : Figures in parantheses represe

Table 1.2 : Island-wise Area and Po

Island	Area of land use
Chetlat	1.04
Bitra	0.10
Kiltan	1.63
Kadamat	3.13
Amini	2.59
Bangaram	0.58
Andrott	4.84
Agatti	2.71
Kalpeni	2.28
Minicoy	4.97
Total	26.9

'Tarawd' isalnds. Melacheries are the descendants of the lower castes.

In Amini, the class distinction is mainly based on property. The Taraws class consists of a few families, which had tenants in early days. The Tanakampranavars were those who possessed property of their own. The Kudiyatis were tenants and Melacheries were tree climbers and labourers. The other four islands of Amini group, i.e., Chetlat, Bitra, Kiltan and Kadmat have only the lower class of people that is Melacheries.

People in Minicoy are divided into four classes. Manikfans are the landowners and they represent the highest caste. The Thakrufans are the sailors and they occupy the second position in the hierarchy. The Thakrus are those who work as sailors but socially inferior to Thakrufans. They work in the boats during voyages. Raveries are the people of the lowest caste and work as tree climbers, toddy tapers and labourers.

Usually the age of marriage in all the islands is 20-25 years for the male and 15-20 years for the female. Child marriage, polygamy and divorces are common in all the islands except Minicoy. Women in Lakshadweep enjoy considerable independence compared to many of their counterparts in the mainland. The obligation of the husband to make an annual payment towards the maintenance of the wife as enshrined in the marriage contract, absence of any ban on remarriage of a widow, freedom to demand a divorce on the grounds of non-payment of maintenance dues by the husband and possibilities of seeking a fresh alliance in case of divorce, have contributed to this commendable situation. To cap them all, the system of Marumakkathayam by which the property descends through the female line, ensures the economic independence of women.

Minicoy enjoys a better position in so far as the position of women in the society is concerned. In Minicoy, the girl has the right to chose her husband. The entire expenditure connected with the marriage have to be incurred by the bridegroom. After the marriage, bridegroom becomes a member of the bride's home. The Minicoyans are monogamous. Early marriage is not allowed. Divorce is quite uncommon in Minicoy. The right of the house is invested with the women and they manage the family matters. The husband takes his wife's family name after the marriage. The fact that most of the men of this island serve in international ships as seamen would have contributed towards this. Apart from dominating the house, the womenfolk have an important role in the village (*Athiri*) administration in this island. It is learnt that the female chief (Boduthatha) is the head of the women's assembly and she organizes women's labour for common purposes in the village (*Athiri*).

Economic System

Fishing, coconut cultivation and coir twisting are the major occupations of the people of Lakshadweep. Tourism also contributes to the economy of these islands. Since coconut husk is the main raw material available, coir based industries are more suitable to these islands. Hence coir-demonstration-cum-training centres, two industrial co-operative societies and seven mechanical decorticating units have been established. Brittle fibre, mattress and mixed fibre are extracted from dry coconut husk. A hosiery factory at Kalpeni produces vests and T-shirts.

The canning factory at Minicoy has been taken over by the Lakshadweep Development Corporation. Apart from commercial manufacturing and marketing of Tuna Cans, marketing of Tuna Pickle Produced under DWCRA units has been taken over by this corporation. A desiccated coconut power unit (at Kadmat), a jaggery vinegar unit (at Kalpeni) and a coconut nursery (at Andrott) have been set up under the auspices of this corporation.

Though tourism has great potential in these islands, with a view to prevent overcrowding and environmental damage, limits have been prescribed on the number of tourists to be admitted. Tourist huts and cottages have been provided at Kadmat, Bangaram, Kavaratti, Kalpeni and Minicoy. Efforts have been made to provide more employment to islanders by establishing tourist cafeteria and floating restaurant.

The system of *Jenmi* (landlord) and *Kudiyan* (Tenant) relationship whereby *Nadapu* (a unit of 30 to 40 trees) used to be handed over to the tenant with the land on which they were planted was found to be feudal in character since it let to absolute misery among the tenants who formed the majority of the population. Hence it was abolished with the enforcement of Lakshadweep Land Revenue and Tenancy Regulation, 1965. Due to this, one-fourth of the land with the trees thereon were reverted to the *Jenmi* and three-fourths of the land held by the tenant were vested with the tenants. It is claimed that this land reform not only changed the economic pattern of the society in the islands but also brought about social changes. The tenant no longer had to work for the landlord in his house nor had to repair his boats to sail them to the mainland[2].

The co-operative movement has taken strong roots in these islands since the late sixties and the entire customer sales are made through co-operatives. It is understood that more than half of the total population of Lakshadweep is members of co-operative societies. There are labour co-operatives and weaving, hosiery, oil mills, bakery, boat building yards and many other activities in the co-operative sector in these islands. The Lakshadweep Co-operative Marketing Federation is the approved wholesaler for the distribution of all essential commodities under Public Distribution System. Primary Co-operative Societies are functioning as the approved retailers.

Literacy and Education

At the time of formation of this territory in 1956, there was only nine primary schools housed in dilapidated buildings. The teaching staff consisted of 28 island teachers mostly untrained or re-employed persons. The percentage of literacy in the territory now forming Lakshadweep according to 1951 census was 15.23. It rose to 43.4 per cent in 1971 and 54.72 per cent in 1981, as against 36.17 per cent in the country in 1981. It is heartening to note that the literacy rate has gone up to as high as 81.78 per cent as per the census. It is a matter of pride to learn that of the total enrolment in the schools, 44.71 per cent are girls. Today the number of educational institutions in the island is 56 including 19 Junior Boys schools, 9 High Schools, 2 Junior Colleges, one I.I.T. and one Navodaya Vidayalaya operating in the island of Minicoy since 1988. With the number of teachers going up to 721, the teacher pupil ratio has become 1 to 22. At present the educational institutions are housed in good buildings and equipped with furnitures and other accessories.

The illiterate and superstitious islanders were deadly against girl's education. Due to continuous efforts of officers and teachers, the islanders began to change their attitude and send their girls for education. The decenial growth rate of female literacy between 1961and 1971 was 176.5 per cent, which was highest in the country. Today Minicoy has the first rank in female as well as male literacy. As per 1991census, percentage of literacy for male and female is 90.18 and 72.89 respectively.

Brief Administrative History

The early history of Lakshadwep is unwritten. What now passes for history is based on various legends. The local traditions attribute the first settlements in these islands to the period of Cheraman Perumal, the last King of Kerala. Though the early inhabitants of these islands were basically Hindus who migrated from the Malabar coast of Kerala at the behest of Raja of Chirakkal, it is universally believed that in the year 41 Hijra (around 14th Century), all the islanders were converted to Islam by St. Ubaidullah from Mecca. Even after the conversion of the entire population to Islam, sovereignty remained in the hands of the Hindu Raja of Chirakkal for some years. In the absence of any written history of the Lakshadweep islands, it is not possible to trace the type of administrative system that was prevailing there. However, it is mentioned that during the days of the rule of Hindu Raja of Chirakkal the islands were administered locally by the people themselves[3]. Apparently, the Raja did not interfere in the administration. Life in the islands seemed to have been peaceful.

The arrival of the Portuguese in the Indian Ocean at the end of the 15th century and their frequent attacks on these islands made it an unhappy possession to the Raja of Chirakkal. So the king bestowed these islands on Ali Raja, his hereditary chieftain as a *jagir* by the middle of the 16th century[4]. In return, Ali Raja had to make an annual payment of 18,000 *fanams* (*fanam* was about one-third of a rupee) as tribute to the Raja of Chirakkal. R.H. Ellis holds that the annual tribute was paid to the Chirakkal House (Raja of Chirakkal) till the middle of the 18th century when the Arakkal family (Ali Rajas) started asserting its own independence. Thereupon the two families became inveterate foes and in 1766, with the help of Hyder Ali of Mysore, Ali Raja became independent of the Chirakkal house. Thus, the Arakkal family virtually got complete control over the islands.

With the advent of the Rule of the Muslim House of Arakkal of Cannannore, a mainlander was appointed in each of the islands (including Minicoy) as *Karyakar* (administrator). The *Karyakar* was directly responsible to the Ali Raja and had exclusive authority in all civil and criminal matters. The help of the *Karyakar* in administration, leading islanders were appointed as jurors to assist the *Karyakar*, and they belonged to the high caste Koyas.

The house of Arakkal ruled the islands for many years. But slowly, the administration deteriorated. There are many stories of atrocities committed by the *Karyakars.* The *Karyakars* received very meagre amounts by way of salary and so they always resorted to extract money from the islanders by misusing their power. They confiscated the property of the poor and heavily punished people for simple offences. People had to pay local taxes for even wearing ornaments or for launching boats.

Gradually, the Arakkal rule became unbearable to the people. The exploitations under the Arakkal rules, especially with regard to the coir monopoly[5], which was enforced with utmost strictness and harshness, gave rise to revolt of Northern islands of Chetlat, Birta, Kiltan, Kadmat and Amini in 1784. Later on, based on the agreements between Tipu Sultan and Cannannore Bibi of Arakkal, in 1787, five islands of Amini group were handed over to Tipu Sultan in return for his territory in Chirakkal. Thus five northern islands came under Tipu Sultan's regime and the rest continued under the Arakkal ruler. The Sultan continued to administer the Amini group of islands till the last battle of Seringapatam. After the last battle of Seringapatam and with the fall of Tipu's kingdom in 1799, the five northern islands went into the hands of the East India Company and were annexed with the South Kanara district in the mainland and administered from Mangalore.

The other islands continued to be administered by the Bibi of Arakkal. After her death, in 1847, a severe cyclone hit the island of Andrott. With the request from the islanders, the Raja of Arakkal decided to visit the island in order to assess the damages and for distributing relief. An officer of the East India Company Sir William Robinson volunteered to accompany the Raja to assess the damage and render relief. On reaching Andrott, the Raja found it difficult to meet all the demands of the people. Sir William then offered to help and send all the requirements in the Company's vessels to the islands in the form of a loan to the Raja. This arrangement continued for about four years. When the loan increased to lakhs and the interest started mounting, the English asked Raja to pay it up immediately which he could not. Finally, in 1854, the islands under the Arakkal ruler were handed over to the East India Company for administration in the name of Raja.

The East India Company changed the administration to the benefit of the people who began to look more towards it for their help than towards the Raja. The Company appointed an *Amin* (the trustee) as the administrator in each of the islands to look after its affairs. The *Amin* was chosen from one of the leading families of the island itself. However, under this system only the landlords (Koyas) could become *Amin.* Thus the administration of the Karyakars who came from the mainland was brought to an end and the islands came to be administered by *Amins* representing their respective islands. Under the agreement signed on 15th November 1908[6], the Arakkal house ceded the full sovereignty over Laccadive and Minicoy islands and they formed part of the British India with effect from 1st July 1905, and were administered by the Malabar Collector stationed at Calicut. Though the entire territory came under the East India Company, the Aminidivi islands continued to be a part of the South Kanara district and Laccadive islands and Minicoy formed part of the Malabar district for administrative purposes.

The government always gave the islands a special status mainly owing to the backwardness of the islands and the peculiar life-styles of the islanders. While the Scheduled District Act of 1874 treated the islands as a 'scheduled district', the Government of India Act of 1919 considered it as a 'backward tract'. Again the Government of India Act 1935 declared the islands as 'excluded areas'.

After Independence

Through a series of historical compulsions, the islanders were left to live in ignorance and poverty for several centuries. The Arakkal house as well as the British Government showed little interest in the progress of the islands. They were interested only in the maintenance of law and order in the territory besides its economic exploitation. Practically no important developmental activity was brought about during these regimes. Moreover, due to their cultural and geographical remoteness and isolation, the islands lagged in development and progress, when compared with the other parts of the mainland.

It was only after India attained independence that the islands began to get positive help and assistance. Considering their economic and cultural backwardness in 1956, the inhabitants of the territory were declared as 'scheduled tribes' by the Government of India and prior to that, in 1950, an islander was included in the Tribal Advisory Council organised by the Madras Government. Finally, it was on 1st November 1956 that under the State Reorganisation Act (1956), all the islands were brought together to form a Union Territory which was named as Lakshadweep in 1973. Meanwhile, the Headquarters of the administration was shifted from Calicut (Kerala) to Kavaratti island in March 1964.

Administrative Set-up

For the sake of administrative convenience, the entire group of islands have been constituted into one district, and it has been divided into four Tashils. Each Tashil (with Headquarters at Amini, Andrott, Kavaratti and Minicoy) is under the control of a Tashildar except in Minicoy, where a Deputy Collector has been appointed since August 1978. The lowest revenue official in each island is known as *Amin.* Practically, the *Amin* manages all the local matters of importance.

The Administrator appointed by the President of India under Article 239 of the Constitution is the head of this Union Territory and he conducts the administration of the Union Territory on behalf of the President of India. The Secretary to the Administrator assists the Administrator at the Secretariat level. Though the departmental offices are working separately, the Administrator's Secretariat and District Administration were functioning as compact units under a single line system of administration till recently. The matters relating to the District Administration, Law and Order and Development Programmes in general are managed by the District Collector-cum-Development Commissioner-cum-District Magistrate, who functions under the administrative control of the Administrator. In discharging his responsibilities, the District Collector-cum-Development Commissioner is assisted by the heads of various departments. Further, to free the Administrator from numerous routine matters, a senior officer of the IAS has been appointed as Managing Director of Lakshadweep Development Corporation since September 1992. This officer functions under the control of the Administrator, and he also works as the ex-officio Secretary of a few major departments such as Fisheries, Industries, Public Works, Medical and Public Health Services.

Under the District Magistrate, there are one Additional District Magistrate and nine Executive Magistrates. To bring the administrator closer to the people, since 1983, all the inhabited islands along with their attached islands and islets have been divided into nine Sub-Divisions/Additional Sub-Divisions, and each one is headed by a Sub-Divisional Officer. These Sub-Divisional Officers function as Executive Magistrates for respective islands. They also function as Block Development Officers or Additional Block Development Officers for those islands, which have been constituted into C.D. Blocks[7]. Co-ordination of all development activities and implementation of all programmes coming under the Community Development Blocks including IRDP, JRY, TRYSEM, NRY etc. and the area development programmes under the Five Year Plan Schemes in these divisions and sub-divisions are the responsibility of these officers. Apart from liasing between the various departmental officers in these islands, the Sub-Divisional Officers also exercise the administrative powers for local administration and head of the official wing of the Island Councils[8] and Block Level Committees in their areas.

From the above discussion it could be understood that there was absolutely no scope for people's participation in administration. This was mainly due to the absence of any democratic institutions in the islands. Though Citizens Committees came into existence in 1956-66, the traditional groups that were in existence prior to the formation of Citizens Committees were known as *Karanavans* in Laccadive and Minicoy groups of islands and *Mukthassors* in Amindivi group of islands. They were consulted in matters relating to local problems in their islands. To advise the Administrator and the Home Ministry (at the Centre) respectively, an Advisory Council and Citizens Committee that continued till 1988 could provide for participation of 'window-dressing type' only. There was no other representation for the people in the administration, because of which it could not fully reflect the aspirations of the people.

DEMOCRATIC DECENTRALIZATION AND DEVELOPMENT ADMINISTRATION

This section deals with the efforts/attempts made by the Central Government (Lakshadweep Administration) in the direction of decentralized governance and development administration in Lakshadweep. An attempt has also been made to bring into light the existence and operation of traditional groups and committees that ensured to some extent people's participation in administration.

Prior to the State Reorganisation and formation of the separate Union Territory of Lakshadweep in 1956, these islands formed part of the Chevayoor Constituency in Malabar District of the erstwhile to the State Assembly and Parliament represented these islands in the Madras Legislative Assembly and Parliament. After the formation of the Union Territory, from 1956 onwards, one member was nominated by the President to represent these islands in the Parliament till 1967 when the Laccadive, Minicoy and Amindivi Islands Parliamentary constituency was formed and a representative was elected to Parliament. Except this the Union Territory had no other democratic institution involving people's participation till 1988. However, some traditional groups existed. They were called *Karanvaran* in the Lakshadweep and Minicoy groups of Islands and *Muktassor* in the Amindivi group. In 1965-66, these groups were given the name of citizen committees that helped the administration in solving local problems. In addition to the above, two committees namely Advisory Council and Advisory Committee were formed to advise the local administration and the Union Ministry of Home Affairs which was in overall charge of the Union Territory. Later, the Island and Union Territory level National Integration Councils were constituted for assisting the local administration.

Advisory Committee

The Advisory Committee attached to the Ministry of Home Affairs (at the Centre) was constituted on 12th June, 1958. The Administrator, the sitting Member of Parliament and five other non-officials are members of the committee. The non-official members are nominated by the president on the recommendation of the Administrator for a period of one-year commencing from first April. This Committee meets twice a year, and gives suggestions and recommendations with regard to planning and budgeting of the administration.

Advisory Council

To aid and advise the Administrator in carrying out the day-to-day administration of the Union Territory an Advisory Council was constituted by the Ministry of Home Affairs on 29th June, 1957. The Council has 13 members including the Member of Parliament and the Members of the Advisory Committee. The members are nominated by the President on the recommendation of the Administrator for a period of one year from first April. This Council holds three sittings in a year to discuss the developmental activities and to suggest ways and means for a smooth functioning of the administration.

Citizen Councils

The Island and Union Territory level Nation Integration Councils were constituted on 30th July, 1970. The Administrator is the Chairman of the Union Territory level Council. These councils were created mainly for assisting the local administration and police to maintain law and order, and to guard the security of the islands to promote national integration. Besides the above Councils and Committees, all the recognised *Karanavans* (village elders) who represented the traditional system of island administration were consulted in all matters of administrative importance.

As expected, these Committees and Councils functioned merely as advisory bodies without any involvement or participation of people in local administration. As referred to earlier, the participation of people, if any, was of 'window dressing type'. Since there was no other institution providing for representation of the people in administration, it could not fully reflect the aspirations of the people.

In the above circumstances, when the rest of the country was experimenting with democratic decentralisation in the form of Panchayati Raj Institutions (as rural local-self government) and various other Urban Local Bodies, people of Lakshadweep were longing for their representation in administration. Obviously, there were popular demands for setting up democratic institutions aimed at popular participation. In this regard, mention may be made that the visit of the former Prime Minister Late Rajiv Gandhi to these islands in December 1986 proved to be a stimulant in this direction. Immediately after his visit, two regulations namely Lakshadweep (Administration) Regulation, 1988 (No.3 of 1988) and Lakshadweep Island Councils Regulation, 1988 (No.4 of 1988) were promulgated to form Island Councils at the island level and Pradesh Council at the Union Territory level respectively.

Island Councils

Accordingly, in pursuance of the Presidential Promulgation of the Lakshadweep Island Councils Regulation, 1988 (No. 4 of 1988), the Island Councils in Lakshadweep came into being from 6th April 1990. Interestingly, this was the first democratic set-up of the Islands that came into being in the fortieth year of Indian Republic. For the first time, democratic institutions in the form of Island Councils were constituted in ten islands. Altogether, 79 members were directly elected to these Island Councils and had a Chairperson and Vice-

Chairperson, who were elected by and from amongst the members of the Island Council in their first meeting after the election. The tenure of the Council and for that matter the term of office of the members, chairperson and vice-chairperson was for a period of four years from the first meeting of the Island Council. The size of these councils in terms of their number of members varied depending upon the population of the islands.

Pradesh Council

Similarly, the Pradesh Council was constituted for the Union Territory as a whole in pursuance of the Presidential Promulgation of the Lakshadweep (Administration) Regulation, 1988 (No. 3 of 1988). It consisted of 21 members who were indirectly elected by and from amongst the members of each island council. The size of the Island Councils and their representation in the Pradesh Council is shown in Table 1.3.

Besides the elected members of the Island Councils, the Administrator of the Union Territory, the Collector-cum-Development Commissioner of Lakshadweep and the sitting Member of Parliament representing Lakshadweep in the Lok Sabha were also made the members of the Pradesh Council. The Administrator was the Chairman of the Pradesh Council, and in his absence, the Vice-Chairman , i.e., the Collector, used to preside over the meetings.

Functioning of Island and Pradesh Councils

The Island Councils that replaced the citizens committees at the island level were assigned with the responsibilities of sanitation and public health, public works, planning and development, administration and social welfare. Sanitation and public health covered sanitation and conservancy, removal of rubbish and keeping the areas of the island in a clean condition, maternity and child welfare, family planning, construction and maintenance of public latrines and regulating checking and abating of offensive or dangerous trade or practice. Lighting of island and establishment and maintenance of public utility places formed part of public works.

Table 1.3 : Composition of the Island Councils and their Representation in the Pradesh Council

Name of the Island/ Island Council	Number of Members in the Island Council	Number of Members Represented in the Pradesh Council
Chetlat	6	1
Bitra	3	1
Kiltan	6	1
Kadamat	8	2
Amini	10	3
Bangaram	—	—
Andrott	10	3
Agatti	8	2
Kavaratti	10	3
Kalpeni	8	2
Minicoy	10	3
Total	79	21

Note : Island Council was not constituted in Bangaram in 1988. It was only in the year 1991 that it was enumerated by the Census of India and was found to have 61 population in total.

Planning and development encompassed preparation and implementation of plans for the development of agriculture, animal husbandry, fisheries, island industries and co-operatives especially (a) distribution of improved seeds, manure and fertilizers; (b) promoting the use of improved agriculture implements and making such implements easily available; (c) improvement and general care of livestock and promotion of poultry keeping; and (d) providing for organization management and development of cottage and small scale industries.

Administration of Island Council property, numbering of premises, maintenance and upkeep of Island Council records and registration of births and deaths were the activities specified under the head administration. Social welfare included relief to the crippled and the destitute, preventive and relief measures in times of natural calamity, promotion of moral and social welfare activities and assisting voluntary organization and agencies engaged in such activities.

The Island Councils were empowered to levy tax on the owners or occupiers of buildings, on vehicles kept within the jurisdiction of the Island Council, lighting tax, drainage tax, establishment tax, octroi tax on boats kept within the jurisdiction of the Island Council including the lagoons attached thereto for fishing or for carrying goods or passengers, licence fee for boats maintained for public transport of goods or passengers and fee for providing protection of crops in the Island Council area. Though the list of functions to be performed by the Island Councils and their taxation were matching with those of the Panchayats in the mainland, these Councils could not exercise powers in a reasonable manner for various reasons that have been plaguing the Panchayats of the mainland. Though most of these schemes were transferred to the Island Councils, due to the reluctance on the part of the bureaucrats to share the powers with the democratically elected people's representatives many of the functions could not be carried out. Secondly, the elected representatives were not having any experience in coping with the powers and functions entrusted to them. Finally, it was felt that there has been absence of training to the elected members in governance.

A study conducted by Jos Chathakulam and V.K. Kurien[9] observes that 'the Island Council' had only very limited functions. A careful reading of the Island Council Regulation Act revealed that the Council had only advisory functions on health, education and matters relating to social and economic well-being of the people in the islands. The political leadership in the Councils were convinced that the various provisions in the Act were designed and incorporated to put the bureaucrats at the top on the one side and control the democratic desire of the people on the other side. A considerable majority of the members, presidents and vice-presidents of the Island Council were not satisfied with the powers and functions assigned to the Island Council.

In a formal group discussion with the researcher, they revealed that not only the financial allocation to Island Councils were very meagre and negligible, but also the Island Councils were under the strict administrative control of the higher officials from the Union Territory of Lakshadweep. Administrative and technical sanctions were denied to a number of local projects. There was no provision for local initiative in the area of development projects. In most cases, proposals of the Island Councils were rejected by the District Rural Development Agency (DRDA) even without mentioning the reasons thereof. DRDA and the Panchayat Directorate acted as a supervising, controlling and checking agency rather than providing any supportive structure to the Island Councils.

The members of the former Island Councils were not given any training by the Administration on matters relating to local administration. Further, they were not provided with the Rules and Regulations for the Island Councils or any handbook or reference book to clarify their doubts as a result of which the business proceedings of these bodies were under utter confusion. Within their financial and structural limitations, a majority of the former Island Councils members observed that they performed relatively well and were committed to local problems and issues of the people and the Islands.

Thus, it could be concluded that even though the constitution of the Island Councils was an improvement over the previous system of Citizens Committee, these Councils could not come up to the expectations of the people and their representatives. However, the silver lining in this exercise was the election of the representatives by the people themselves rather than that of appointment of the recommendation of the Administrator as it used to be in the case of Citizens Committee.

As regards the composition and functions of the Pradesh Council, the major difference between the erstwhile Advisory Council and this Pradesh Council was that while the members of the former were appointed on the recommendation of the Administrator, in the latter, membership was based on the indirect election by the Island Councils. Even then, the Administrator had powers to nominate one woman member to the Pradesh Council, if there was no presentation from the women category. Further, he was empowered to appoint three councillors from amongst the 21 elected members of the Pradesh Council, who were allocated different departments. With the exception of matters concerning the service (including matters relating to persons, police and public order, vigilance, judiciary and election) all matters relating to foreign nationals and also matters relating to restriction on entry and residence in Lakshadweep, the business of the administration was allocated to these three councillors at the discretion of the administrator. The provisions of the regulation based on which the Pradesh Council was constituted made it essential to have at least two meetings of the council in a year.

Since the Chairman and Vice-Chairman of the Pradesh Council were bureaucrats from the islands, the 21 elected members from different councils had little space to perform their 'legislative' functions in the Pradesh Council. Moreover, the 21 members in the Pradesh Council were not a homogeneous political and economic group. The divisions in the Pradesh Council based on party politics, strengthened the bureaucratic control over the elected members in the council. So, it continued as an advisory body without much executive functions. It may be noted that unlike the Island Councils that were constituted for the local governance, the Pradesh Council was constituted to work as a mechanism for 'administrative decentralisation' though both the institutions had a pseudo political image.

The indirect election of members of Pradesh Council by the Island Councils and the indirect election of members of the Advisory Committee of the Ministry of Home Affairs provided a vertical linkage among all the three institutions. However, reducing these bodies as advisory in effect had dampened the spirits of the elected representatives. Further, the making of the Administrator as the Chairman of the Pradesh Council was against the principles of democracy. Without any hesitation one can say that the Pradesh Council had very little scope to shape their urge for 'self realisation' and 'self determination' for the people of Lakshadweep.

LAKSHADWEEP PANCHAYATS REGULATION 1994 AND BUILDING OF DEMOCRATIC INSTITUTIONS

Following the enactment of the Constitution (Seventy-third Amendment) Act, 1992, on 24th April 1993, many States and Union

Territories had either framed new Panchayati Raj Acts/Regulations or had gone in for suitably amending their existing Acts in order to make it in conformity with the 73rd Amendment Act, 1992. Accordingly, in pursuance of the Constitution (Seventy Third) Amendment Act, 1992 and in exercise of the powers conferred by Article 240 of the Indian Constitution, Lakshadweep Panchayats 1994 (No. 4 of 1994) was promulgated by the President of India on 23rd April 1994.

The Constitution (Seventy-third Amendment) Act, 1992 under Article 243B (1) enjoins upon the States to constitute a three-tier system of Panchayats at the village, intermediate and district levels. However, under Article 243B (2) it also specifies that notwithstanding anything in clause (1), Panchayats at the intermediate level may not be constituted in a State having a population not exceeding 20 lakhs. Since Lakshadweep happens to be uni-direct Union Territory with a total population of 51,707 persons spread over 11 inhabited islands, Lakshadweep Panchayats Regulation 1994 provided for a two-tier system for of Panchayats at the Village (*Dweep*) and district levels with Gram Sabhas at the bottom. In addition, the Regulation also provides for various revolutionary provisions such as direct election of members to both district and village (*Dweep*) Panchayats, reservation for women (not less than 33 per cent) and SCs/STs (proportionate to their population) for a broad-based participation of the people, especially the rural poor and the deprived, in the process of their development. It also makes provision for institutions like District Planning Committee, Independent Election Commission and Finance Commission for ensuring the sustainability and smooth functioning of the Panchayati Raj Intitutions in the Islands.

In what follows, presents a critical examination of various provisions in the Lakshadweep Panchayats Regulation 1994 in the light of the Constitution (Seventy-third Amendment) Act, 1992 and the progress made in building up institutions of democratic decentralization in Lakshadweep.

Gram Sabha

Even prior to the 73rd Constitutional Amendment, provisions for 'Gram Sabha' as an institution of 'direct democracy' were there in a majority of Indian States except Kerala and Tamil Nadu[10]. There were broadly three categories of membership in Gram Sabhas in different States, i.e., all the voters in the concerned village, a list of voters to be prepared for the purpose and all adult residents of the village.

As per the Lakshadweep Panchayats Regulation 1994 (LPR 1994), the Gram Sabha shall consist of persons registered in the electoral rolls relating to an island or group of islands comprising the area of the Village (*Dweep*) Panchayat. As Gram Sabha (GS) is considered as the only means of 'direct democracy' where many important decisions have to be arrived at, it may serve the purpose of training ground for all people, especially the younger generation[11]. Hence, it would have been better if all those who are interested in attending the Gram Sabha meetings would have been allowed to do so. This could have been done by restricting the actual participation in deliberations (giving suggestions, taking decisions and casting vote) to the persons above 18 years of age in consonance with the voting age at Panchayat, Assembly and Lok Sabha elections. It may be recalled that one of the reasons for the failure of Island Councils and Pradesh Councils was that the popular leadership was lacking experience. If the above mentioned suggestion is considered, it may provide opportunity for everyone to observe and learn the administrative processes.

As per Section 4 (1)(a) of the said Regulation, a member of Gram Sabha shall cease to be a member, if he is disqualified under Section 12 of the Lakshadweep Panchayats Regulation 1994[12]. Apparently, these conditions were imposed with regard to the membership of the Gram Sabha needs consideration. It is felt that they have to be applied only in case of Village (*Dweep*) Panchayat and District Panchayat, and not to Gram Sabha.

While analyzing the Panchayat Acts of various States as they were prevailing prior to the Constitution (Seventy-third Amendment) Act, 1992, it could be observed that the functions of the Gram Sabha generally included considering and making recommendations with regard to matters such as the annual statement of the accounts, administrative report of the preceding financial year, the last audit report note and replies, report of the development programmes of the preceding year, development programmes proposed to be undertaken during the current year, mobilizing voluntary labour and contributions in kind and cash for the community welfare programmes and identification of beneficiaries for the implementation of development schemes pertaining to the village. However, it is noticed that no such specific function has been assigned to Gram Sabha as per the Regulation under discussion.

Section 6 (1) of the Lakshadweep Panchayats Regulation makes it mandatory for the Gram Sabha to meet at least twice in a year, one before the harvesting of the crop and the other after the harvesting of the crop. However, the Pradhan (Chairperson of the Village Panchayat) can call extraordinary meeting of the Gram Sabha upon a requisition in writing by not less than one-fifth of members of the Gram Sabha, within thirty days of the receipt of such a requisition. This provision is a novelty and it may be helpful in convening the Gram Sabha to consider any matter requiring urgent attention. The quorum for a meeting of the Gram Sabha is fixed at one-tenth of its total membership and this has been considered reasonable.

General opinion with regard to the functioning of the Village Panchayat and Gram Sabha relating to a particular village has been to compare the Gram Sabha with the 'Legislature' or 'Parliament' and the Village Panchayat to the Executive', i.e., the Council of Ministers. In such a situation, the Panchayat has to be 'accountable' to the Gram Sabha consisting of all the people of that panchayat area.

It is true that other than constitution and meetings, the LPR, 1994 has been silent about the powers and functions of the Gram Sabha. Keeping in view the islands' small and compact nature, higher rate of literacy and the instances of voluntary mobilisation of labour purposes, if the provision for 'recall' of Pradhan or members of the Village (*Dweep*) Panchayat by the Gram Sabha is incorporated in the Regulation, it may be judiciously and effectively used by the people of Lakshadweep. It may help Gram Sabha to play a very effective role and function better than its counterparts in other parts of the country, and emerge as a trendsetter in this regard.

Village (Dweep) Panchayat

As per Secion 8(1) of the LPR 1994, Village (*Dweep*) Panchayat shall be constituted in each of the isalnds of Chetlat, Bitra, Kiltan, Kadmat, Amini, Andrott, Agatti, Kavaratti, Kalpeni and Minicoy. Based on the criteria fixed for number of seats in the Panchayats, Minicoy, Andrott, Kavaratti and Amini will have 10 numbers each since their population is between six and ten thousands. Kalpeni, Kadmat and Agatti will consist of 8 members each as their population lies within the range of six thousand and three thousands five hundred. Kiltan and Chetlat are likely to have six members as their population fall within the group of not less than two thousand but not three members, as its population is less than two thousand. Perhaps this will be the smallest Panchayat in terms of its population.

Reservation for Scheduled Tribes and women in membership as well as in positions of chairperson have been ensured in accordance with the Constitutional (Seventy-third Amendment) Act, 1992. While the election of the members of the Village (*Dweep*) Panchayats has been made direct by the people, the Chairperson (Pradhan) and Vice-Chairperson (Up-Pradhan) will be indirectly elected, i.e, by and from amongst the members of the Village Panchayat. This is likely to create a piquant situation in case of a very small Panchayat such as Bitra where there are only three members. As per the Regulation, one of them will be elected as the chairperson and the other will be the vice-chairperson. If the imagination is stretched a little, at the time of absence of the Chairperson, the Vice-Chairperson has to preside over the meeting to be attended by the lone member. In such a situation what type of deliberations will take place therein? Considering the compact nature of the islands and their respective population, it would have been better if the election of the Chairperson have been made direct. Apart from helping in overcoming the problem of paucity of members, it may arouse greater interest in the Panchayat affairs, as more leadership positions will be created.

There is no clear-cut definition of quorum for a meeting and the number of meetings to be conducted in a year. Similarly, the staff to be allocated to the Panchayats has to be specially mentioned before conducting the elections to the Panchayats.

District Panchayat

Section 8 (1) of the LPR, 1994, provides for the constitution of a District Panchayat for the whole of the Union Territory. The District Panchayat consists of directly elected members from territorial constituencies (determined by the Election Commission) at the rate of one for every two thousand five hundred of population of a Village Panchayat and if the reminder is more than one thousand two hundred and fifty, then the number of such seats shall be measured by one. However, at least one seat has been allotted to a Village Panchayat to facilitate the representation of smaller Village Panchayats such as Chetlat and Bitra in the District Panchayat. In addition to these, the Pradhans of the Village Panchayats and the Member of the House of People representing the Union Territory have also been made as members of the District Panchayat with voting rights. As regards reservation of seats for STs and women, reservation for Scheduled Tribes and Women in membership as well as in positions of President-cum-Chief Councillor have been made in conformity with the Constitutional Seventy-third Amendment Act, 1992.

As per Section 24 of the LPR 1994, the President-cum-Chief Councillor and two Vice President-cum-Councillors shall be elected from amongst the directly elected members, by the directly elected members and Pradhans of the Village Panchayats, who happen to be the ex-officio members of the District Panchayat. Such provisions have been made with a view to enable a strong structural linkage between the Village Panchayats and District Panchayat. It is learnt that the creating of two Vice President-cum-Councillor positions has its origin in the composition of the erstwhile Pradesh Council. However, it is suggested that to provide more freedom to the President-cum-Chief Councillor, provision may be made for his direct election by the people of the entire Union Territory in view of the above mentioned facts and the smallness of the Union Territory itself. Further, the reasons advanced for direct election of Pradhan Village Panchayat are also applicable to the position of President-cum-Chief Councillor too.

POWERS AND FUNCTIONS OF DISTRICT AND VILLAGE PANCHAYATS

While the functions of the erstwhile Island Councils have been transferred to the Village Panchayats, it has been empowered to make provision for carrying out any other work or measure which is likely to promote the health, safety, comfort or convenience, social, economic or cultural well-being and education of the residents of the islands. Apart from that the Administrator of the Union Territory under Section 46 of the Regulation may entrust to the Village Panchayat the execution, maintenance or repair of any work including implementation of schemes of economic development and social justice. Under the same Section, the Administrator may also place the management of institution at the disposal of the Panchayat.

District Panchayat has been assigned the responsibility of implementing the matters specified in the Fourth Schedule (Eleventh Schedule of the Constitution Seventy-third Amendment Act 1992) of the LPR, 1994.

As per the Section 61 of the LPR 1994, where the functions and duties assigned to a Village (*Dweep*) Panchayat and to the District Panchayat relate to the same subject, then in order that the functions and duties may not overlap or that the responsibility for performing any such function or duty is not shifted by one panchayat to another on account of any ambiguity or misunderstanding, the Administrator may from time to time, by an order in writing, issue to all or any of the Panchayats, such directions, as he may think responsibility and the Panchayats shall be bound to exercise their powers and perform their functions and duties in conformity with such directions.

Though the above mentioned clause may be useful in resolving the conflicts between the Panchayats at different levels, it would be better to clearly demarcate the areas of operation of these Panchayats to ensure their effective functioning and accountability.

Finances

It may be surprising to learn that no form of taxation was prevalent in Lakshadweep till 1988. However, the Island Councils that were constituted after 1988 following the Lakshadweep Island Councils Regulation, 1988, levied a few taxes. Under such a kind of situation, it would be a difficult task for the village and district Panchayats to impose the taxes assigned to them as per the Regulation under discussion.

While most of the taxes assigned for the Island Councils have been transferred to the Village Panchayats *in toto*, a few items such as a license fee for boats and fee for providing protection of crops in the Island Council have been dropped.

The taxation of the District Panchayat covers a tax on profession, trade , callings and employments, a duty on transfer of immovable property in the form of surcharge on the duty imposed under the Indian Stamps Act, 1899 and a theatre tax in respect of every cinema theatre and other place of entertainment to which persons are ordinarily admitted on payment for performances or shows held or conducted thereat and fees on the registration of vehicles including boats or sailing vessels.

However, as per the Section 53, the Administrator may, by notification, suspend the levy or imposition of any tax or fee and may at any time in like manner rescind such suspension. This is likely to have a negative impact on the psyche of the people's representatives who are already considered to be averse to impose too many taxes on their citizens.

Executive Authorities

Under Section 25 of the LPR, the executive powers of the Village (*Dweep*) Panchayat and District Panchayat have been vested with the Chairperson and the President-cum-Chief-Councillor respectively. Section 33 (1) of the said Regulation makes provision for the appointment of an Executive Officer for every Village (*Dweep*) Panchayat and a Chief Executive Officer for the District Panchayat have the right to attend the meetings of the Panchayats and take part in the discussions without any right to move any resolution or to vote. Though, they have been assigned the duty of carrying into effect the resolutions of the Village and District Panchayats, the position of the Executive Officer *vis-à-vis* the Pradhan and the Village Panchayat and the Chief Executive Officer *vis-à-vis* the President-cum-Chief Councillor and the District Panchayat has not been made clear. Conferring the executive powers of the Village Panchayat and the District Panchayat on the Pradhan and President-cum-Chief Councillor respectively may be an indicator which points out that the elected representatives are likely to have a greater say in the decision making and implementation.

In addition to the Executive Officers and the Chief Executive Officer, though Section 36 (1) of the Lakshadweep Panchayats Regulation 1994 provides that every Village (*Dweep*) Panchayat and the District Panchayat shall have such other officers and employees, nothing has been done in this direction yet. It is reported that when the Island Councils were constituted sufficient staff were not transferred to them and that was also one of the reasons for the failure of those Councils. Unless suitable measures are initiated to provide adequate personnel to the village and district Panchayats, they may also end up with similar situation.

District Planning Committee

Section 85 (1) of the LPR, 1994, empowers the Administrator to constitute a District Planning Committee to consolidate the plans prepared by the Village (*Dweep*) Panchayats and the District Panchayat and to prepare a draft development for the Union Territory as a whole. The District Planning Committee is to be constituted by the Member of Parliament representing the Union Territory, the President-cum-Chief Councillor of the District Panchayat and such number of persons, not less than four-fifth of the total number of members of the Committee, as may be prescribed by the Administrator, elected by and from amongst, the elected members of the District Panchayat. The Regulation provides for the Administrator or such other officer as may be designated by him to be its ex-officio Chairman.

The exclusion of the Pradhans of the Village Panchayats from the District Planning Committee and the provision which enables the Administrator or such other officer designated by him to become the Chairman of this Committee are the grey areas in this regard. It is hoped that a rethinking will take place about these aspects.

Finance Commission and Election Commission

While Article 243-I (1) of the Constitution (Seventy-third Amendment) Act, 1992, provides for the constitution of a Finance Commission to review the financial position of the Panchayats and to make recommendations to the Governor, Article 243-K (1) provides for the constitution of a State Election Commission consisting of a State Election Commissioner to be appointed by the Governor of a State for the superintendence, direction and control of the preparation of electoral roles for and conduct of all elections to the Panchayats at all levels. Though Lakshadweep Panchayats Regulation, 1994, provides for a Finance Commission and Election Commission, in doing so, it has followed the Constitution (Seventy-third Amendment) Act, 1992, in letter but not in spirit. The Regulation under Section 86 and 87 has just extended the coverage of the Finance Commission and Election Commission of Andaman and Nicober Islands to Lakshadweep. Since the Constitution (Seventy-third Amendment) Act, 1992, provides for an independent Finance and Election Commission for the States and UT, it is doubtful if a common finance and Election Commission sitting in Andaman and Nicobar Islands in the Arabian Sea, can do justice to the people of Lakshadweep with their different socio-economic and geographical background.

Though most of the above-described provisions have been brought in as per the mandate of the 73rd Amendment, there are a few aspects wherein the Lakshadeep Panchayat Regulation has gone many steps ahead of this Amendment Act. For instance, the provision that enables the revision of the electoral rolls of Gram Sabha at least once in a financial year. Such a provision electoral rolls of Gram Sabha at least once in a financial year. Such a provision will definitely facilitate participation of more number of persons in Gram Sabha meetings, as one need not wait until the revision of the electoral roll for the Parliament elections. Similarly, another provision makes every Police Officer or the Chief Executive Officer, as the case may be, of a Panchayat of an offence coming to his knowledge which has been committed under this regulation or any rules or bye-laws made thereunder and shall assist him in the exercise of his lawful authority. Specifying the role of the Police has brought in a refreshing change where in the importance of the Panchayats has been duly recognized.

Despite such a farsightedness, a few irritants have also found a place in the Regulation. It has already been brought out that the Administrator has overriding powers in respect of suspension of levy of a tax or fee. Similarly, any officer authorized by the Administrator may suspend the execution of order or resolution of the Panchayat if he feels that the execution of any order or resolution or the doing of anything which is about to be done, or is being done by or on behalf of the Panchayat is causing or likely to cause injury or annoyance to the public or to lead to breach of peace or is unlawful. At the same time, such as authorized officer has to send a copy of the order and a statement of the reasons to the Panchayat concerned. Further, a report of the circumstances in which the order was made has to be submitted by him to an authority to be specified by the Administrator. Such as authority may after making such inquiry an deem fit by him, rescind, modify or confirm the order.

The power of suspension of the execution order or resolution of the Panchayat by an officer authorised by the Administrator will not only curtail the autonomy of Panchayati Raj Institutions, but also will dampen the spirit of self-governance. In the same way, provision regarding the appeal against the order of the Panchayat also undermine the authority of democratic institutions.

Though it is felt that there should be some safeguards against any possible unlawful action on the part of the Panchayats at any level, it appears that there are a few shortcomings in the methods prescribed as mentioned above. While in the former case of suspension of execution order or resolution of the Panchayat, suitable provisions have been made available for giving notice to the Panchayat and making an inquiry before arriving at a final conclusion, such provisions are not at all provided in considering an appeal against the order of a Panchayat. Hence, it would be appropriate if an institution similar to that of ombudsman is brought in to provide suitable remedies to any aggrieved individual or institution due to the order of any Panchayat. Further such an ombudsman may be authorized to study the resolutions or orders of any Panchayat, on a representation made to it by any individual or institution or *suo moto*. This ombudsman may be appointed by the Parliament as there is no Legislature for this Union Territory. Every decision of this ombudsman may be laid before each House of Parliament, as soon as it is made, similar to that of the Section 83 relating to rules and bye-laws to be laid before parliament. We hope that such provisions will satisfy those who sound cautious in view of the strategic location of this Union Territory[13].

Building up institutions of Democratic Decentralization

Though Lakshadweep Panchayats Regulation, 1994 was promulgated on April 23, 1994 in order to bring in conformity with the Constitution (Seventy-third Amendment) Act, 1992, the Regulation came into force only with effect from April 24, 1995. Subsequently, the Lakshadweep Island Councils Regulation, 1988 and the Lakshadweep (Administration) Regulation, 1988 were repealed. Though the Island Councils and the Pradesh Council were dissolved on 5th May 1995, elections to the village and district Panchayats under the new regulation were not held till December 1997. For a period of more than two and a half years, there occurred an institutional vacuum in the process of decentralised governance in the Union Territory. Expressing their dissatisfaction, the scholars and experts in the field stressed on the need for constituting the Panchayats as early as possible as per the provisions of the Lakshadweep Panchayats Regulation, 1994. As a custodian of democratic decentralisation and decentralised governance, Rajiv Gandhi Foundation, New Delhi in collaboration with the Centre for Rural Management, Kottayam, Kerala, organised a Sub-Regional Workshop on "Panchayati Raj" in Kavaratti (Administrative capital of Lakshadweep) from March 8-10, 1996, in order to look into the anomalies, lacunae in the Lakshadweep Panchayats Regulation, 1994 and suggest measures for amending the Regulation and holding elections in as short a time as possible. Participating in the workshop, most of the former members, Presidents and Vice-Presidents of the earlier Pradesh Council and Island Councils observed that it was undemocratic to dissolve the former Pradesh and Island Councils without creating any alternative democratic institution at the island level.

Apart from making amendments to the new Regulation, all the participants in the new workshop including the academics stressed on holding of early elections to the panchayats to remove the vaccum. Nothing seemed to bother the Island Administration in conducting early elections to Panchayati Raj Institutions.

Finally, it was in the middle of 1997 that the delay in conducting the election to the Panchayats was questioned by M.P. Cheriyakoya, an Ex-councillor from Kavaratti, in High Court of Kerala. The Court gave the judgement to conduct the Panchayat elections in Lakshadweep on or before December 31, 1997. Accordingly, the election to the Village (*Dweep*) Panchayats and District Panchayat was held on December 14, 1997, in all the islands. The election to the two-tier system of Panchayats in Lakshadweep was held simultaneously after a gap of roughly two and a half years from the date of the notification of the Panchayat rules. The arrangements for the panchayat elections were foolproof and the election was free and fair. There was no serious complaint on any of the poll related issues in the election. For the first time, people of Lakshadweep exercised their democratic right to form local self-government institutions in a big way, electing 79 members to the Village Panchayats and 22 members to the lone District Panchayat. The people were very much enthusiastic, which had resulted in a higher percentage of voter's turn-out. Tables 1.4 and 1.5 given below show the details of voter turnout and the election in terms of seats won by various political parties.

As it is evident from Table 1.4, the large scale participation of people in the elections to district and village Panchayats in almost all the islands speaks of the enthusiasm and interest of the people of Lakshadweep in elected Panchayats for decentralised governance. As regards the representation of political parties in these institutions, while both Congress and Janata Dal begged equal number of seats in the twenty-two (22) member District Panchayat, Janata Dal established its supremacy in the Village Panchayats by capturing more number of seats in 5 out of 10 Village Panchayats. Congress had a lead over 4 Village Panchayats, while the result of Kadamat Village Panchayat was tied with both Congress and Janata Dal securing equal number of seats in the eitht-member Village

Table 1.4 : Percentage of voter's turnout

Sl.No.	Island	Total Voters	Total Votes Polled	Percentage
1.	Chetlat	1273	1084	85.15
2.	Bitra	149	124	83.22
3.	Kiltan	2147	1787	83.31
4.	Kadamat	3028	2441	80.6
5.	Amini	4383	3753	85.62
6.	Andrott	6205	4993	80.46
7.	Agatti	3884	3036	78.16
8.	Kavaratti	5081	4380	75.5
9.	Kalpeni	2919	2100	81.0
10.	Minicoy	6752	4459	63.83
	Total	35821	28157	78.6

Source : Lakshadweep Secretariat, Kavaratti.

Table 1.5 : Results and Party Position in Lakshadweep Panchayats Election, 1998

Sl. No.	Island	District Panchayat			Village Panchayat			
		Total Seat	Cong-ress	Janata Dal	Total Seat	Cong.	J.D.	Ind.
1.	Chetlat	1	1	-	6	4	2	-
2.	Bitra	1	1	-	3	3	-	-
3.	Kiltan	1	-	1	6	1	5	-
4.	Kadamat	2	2	-	8	4	4	-
5.	Amini	3	1	2	10	4	6	-
6.	Andrott	4	1	3	10	6	4	-
7.	Agatti	2	2	-	8	4	3	1
8.	Kavaratti	3	1	2	10	3	7	-
9.	Kalpeni	2	-	2	8	-	8	-
10.	Minicoy	3	2	1	10	4	6	-
	Total	22	11	11	79	35	43	1

Source : Lakshadweep Secretariat, Kavaratti.

Panchayat. While Congress secured all the three seats in the Bitra Village Panchayat, Janata Dal captured all the eight seats in the Kalpeni Village Panchayat. Of the total 79 seats in ten Village Panchayats of Lakshadweep, Janata Dal secured 43 seats, Congress 35 and one independent won seat, which went to a woman candidate in the Agatti Village Panchayat.

Though majority of the former Pradesh Council members was not happy with women's reservation, there was lots of enthusiasm among the women folk for contesting elections. This was the first time the women folk of these islands had the opportunity of contesting public elections. Though women candidates contested the election in large numbers from the reserved constituencies. However , in certain reserved constituencies, women candidates contested the election independently. But only one independent women candidate won the election in the Agatti Village Panchayat.

FUNCTIONING OF PANCHAYATS AND OTHER INSTITUTIONS LIKE DPC, SFC, AND SEC

The performance of the Panchayats and other institutions could be assessed only when they are in operation for more than a year or so. Though more than two years have passed since Panchayats were constituted both at the island and district level, they are yet to operate in full scale both in implementation of schemes and appointment staff. Gram Sabha, which works as the 'legislature' at the village level, is yet to be constituted. Even some of the island Panchayats are not convening meeting in time and recording the minutes as required under the provisions of the regulation. Decisions have been taken to transfer about 40 per cent of the fund of the Administration to the District/Village Panchayats. The pattern of finance and devolution etc. has been worked out by the Finance Commission. As has been mentioned, a true picture of the functioning of the newly created Panchayati Raj Institutions could be obtained only when an intensive study is carried out.

CONCLUDING OBSERVATIONS AND REFLECTIONS

Decentralisation – the assignment of fiscal, political and administrative responsibilities to lower levels of government is occurring world wide for different reasons, at different paces, and through different means. Political changes world wide have given voice to local demands and the need to bring economic and political systems closer to local communities. In some cases the very preservation of the national political system has forced the Central Government to go in favour of decentralisation of power. Whatever may be the reason for decentralisation of power and whatever may be its form, the fact is that decentralisation has become the focus of administration, economy and the policy and is being seen as a broader process of political and economic reform.

Panchayati Raj Institutions (PRIs) in India, which are otherwise known as the institutional mechanism for democratic decentralisation and decentralised governance have had a checkered history. These institutions of rural local self-government during the last 40 years or so of their existence have moved through many ups and downs, twists and turning points. And the very nature, scope and functioning of these institutions have undergone many changes depending upon the attitude of the ruling elites, the quality of their leadership and the bureaucratic control exercised over these institutions. Their capacities for effective mobilization of the rural material and human resources have been very much dependent on the functioning of the governments and the way they have looked at it. Though some states have achieved greater success in the functioning of Panchayati Raj system, it has been a total failure in some other states.

As such, while analysing the process of democratic decentralisation or for that matter the 'major shifts' in the direction of decentralised governance in Lakshadweep, it is very important to make a distinction between Lakshadweep as a centrally administered Union Territory and the States that enjoy a definite political autonomy and have a decentralised administrative set-up as federating units of the union. Then only one can make a sound analysis of the process of democratic decentralisation and the shifts that have taken placc in the direction of decentralised governance.

The States in the mainland are governed by governments of their own with adequate political, administrative and financial autonomy under the Constitution, whereas the Union Territory of

Lakshadweep is administered centrally by an Administrator appointed by the President of India under Article 239 of the Constitution. While PRIs have been in operation in almost all the States since indpendence (institutionalised in the year 1959 as local governments at the third tier), democratic decentralisation in Lakshadweep had its beginning in the year 1990, when Island Councils and Pradesh Councils were constituted in Lakshadweep following the promulgation of the Lakshadweep Island Councils Regulation 1988 and the Lakshadweep (Administration) Regulation 1988. Interestingly, this was the first democratic set-up of the Islands that came into being in the fortieth year of Indian Republic. The Citizens Committees, Advisory Council and Advisory Committee that existed earlier to help facilitate Lakshadweep administration and solve the local problems had only nominated members and functioned as advisory bodies without any involvement or participation of he people in local administration.

Put in the framework of four forms of decentralisation, i.e, deconcentration, delegation, devolution and privatisation, the creation of Island and Pradesh Councils could be identified with delegation wherein specific functions and duties were transferred to these newly created institutions, while the ultimate responsibility and control remained with the Administrator of Lakshadweep.

Quite similar to the experiences of the States in the mainland, the Island Councils of Lakshadweep could not exercise their powers in a reasonable manner for a variety of reasons. Though some functions and responsibilities were transferred to the Island Councils, the ultimate control rested with the Administrator, which gave bureaucracy an upper hand, and finally rendered these institutions ineffective. Then came the Constitution (Seventy-third) Amendment Act 1992, following which Village and District Panchayats were constituted in 1998 as per the provisions of the Lakshadweep Panchayats Regulation 1994.

Promulgation of the Lakshadweep Panchayats Regulation, 1994 by the President of India and the constitution of a two-tier structure of Panchayats at the Island and district level could be considered as a step in the direction of devolution but to a limited extent.

Though devolution of power to the people through the creation of Village and District Panchayats under the Lakshadweep Panchayats Regulation 1994 has been hailed as a significant step in the direction of decentralisation, still there are some constraints and anomalies in the said regulation which raise doubt about the smooth functioning of the system. Structurally when Lakshadweep Panchayats Regulation 1994 has taken into account the major mandatory provisions[14] of the Constitution (Seventy-third) Amendment Act, 1992 a closer look at some of the provisions of the Regulation shows that like many other State Panchayati Raj Acts formed or amended in conformity with the Constitution (Seventy-third) Amendment Act, 1992, Lakshadweep Panchayats Regulation 1994 do not reflect 'the spirit' of the Constitution (Article 243G) which envisages panchayats as institutions of self-government enjoying optimum political, administrative and financial autonomy.

Making the Gram Sabha Effective

Like most of the State acts, other than constitution and meetings, Lakshadweep Panchayats Regulation 1994 has not assigned any specific functions to the Gram Sabha. As such, it just remains as a mere recommendatory body. Since Gram Sabha is seen as the only institutional forum through which people can directly participate and play a meaningful role in the governance and development of their village, the jurisdiction of Gram Sabha needs to be sufficiently enlarged so as to cover all aspects of governance including revenue, regulatory and developmental functions. As Gram Sabha is seen as a general body, the Gram Panchayat (as executive organ of the village government) should be made accountable to the Gram Sabha for all its actions of omission and commission. Further, Gram Sabha should be entrusted with the power to have its committees consisting of non-Panchayat members to play a supervisory role over the functioning of the Gram Panchayat. It should have the power to approve the plan, the budget, and the list of beneficiaries, sites for different developmental works/projects and accounts of the Panchayat. Social auditing by the Gram Sabha could bring about a qualitative change in the functioning of the Gram Panchayats. Some of the non-Panchayat members should be authorised to look into the accounts and put their signature as a token of verification by them. All said and done would definitely strengthen the Gram Sabha and help it play an effective role in the functioning of the Lakshadweep Panchayati Raj System.

Powers and Functions of Panchayats

Under the Lakshadweep Panchayats Regulation 1994, when the functions of the erstwhile Island Councils have been transferred to the Village Panchayats, the District Panchayat has been assigned with the 29 functions as specified in the Eleventh Schedule to the Constitution. On the one hand, when the Panchayats have not been provided with adequate functions, on the other they have overlapping powers and functions which not only undermines the efficiency of the Panchayats but also creates scope for confusion and conflict. Hence, to avoid unnecessary confusion and overlapping in the functions of the panchayats and to ensure the accountability in their functioning, provision should be made to have a clear-cut demarcation of functions between the Panchayats at both the levels.

Though the Chief Executive Officer and Executive Officers have been assigned the duties of carrying into effect the resolutions of the District and Village Panchayats respectively, the position of the Executive Officer *vis-à-vis* the Pradhan and the Chief Executive Officer *vis-à-vis* the President-cum-Chief Councillor has not been made clear. Further, it has been found that on matters relating to functions of the Village Panchayats (Section 46) and many others, the Administrator of the Union Territory enjoys a overriding position over the panchayats. This will not only have a negative impact on the psyche of the people's representatives but also will encourage the bureaucratic control over the functioning of Panchayati Raj Institutions. Provisions must, therefore, be made to ensure full financial administrative and political autonomy of the Panchayats to allow them to function as 'institutions of self-government' (Article 243G)[15].

In addition to the Executive Officers and the Chief Executive Officer, the Regulation also provides for other officers and employees for the Village Panchayats and District Panchayat. But nothing substantial has been done yet. Steps must, therefore, be taken to provide adequate to the Village and District Panchayats failing which they may end up with the similar situation that had led to the failure of Island Councils.

District Planning Committee

Under the participatory approach to development now in operation, a lot of emphasis is being given to decentralised planning. Though some kind of district planning has been in vogue for long, plans received from below do not get due weightage in the preparation and finalisation of the state plan. Though Lakshadweep Panchayats Regulation 1994 makes provision for the constitution of the District Planning Committee (hereafter DPC) to consolidate the plans prepared by the urban and rural local governments at different levels and to prepare a draft development plan for the district as a whole, the exclusion of the Pradhans of Village Panchayats from the DPC and the provision of that enables the Administrator or such other officers designated by him to become the chairman of the DPC, raise doubts about the efficiency and effective functioning of the DPC.

In addition to identification of local needs and priorities, successful planning and implementation also requires the expertise and technical know-how of the technocrats, experts in finance and banking and the environmental specialists. Keeping this in mind, provision must be made for the representation of the Village Pradhans and the inclusion of people from different field of specialisation having a definite bearing on development planning.

State Election Commission and Finance Commission

The Constitution (Seventy-third) Amendment Act 1992 has made provision for the Constitution of independent Finance and Election Commission, for ensuring independence in the functioning of these commissions. By constituting the Finance Commission and Election Commission of Andaman and Nicobar Islands to

Lakshadweep, the Lakshadweep Panchayats Regulation 1994 has just fulfilled the constitutional requirement but not its purpose. It really raise doubt if a common Finance Commission and Election Commission sitting in Andaman and Niccobar Islands in the Bay of Bengal could do justice to the people in terms of assessing the financial requirements of the people of Lakshadweep with their very different nature of socio-economic and geographical background.

Continuity and Sustainability of Panchayats

Conducting periodic and regular elections to the Panchayats is essential for the existence, continuity and sustainability of the PRIs. And the constitution has been very clear about it. Though almost all the States including Lakshadweep have followed the constitution (Seventy-third) Amendment Act, 1992, in reproducing the provisions relating to duration of Panchayats (243E)[16], a few States have shown interest in conducting regular elections to the Panchayats, when it is due.

Following the Constitution (Seventy-third) Amendment Act, 1992, Lakshadweep Panchayats Regulation was promulgated on 23rd April 1994. Subsequently, the Island and Pradesh Councils which existed prior to the coming into effect of the Lakshadweep Panchayats Regulation, 1994, were dissolved on 5th May 1995, creating a vacuum in the process of democratic decentralisation and decentralised governance. Mention must be made here that though the Regulation has made it explicitly clear that in case of dissolution, the elections to constitute the new PRIs should compulsorily be completed before the expiry of six months, the elections to constitute the new Panchayats at the village and district level were finally held in December 1997 after a period of two and half a years from the date of dissolution. This happened despite the fact that Lakshadweep is administered by the central government with the help of an Administrator appointed by the President of India.

This certainly amounts to the violation of the Constitution. When Constitution has been very clear about the prescriptions, it has not spelt out any sanctions in case of violation of the provisions of Constitution. In order to provide continuity and sustainability to the functioning of Panchayati Raj Institutions, the Central Government has to initiate some stern but practical measures in this direction.

Finally, democratic decentralisation as a process of governance results in greater participation in development activities, more effective and efficient administration of local and rural development programmes and expanded administrative capacity outside of the national capital. But in most cases it faces problems at the time of implementation. Sometimes problems arise from insufficient political and bureaucratic support and sometimes from ingrained centrist attitudes and behaviour on the part of political and administrative leaders. Sometimes decentralisation policies and programmes are inappropriately designed, organised and carried out and ultimately fail, due to lack of insufficient transfer of financial resources to the organisations and institutions to which responsibilities have been transferred. This is what exactly has happened in the country. Like most of the states in the mainland, the efforts of the Lakshadweep Administration in the direction of decentralised governance through the building of grass roots democratic institutions have been *ad hoc* and inappropriately designed. It has not been accompanied by sufficient political, administrative, financial and bureaucratic support.

Democratic decentralisation is an attempt to counteract, not to reinforce ingrained bureaucratic and managerial behaviour. Its success depends in large part on changes in attitudes and behaviour that have been bred by and maintained through highly centralised structures and procedures. It requires a thorough design, analysis and preparation, a strong and sustained political commitment, extra resources, new patterns of administrative behaviour, a reorientation of attitudes and relationships and indeed a long period of time for implementation before positive results could be derived. Further, along with the devolution of powers and responsibilities, democratic decentralisation, for its success, requires transfer of adequate financial resources to the local bodies and also a component of training for the central administrators, local staff, officers and the people at large. Decentralisation of any sort imposes additional (or at least different) burdens on administrators and institutions, which requires extra staff for the purpose. In addition, existing staff and people's representatives must be informed of their new responsibilities and instructed on how to carry them out. Moreover, decentralisation implies a new set of roles for central administrators, requiring less central initiatives and greater facilitation of decentralized planning, decision making and management. Training, therefore can help in reorienting central administrators to their new tasks of supervision and support.

Hence, to strengthen the Panchayati Raj Institutions and to have a successful and sustainable Panchayati Raj System of decentralised governance, the latest effort/attempt of Lakshadweep Administration in the direction of democratic decentralisation and decentralised governance should take into account the above principles.

As mentioned earlier, despite their inherent central tendencies (because of the political and administrative set-up) the Islands of Lakshadweep have, in comparison to the States in the mainland, the advantage of having the most fertile land for the democratic seed-drilling process and developing a strong Panchayati Raj structure. In view of Islands' small size, less and homogeneous population (100 per cent Muslims with just four castes), higher literacy rate including that of women (81.70 per cent male and 72.89 per cent female) and the instances of voluntary contribution of labour for community purposes, Panchayati Raj Institutions in Lakshadweep are likely to function better than their counterparts in other parts of the country and could emerge as a trend-setter in this regard. Further, keeping in mind the above characteristics of the Islands which take them closer to the Swiss Cantons (in comparison), if the provision of 'recall' of the chairpersons and members of the Village Panchayats by the Gram Sabha could be incorporated in the Lakashadweep Panchayats Regulation, 1994, it might be judiciously and effectively used by the people, thus making the representatives of the people more accountable and heralding a new era of decentralised governance in Lakshadweep.

NOTES

1. N.S. Mannadiyar (ed.); "Administration of Lakshadweep" in *The Gazetteer of India, Union Territory of Lakshadweep*, Kavaratti, 1977.
2. M. Ramunny, "*Laccadive, Minicoy and Amindivi Islands*", Publications Division, Ministry of Information and Braodcasting, Government of India, New Delhi, 1972, p. 32.
3. R.H. Ellis, *A Short Account of Laccadive Islands and Minicoy*, Madras, 1924.
4. *Jagir* means a grant of the public revenues of an area to a person with power to collect and enjoy them and to administer the government there.
5. Coir monopoly was introduced in 1765 by Bommaly Raja by which he established a monopoly of purchase of coir products of the islands.
6. R.H. Ellis, *A Short Account of Laccadive Islands and Minicoy*, Madras, 1924.
7. Initially there were four special types if C.D. Blocks which started functioning from January 1971 with their headquarters at Amini, Andrott, Kavaratti and Minicoy. The Amini block was later bifurcated into two from 2nd October 1976, i.e, C.D. Block Amini (consisting of Amini and Kadmat Islands with Headquarters at Amini) and C.D. Block Kiltan (consisting of Chetlat, Bitra and Kiltan with Headquarters at Kiltan). Thus, there are five blocks in this Union Territory now.
8. The Island Councils in Lakshadweep came into existence in 1990 as a result of the Lakshadweep Island Councils Regulation, 1988 (No. 4 of 1988).
9. Jos Chathkulam and V.K. Kurien, *Political Economy of Development Administration: A Study of Jawahar Rozgar Yojana in Lakshadweep Island*, (mimeo), Centre for Rural Management, Kottayam, 1995, p. 5. Also see, Centre for Rural Management (1996), Report of the Sub-Regional Workshop on Panchayati Raj, Organised by the Centre for Rural Management from 8-10 March, 1996, at Kavaratti Island, Kavaratti, Lakshadweep. The workshop was sponsored by Rajiv Gandhi Foundation, New Delhi : Chathukulam Jos C (1996), "Panchayati Raj in Lakshadweep : A Non-Starter", *Kurukshetra*, Vol. XLIV, No. 12, September.
10. Henry Maddick, *Panchayati Raj : A Study of Rural Local Government in India*, Longman, London, 1970, p. 75.

11. B.S. Bhargava and V. Venkatakrishnan, "Constitutionalisation of Panchayati Raj" in G.Palanithurai (ed.) *New Panchayati Raj System : Status and Prospects*, Kanishka, New Delhi, 1996. Also see, B.S. Bhargava and V. Venkatakrishnan (1996), "The Process of Democratic Seed-Drilling in Lakshadweep : The Case of Panchayats", *Madhya Pradesh Journal of Social Sciences*, Vol.1, No. 2, July-December; B.S. Bhargava and V. Venkatakrishnan (1996), "The Process of Democratic Seed-Drilling in Lakshadweep : The Case of Panchayats", Institute for Social and Economic Change, Bangalore (A Research Working Paper).

12. According to Section 12 of the Lakshadweep Panchayats Regulation 1994, a person shall be disqualified for being chosen as, and for being, a member of a panchayat if he – (a) is not a citizen of India; or (b) has not attained the age of twenty-one years; or (c) holds any office of profit under the Central Government; or (d) any local authority for misconduct unless a period of five years has elapsed from such dismissal; or (e) any person who has directly or indirectly any share of monetary interest in any work done by or to the panchayat or any contract or employment with, under or by or on behalf of the panchayat or any contract or employment with, under or by or on behalf of the panchayat; (f) is an undischarged insolvent; or (g) is of sound mind and stands so declared by a competent court; or (h) sentenced to imprisonment for not less than six months and five years have not elapsed since his release; (i) is in arrear for such period as may be described of any tax, fee or other sum due to the panchayat; or (j) is so qualified by or under any law for the time being in force for the purpose of election to the House of People, provided that no person shall be disqualified on the ground that he is less than twenty five years of age if he has attained the age of twenty one years' or (k) is so qualified by or under any law made by the Parliament.

13. For some interesting details, see Jos Chatukulam *et al.* (eds.), Bemidukalude Punaravatharam Lakshadweep Pancahayat Rajum (Malayalam), Centre for Rural Management, Kottayam, 1996.

14. Direct election of members of panchayats at all levels, uniform term of five years, reservation for Scheduled Tribes in proportion to their population, one-third reservation for women, similar reservation for chairpersons, provision for State Finance Commission, provision for State Election Commission, reconstruction of Panchayats within six months in case of their dissolution etc. are some of the major mandatory provisions of the Constitution (Seventy-third) Amendment Act, 1992.

15. Article 243G of the Constitution leaves it to the State Legislatures to endow the panchayats with such powers and authority as may be necessary to enable them to function as institutions of self-government and such law may contain

provisions for the devolution of powers and responsibilities upon panchayats at the appropriate level, subject to such conditions as may be specified therein, with respect to (a) the preparation of plans for economic development and social justice, and (b) the implementation of schemes for economic development and social justice as may be entrusted to them including those in relation to the matters listed in the Eleventh Schedule.

16. Article 243E of the Constitution (Seventy-third) Amendment Act, 1992 states that :

    (1) Every Panchayat, unless sooner dissolved under any law for the time being in force, shall continue for five years from the date appointed for its first meeting and no longer.

    (2) No amendment of any law for the time being in force shall have the effect of causing dissolution of a panchayat at any level, which is functioning immediately before such amendment, till the expiration of its duration specified in clause (1).

    (3) An election to constitute a Panchayat shall be completed

        (a) before the expiry of its duration specified in clause (1);

        (b) before the expiration of a period of six months from the date of its dissolution;

    Provided that where the reminder of the period for which the dissolved panchayat would have continued is less than the reminder of the period for which the dissolved panchayat would have continued is less than six months, it shall not be necessary to hold any election under this clause for constituting the panchayat for such period.

    (4) A panchayat constituted upon the dissolution of a panchayat before the expiration of its duration shall continue only for the remainder of the period for which the dissolved panchayat would have continued under clause (1) had it not been so dissolved.

2

NEW PANCHAYATI RAJ SYSTEM IN BIHAR

CHANDAN DATTA

Bihar occupies a unique position in the map of India. It is one of the highest populous State in the country. (Second highest based 2001 census). The density of population is nearly double of all India average. Literacy level is well below the national average. The infant mortality rate is higher than Indian average.

The rural population is higher than national average. In some districts of north Bihar rural population accounted for over 90 per cent. The higher concentration of population in rural areas led to over dependence on agriculture. The average size of holding is almost half of all India size. The north Bihar is highly flood prone. The absence of viable strategies of flood control and water management led to backwardness of the region and the state. The agriculture growth of the state is well below the national growth.

The economic and social infrastructure as judged by per capita electricity consumption, road length per lakh population and hospital beds per lakh compared unfavourably with the national average.

The State so far could not procure its due share of funds available with various financial agencies. This was evident from the fact that till March 1996, the share of Bihar in total sanctions from the financial institutions was only 1.32 per cent. The increase in advance to them. The credit deposit rate in the State was abysmally low (27%) as compared to all India (60%).

In Bihar large proportion of population living below the poverty line. Employment in agriculture sector is increasing. Bihar witnessed a large scale migration of labour since late seventies of the states of Punjab, Haryana, Delhi, etc. This is due to high fluctuation in the availability of employment in the State.

From early sixties till the end of eighties for almost three decades not a single chief minister lasted full terms resulting into constant political maneuverability and leg pulling. As such they did not find time to think for the State and feel the pulse of the flight. The uncertain tenure of the chief minister had a demoralizing and adverse impact on the bureaucrats functioning longer remained answerable. Responsibility was the first casualty in this period. By and large people also become unconcerned. Though Bihar was the seat of Jaiprakash Narayan who led student and youth movement during 1974-75. But its momentum and impact was short lived.

"Caste" remained the only factor for the politicians to align with the people. Then came in canalization of the system and the politicians played the caste card to their advantage and the state's development was given a back seat. The work culture was the worst victim in the newly developed socio-political and economic scenario. No one thought of economic issues inflicting the State, everyone conveniently forget that only by addressing the economic issue, a vibrant and sustained development could be brought about. The zamindary system in the state introduced by the British Government was described as the victim of the peace, which strengthens feudal framework and was not condncive to the industrialization or modernization of state's economy. In the post-Independence era, the zamindary system was abolished in 1955. This meant that the system which was rightly or wrongly accepted by the tillers of the soil came to an end and no system was introduced to fill in the void thus created.

Though the community development programme started in early fifties, it could not meet the aspirations of the people to identify themselves with the people. The Government aids and subsidies in the subsequent years made the people dependent on the government, though the subsidized inputs helped the large farmers in a big way. Everybody started looking at the government for anything and everything. This led to lack of initiative on the past of the people. There were no new avenues opened up and no new ideas innovated in the State. The net result was an over crowded and underdeveloped agriculture sector, an almost non-start industrial sector and slowly moving tertiary sector with a huge army of unemployed youths.

There was a need felt for introduction of democratic institutions at the grass root level to ensure people's participation in planning and implementation of rural development activities. The Constitution was amended to strengthen Panchayati Raj Institutions. It was a strange that on some pretext or other, Panchayat elections were not held for a pretty long time/period. At last election held in April 2001. The Zamindary system in the State introduced by the British Government was described as the victim of the peace, which strengthens.

Panchayat History in Brief

Soon after Independence, the Bihar Government enacted the Bihar Panchayat Raj Act, 1947, and it was implemented throughout the state in the following year, the aims and objectives of the legislation noted that the Act was enacted to establish local self-governance in the rural communities so that they could make their social and economic development. The legislative measure got a boost from the provision in Article 40 of the Constitution enacted a few years after the enactment of the Bihar Panchayati Raj Act, 1947. The Article 40 mentions that the State governments shall make efforts to constitute Panchayat and to provide them requisite powers and responsibilities so that they can act as institutions of local self government.

When the Constitution was adopted in 1950 the Panchayats all over the country got constitutional sanction. That is another thing that at that time no mention was made on the structure and functions of Panchayats. As a result the Panchayati Raj Institutions (PRIs) could not work in an effective fashion in the State and the concept of rural development could not be met.

Planned development started in the country in 1952, when the first elected government headed by the Prime Minister Jawaharlal Nehru took reins of the country. Alongside the implementation of the First Five Year Plan blocks were set up all over the country to implement community development projects. But since there was no participation of panchayats in the community development projects, no significant progress in rural development could be made. A committee headed by Balwantrai Mehta recommended in 1957 set up three-tier Panchayat Raj system throughout the country The three-tier Panchayati Raj system included constitution of Zilla Parishad at the district level, Panchayat Samiti at the Block level and Gram Panchayat at the village level. Various experiments were carried out through these Panchayats, but they failed to bring about desired results.

Since there was no participation of all sections of the society like weaker sections and women in the Panchayats, a large section of the people remained deprived of benefits of development. In view of this parliament enacted 73rd Constitutional Amendment in 1992 following acceptance of the report of Ashok Mehta Committee constituted in 1978. All the State government were directed to implement provisions of the 73rd Constitutional Amendment in their respective States with immediate effect. The amendment not only provided the Panchayats rights pertaining to development but also provided them political importance. Following the directives of the Central Government the Bihar Government enacted the Bihar Panchayati Raj Act, 1993.

Probably the greatest achievement of the new Panchayati Raj system is that it has made elaborate arrangement to provide reservation to those very people who were left outside earlier in the Panchayati Raj system. Thus reservation was made for scheduled for each of them were reserved for women of these disadvantaged groups.

73rd Amendment and After

The Bihar Government implemented Bihar Panchayati Raj Act, 1993, throughout the State by an order issued by the Panchayati Raj directorate. Accordingly the old Panchayati Raj Act, 1947, was cancelled. But to maintain continuity the new Act has provision in section 157(f) the existing Panchayats will continue to function as per new Act till elections to the Panchayats are held.

The state government took benefit of this lacuna, and silence of the 73rd Amendment to the Constitution of India regarding the first election after the enactment of States Panchayati Raj laws, to put off elections to the Panchayats. While elections were held twice in almost all the States, in Bihar the first election could not take place till April, 2001.

Delimitation of the Panchayats was first issue and the State government referred the case to the State Election Commission. The real problem, however, cropped up on the issue of reservation. Though the constitution has provision for the reservation posts for scheduled castes and scheduled tribes, it is silent on reservation of posts for Backward Classes and has left this to the discretion of State. Accordingly, Bihar legislature passed a law to fix quota for the Backward Classes. This infuriated a section of society and they moved to the Patna High Court with a petition. After lengthy hearing the Patna High Court ruled on March 18, 1996, that single posts like Mukhiya, Sarpanch, Pramukh and Adhyakshas would not be reserved. It also ruled that reservation would not exceed 50 per cent of the total seats in different tiers of Panchayats. It was against this decision that the Bihar Government filed a petition in the Supreme Court. On February 24, 1997 the bench of judges hearing the case dissolved the Panchayats for which the elections were held in 1978. It vested the work of Gram Panchayats on Gram Sewaks and that of Panchayat Samiti on Block Development Officers.

On July 22, 1997 the Supreme Court bench ruled that no election could be held till it gave the verdict. This created a peculiar situation as funds for rural development continued to lapse. The Central Rural Development Secretary made it clear that no fund would be allocated till elections were held.

Meanwhile, another case was filed by the Panchayat Parishad, a network of Mukhiyas of the State, over the delay on ruling. After that the Panchayat Bachao Abhiyan was formed with a view to fighting the cause of the people who had been deprived of their rights. To press the point further various social organizations of the State launched a signature and postcard campaign. Their target was to collect one lakh signatures. The postcards were addressed to Supreme Court and a copy of each was sent to the President, the Prime Minister, the Government, the Chief Minister and the State Election Commission.

In another development the Rural Development Minister announced in July 1998 in the State Legislative Assembly that the government would hold Panchayat elections in the State only after the Supreme Court disposed of the petition challenging the Patna High Court order striking down certain provision of reservation in the Bihar Panchayati Raj Act, 1993.

On March 28, 1999, activists of the Bihar Pradesh Lok Samiti and the Manav Jodo Abhiyan decided to organize *dharnas* at all the district headquarters on April 8 to mount pressure on the government to hold Panchayat elections at the earliest. Due to joint efforts of several NGOs *Panchayat bachao abhiyan* and several activists the Patna High Court ordered the Bihar government announced that it would hold elections to Panchayats and local bodies in February 2001. But the High Court order put the State Government in a fix as it ruled out any reservation for single posts. Thus, it kept posts of Mukhiya and Sarpanch at the Gram Panchayat level, Pramukh at the Block level and Adhyaksha at the District level out of ambit of reservation. Besides it directed the government to keep the reservation within 50 per cent. Then government decided to make suitable amendment in the Panchayati Raj Act, 1993. After the amendment it took several months and lastly panchayat election took place in April 2001.

MAIN PROVISION IN BIHAR PANCHAYAT RAJ ACT, 1993

GRAM SABHA

The Gram Sabha shall meet form time to time but not more than three months shall interview (gap) in between two meetings. It is the responsibility of the Mukhia convene the meeting. If Mukhiya (President of Gram Panchayat) fail to convene the meeting the

Executive Officer of the Panchayat Samiti shall convene the meeting. The quorum for Gram Sabha shall be one- tenth of the total members of Gram Sabha.

One important features of Bihar Act is that the Gram Sabha can also form one or more vigilance committees consisting of persons who are not members of the Gram Panchayat to supervise the Gram Panchayat activities relating to the Gram (village). Reports of these committees are also to be placed before the Gram Sabha.

GRAM PANCHAYAT (G.P.)

The District Magistrate (DM) declares the area of G.P. The population of GP is normally 7000.

The President of G.P. (Mukhiya) to be elected directly. The Vice President (Up-Mukhia) to be elected/selected among the elected members of G.P.

Functions of G.P

The G.P. has been assigned 31 functions ranging from preparation of Annual Plans to the Public Distribution System (PDS). However, the real devolution yet to took place. The G.P. shall meet at least once in two months. President can also call the meeting. Special meetings can be called in three days notice. The Quorum for a meeting of G.P. shall be at least half of the total number of members.

Functions and Powers of Gram Panchayat

1. Preparation of annual plans for the development of the Panchayat area.
2. Preparation of annual budget.
3. Power for mobilizing relief in natural calamities.
4. Removal of encroachments on public properties.
5. Organizing voluntary labour and contribution for community works.
6. Maintenance of essentials statistics of Gram Panchayat.

7. Agriculture including Agriculture extension.
8. Animal Husbandry, Dairy and Poultry.
9. Fisheries.
10. Social and Farm Forestry, Minor Forestry Produce, Fuels and Fodder.
11. Khadi, Village and Cottage Industries.
12. Rural Housing.
13. Drinking Water.
14. Roads, Building, Culverts, Bridges, Ferries, Waterways and other means of communication.
15. Rural Electrification.
16. Non-Conventional Energy Source.
17. Poverty Alleviation Programme.
18. Education including primary and secondary schools.
19. Libraries.
20. Cultural Activities.
21. Public Health and Family Welfare.
22. Women and Child Development.
23. Welfare of weaker sections and in particular the schedule castes and scheduled tribes.
24. Public Distribution System.
25. Construction and maintenance of Cattle Sheds, Pounds and Cart Stands.

Assigned Functions

According to Act, Government may transfer the management and maintenance of forest situated in the Panchayat area, management of wastelands, grazing lands or vacant land, "belonging to the Government", collection of land revenue "on behalf of the Government" and the maintenance of such records.

Standing Committee

Every G.P. shall constitute the following three Committees by election of selection. These Committees are:

- Production Committee.
- Social Justice Committee.
- Amenities Committee.

Each Committee shall consist of not less than three and not more than five members. The President shall be an ex-officio chairperson of all the three committees. The Social Justice Committee shall include at least one woman member and one SC. However, the G.P. have power to revise or modify any decision of these committees.

Taxation Power of G.P.

The G.P. may impost yearly tax on the following:

- House Tax.
- On Professionals, trade, etc.

The G.P. can also realize the following fees

- Fees on registration of vehicles
- Fee for providing sanitary arrangements at such places of pilgrimage, fares and means.
- Water tax.
- Lighting fee.
- Conservancy tax.

The G.P. can make Bye-Laws

Thc GP has the power to make bye-laws with the approval of Z.P.

G.P. to prepare annual budget

The G.P. shall prepare annual budget of its estimated receipts and disbursements for the following year and shall get it approved in its meeting by a majority of its members present.

Staff of G.P.

According to Act each G.P. shall have a Government appointed secretary.

Power of Government to dissolve and reconstitute Panchayats

The Government by an order published in the officials Gazette, dissolve a Gram Panchayat on the grounds that its area has been altered and it needs to be constituted a fresh. This clearly shows the powerful role of the State Government has in the G.P.

PANCHAYAT SAMITI (PS)

For every development Block there shall be a Panchayat Samiti (PS). It shall consist of directly elected members, each members representing a population of approximately 5,000. The elected members of the PS shall elect/select two members from among themselves as its President (Pramukh) and Vice-President (Up-Pramukh). The PS shall meet at least once in every two months. Half of the total number of its members shall form the quorum for the ordinary meetings.

Besides the directly elected members, the PS also have GP presidents under their PS, MP, MLA and MLC of their areas are the ex-officio members.

Functions of PS

According to Act PS has been assigned 27 functions. But this assignment of the functions is subject to such conditions as may be prescribed by the government from time to time. This clearly shows governments control over the PS.

Functions and Powers of Panchayat Samiti

1. Subject to such conditions as may be prescribed by the Government, from time to time, the PS's shall undertake the following:

   (i) Preparation of the annual plans in respect of the schemes entrusted to it by virtue of the Act and these assigned to it by the Government or the Z.P. and submission thereof the Z.P. within the prescribed time for integration with the District Plan.

(ii) Consideration and consolidation of the Annual Plans of all Gram Panchayats in the PS and submission of the consolidated plan to the Z.P.

(iii) Preparation of annual budget of the Panchayat Samiti and submission of the consolidated plan to the Zilla Parishad.

(iv) Performing such functions and executing such as may be entrusted to it by the Government or the Z.P.

2. Agriculture including agriculture extension.
3. Land improvement and soil conservation.
4. Minor irrigation, water management and watershed development.
5. Poverty Alleviation Programmes
6. Animal Husbandry, Dairying and Poultry.
7. Fisheries.
8. Khadi, Village and Cottage Industries.
9. Rural Housing.
10. Drinking Water.
11. Social and Farm Forestry, Minor Forest Produce, Fuel and Fodder.
12. Roads, Building, Bridge, Ferries Waterways and other means of communication.
13. Non-Conventional energy sources.
14. Education including primary and secondary schools.
15. Technical training and vocational education.
16. Adult and non-formal education.
17. Cultural Activities.
18. Markets and Fairs.
19. Health and Family Welfare.

20. Women and Child Development.
21. Social Welfare including welfare of the handicapped and mentally retarded.
22. Welfare of the weaker sections and in particular of the SC and ST.
23. Maintenance of community assets.
24. Public distribution system.
25. Rural electrification.
26. Co-operation.
27. Libraries.
28. Such other functions as may be entrusted.

Standing Committee

The PS shall have the three Standing Committees. These are :

- General Standing Committee.
- Finance, Audit and Planning Committee.
- Social Justice Committee.

The President and the Vice-President are the members of each committee while Executive Officer of PS (Block Development Officer) shall be the ex-officio Secretary of all the standing committee. The functioning of these committees shall follow the "Guidelines laid down by the "Government from time to time". Therefore, these committees are not really empowered to take their own decisions.

Executive Officer

The Government shall appoint an officer not below the rank of a Deputy Collector as the Executive Officer of the PS.

The Executive Officer among other work "supervise and control" the execution of all works of PS.

Taxation Power

The PS can levy tolls in respect of any ferry established by it or under its management. The PS can also levy the following fees :

- Fee on the registration vehicles.
- Fee for providing sanitary arrangements.
- Fee for license for a market.
- Water rate.
- Light up rate.

Budget of PS

Every PS shall prepare in each year a budget of its estimated receipts and disbursement for the following year and shall get approved in its meeting by a majority member present.

THE ZILLA PARISHAD (ZP)

For each district there shall be a Z.P. having jurisdiction of entire district excluding urban areas included in a Municipality or Municipal Corporation.

Corporation of Z.P.

The Z.P. consist of directly elected members, all Presidents of PS, Local MP, MLAs, MLCs. Each 50,000 population elects a ZP member.

The elected members of ZP elect/select President (Adhyaksha) and Vice-President (Upadhyaksha).

The Z.P. shall meet at least once in three months.

Functions of Z.P.

The Z.P. is to make plans for economic development and promotion of Social Justice in the district and ensure co-ordinated implementation of such plans. According to Act, the Z.P. assigned 24 functions.

Normally District Magistrate (DM) is the Chief Executive Officer of ZP. The Chief Planning Officer and the Chief Accounts Officer of the Z.P shall be appointed by the Government and shall be drawn from the All India Services.

Functions and Power of Z.P.

It shall be the function of a Z.P. to prepare plans for economic development and social justice of the district and to ensure the co-ordinated implementation of such plans those enumerated below:

1. Agriculture
2. Irrigation, ground water resources and watershed development
3. Horticulture
4. Statistics
5. Rural Electrification
6. Distribution of essential commodities
7. Soil Conservation
8. Horticulture
9. Social Forestry
10. Animal Husbandry and Dairy
11. Minor Forest Produce, Fuel, Fodder
12. Fisheries
13. Household and small scale industries
14. Health and Hygiene
15. Education
16. Poverty Alleviation Programes
17. Social reform activities

Standing Committees at the Z.P. Level

There are provisions of five standing committees in Z.P. These are:

- A General standing committee
- A finance Audit and Planning Committee

- A Social Justice Committee
- An Education and Health Committee
- An Agriculture and Industries Committee

The Z.P. president is the Chairperson of general and finance committee. Chief Executive Officer is the ex-officio secretary of all the standing committees.

Budget

Every Z.P. shall prepare in each year a budget of its estimated receipts and disbursements for the following year and the same to be passed by the majority of the members present.

Taxation

"Based on Government prescription" Z.P may levy tolls in respect of any ferry established by it or under its management. Also levy the following:

- Fees on the registration of boats or vehicles
- A fee for providing sanitary arrangements
- A fee for license for fair or *mela*
- A lighting rate
- Water rate

At each tier there are reservation of seats for women and backward classes. However, G.P. President from the constitutional provisions.

NGO EFFORTS TO STRENGTHEN PANCHAYATI RAJ INSTITUTIONS IN BIHAR

Gaya Experience

The whole process of interventions was discussed with VOs in an organization workshop organized jointly by Bihar Panchayati Raj Samiti and Cencored (an NGO based at Patna) at Gaya in which 18 VOs participated. During the workshop a joint decision was taken to work on Panchayati Raj Institution issues. The workshop also stressed the need for creating a team of field level workers to transmit the messages. During the workshop two methods for message transmission were agreed upon; one was lecture and another was the use of local folk and cultural media. It has been a well-recognized fact that use of folk culture as a medium of communication is very effective; especially among weaker and marginalized sections of society. The need for popular communicating media emerged from the workshop.

Outcome of Gaya Experience

During the workshop, two methods of communicating messages, one the lecture method and second the folk media through songs were tested in the nearby village in small groups where the training was organized. It was the finding of the participants that the message given in form of song was well received by the community. This workshop proved as an event which strengthen the above stated beliefs. In this light VOs participating in that workshop stressed the need for developing communication resources for wider application in Panchayati Raj Institution awareness. In the light of resolutions in the workshop it was decided at NGO level to work in that direction.

Creating Cultural Team

Subsequently, it was felt at NGO level that so far communication through folk media was concerned it could not be achieved without training, specially of those who were identified at community level and were ready to get involved in it. To meet this need to organize a separate training programme on media it was decided linkages with local (grass root) Mandals which constituted the cultural team got developed at different organizational level. Savera, Ujala, Deep of Bettiah (West Champaran), Mahila Shishu Kalyan Sansthan, Gopalganj are some good examples.

The formation of cultural team and its internal linkages with VOs and Support Organization proved quite effective tool to communicate the messages of the 73rd Amendment. In the early phase of Panchayati Raj Institution programme the first printed materials published was *Apna Gaon Apna Desh,* a simple illustration of Panchayati Raj including the new provisions of 73rd Constitution Amendment. This book was used for orienting VOs regarding Panchayati Raj—preparing reading materials for the grass root community as well as for the VOs and the workers on Panchayati Raj Institution and related activities. On the strength of the indications received from the field experiences and from different workshops and trainings CENCORED developed more materials which is heartily used by the VOs.

Madhpur Experience

Based on Gaya experience CENCORED organized its first State level training of trainers of Panchayati Raj aided with communication and folk media at Lot Jagiriti Kendra, Madhpur. The first session was on theoretical understanding on Panchayati Raj and second half dealt with converting the messages into the media in the form of Nukkad Natak, Puppetry, Story Telling Slogans, Posters, etc. Field demonstration and feedback from community was apart of curriculum. In the whole process the responses which come from the community was very positive and encouraging. Based on Madhpur experience communication and development of folk media (songs, nukkad etc). was conceptualized as integral part of Panchayati Raj Institution programme and as an innovative tool providing joyful understanding of the intricate legal provisions of 73rd Constitutional Amendment in favour of *dalits* and woman.

BDVS (Barh) Experience

Bihar Dalit Vikas Samiti working for the *dalits* having a very large network in North and Central Bihar, requested CENCORED to organize a training on Panchayati Raj for their Chief Organizers (Pramukh) and Community Workers. The first training was held in December 1995 which was attended by participants from 12 districts. It was a memorable experience for CENCORED training team because it was a learning process for them too. Training was designed for VOs staffs but the participants were not up to the level expected. It was observed that participants did not follow the lessons imparted through lectures. Subsequently the training design was changed and posters were made simultaneously covering different messages of Panchayati Raj Institution and through these posters training was conducted. Approximately 51 posters were prepared and deliberated through lectures. On evaluation, it was found that this method proved very effective to pass on the messages to the participants having lower level of education.

After the training BDVS requested CENCORED to prepare the book, based on those posters with simple sentences. "Asthniya Swasashan ka Paigam" was thus prepared and was in the form of a folder and this folder was effectively utilized by the trainers and workers of Panchayati Raj Institution in small group contact and proved to be very effective.

Audio cassettes were developed in Maghai, Bhojpuri (Regional language) from the songs prepared and composed by the participants in various trainings and workshops on Panchayati Raj Institution. Songs were also collected from VOs who were given training in effective use of folk media. These songs were compiled and recorded by CENCORED and the cassettes were prepared which was purchased by VOs for their use. It proved to be very popular in the field. In this process cassettes in three regional languages were prepared and these songs were also compiled in a form of a booklet for distribution to VOs for their use in group meetings and field programmes.

Innovation in Panchayati Raj

Information Centre

Information must be accessible to the common people so that they can intelligently and effectively participate in the development processes of their area. Information available today is confined to those information. The government mechanism has made the problem more difficult, moreover the irony is that middle men, local workers, political leaders are exploiting innocent and ignorant masses due to non-accessibility of information.

Origin

A workshop was organized on the role of voluntary organizations in Panchayat by CENCORED immediately after the passage of 73rd Constitutional Amendment. After this amendment in 1993, anticipating early Panchayat election, it was difficult to inculcate among the masses in simple way the intricacies of legal aspects of Panchayati Raj enactment. In this context voluntary organizations felt the need of a centre, through which the common men of society and intending candidates contesting election could be provided with messages of New Panchayati Raj, as well as to provide information regarding the casting of six votes, filling up nomination form, rectification of voters list, demarcation of constituency. To make available details on these counts the concept of Information Centre was developed. The intention behind the implementation of Information Centres was also to strengthen women folk, especially women of deprived and backward class, in discharging their roles in sharing power in Panchayati Raj under the provision of reservation for them for the first time in Panchayat history.

Role of Information Centres has been envisaged at three levels.

(a) Before Election

(b) During Election

(c) Post Election Period

(a) Before Election Period

- Voters' awareness dissemination of messages of New Panchayati Raj.
- Rectification in Voters' List delimitation of Ward and Panchayat constituency to help communities know about their placement in this respect.
- To make voters and would-be candidates, aware regarding the process of casting votes and filling up nomination forms.
- To make available the various Nomination Forms for the various Panchayat positions.

(b) During Election Period

- To help in conducting clear, impartial and peaceful Panchayat elections.
- To encourage and motivate voters to cast their votes.

(c) Post Election Period

- Training and capacity building of elected representatives of Wards and Panchayat. In the light of above circumstances, following objectives were set for the Information Centres.
- To disseminate the information related to 73rd Constitution Amendment in simple language.
- To ensure the community participation in rectification of voters, list, demarcation of ward and Panchayat Constituencies.
- To enable the candidates, intending to contest election, to fill up the different nomination forms for different Panchayat position.
- To provide information regarding value of Panchayat election and six votes to common voters.
- To ensure the decrease in the cases of invalid and cancelled votes.
- To act as a link between community and government in holding clear, impartial and peaceful election.
- To act as a facilitator for *dalit* and women during election period.

Considering the immediate Panchayat election, duration for Information Centre was considered as one month after the Panchayat election and its structural process was started.

Efforts in Panchayat Raj Advocacy Programme in Bihar (1998-2000)

Year	Activities	Objectives	Achievements
1	2	3	4
May 1998	Contact with some VOs Intellectuals and enlightened citizens. Meeting of active members Press Correspondents meet.	Search of active citizen to establish coordination committee or forum by enlightening understanding of election of nearly dead Bihar Panchayat. To initiate regarding political discourse for early Panchayat election in Bihar and to take initiative in formation forum. Wide declaration of nature of campaign.	Acceptance for setting up a team of active members. General consensus for Panchayati Raj forum. Dissemination of campaign programme in village through press.
July 1998	• Public contact through representative of Regional Organizations. • State level programmes of post card writing to Honourable Supreme Court. • Signature Campaign at State level.	• People's awareness • To put pressure for early disposal of dispute. • To activate High Court regarding the gravity issue and to solicit advocate's cooperation through distributing printed materials.	• Development of understanding regarding Panchayat election among people, media and other under arbitrational banner of campaign. • Submission of memorandum before Honourable High Court consensus regarding

Contd......

Contd......Efforts in Panchayat Raj Advocacy Programme

1	2	3	4
	• Demonstration by 200 women and VOs representatives before Honourable Patna High Court. • State level meeting. • Contact and meeting with Delhi based gentries and organizations. Topic–Election in Bihar who is culprit.	• Wide endorsement of wider campaign for Bihar Panchayat Election. • To prepare design for the National Level Campaign for drawing attention, through public movement at State level and to review the progress.	future action plan through advocates of network.
August 1998	• State level public contact. • Press conference. • Protest demonstration, rally, Natak, Seminar, Foot March Cycle rally and signature campaign at District and Block levels. • Meeting of Delhi level Implementing Committee at CSDS. • Meeting of Mr. Amarendra Sharan, Advocate, Supreme Court with active member of campaign committee.	• To mobilize resource for programme implementation. • To make aware regarding programme. • To organize Press conference at Delhi. • To organize seminar and Jan Panchayat at Rajghat New Delhi. • To prepare for Seminar, Press conference. • To provide information of seminar and Jan Panchayat programme.	• Success in contact campaign. • Appreciation by the representative of all Newspapers, committed to highlight the issue. • Sensitization of people of state towards the issues. • Consensus decision was taken. • Seminar and Jan Panchayat were organized under leadership of Mr.V.M. Tarkunde.

Contd......

Contd......*Efforts in Panchayat Raj Advocacy Programme*

1	2	3	4
	• Contact with Mr. Ramanuj Sharma, petitioner of Panchayat Parishad.	• To demand justice from Bapu (Mahatma Gandhi) to sensitize journalists, and intellectuals for early panchayats election in Bihar. • To pressure the case of petitioner as per decision of Jan Panchayat. • To get NOC.	• Nearly 300 men and women participated in Jan Panchayat. • It was decided to procure NOC from previous advocate and to mention the case. • Determination of date for Delhi departure.
September 1998	• To procure NOC for Amarendra Sharan Advocate Supreme Court. • To participate in the meeting of and formation of joint coordination committee of CENCORED and Bihar Rajya Panchayat Parishad.	• To mention the case • To sensitize the members of Parishad regarding the issue and decide the future linkage.	• NOC and affidavit were made available on 07.09.98 to the advocate. • A joint coordination committee of CENCORED and Parishad was formed.
October 1998	• To have contact with elightened citizen politicians and media people through coordination committee and to appeal through Akhil	• To sensitize people regarding the issue • To mention the case.	• Bihar government filed before Honourable Supreme Court for early hearing. • Available documents were presented to advocate.

Contd......

Contd......Efforts in Panchayat Raj Advocacy Programme

1	2	3	4
	Bhartiya Jan Vigyan Congress for early Panchayat Election.		
November 1998	• Advocate to mention the case before Honourable Supreme Court • Meeting with retired Judge and Advocates	• Early disposal of pending cases. • As above.	• The case was mentioned on behalf of Government of India on 10.11.98 and by Amarendra Sharan on 21.11.98 • Meeting was held at the residence of Mr. V.M. Tarkunde and emphasis was laid down on organizing national level seminar.
December 1998	• To procure relevant documents. • To available all sorts of documents relevant to Panchayati Raj.	• To prepare the material for National Seminar.	• Following materials were prepared and produced: • Main Paper. • Panchayat Election and Bihar • Panchayati Raj system in Bihar up date status. • Rural Justice system in Bihar. • Chronology.

Contd

Contd......Efforts in Panchayat Raj Advocacy Programme

1	2	3	4
			• Bihar Panchayati Raj Act, 1993 and Panchayati election a reality. • Panchayati Raj Act in Bihar and its electoral problems. • Present status of Panchayat in Bihar–Election and enact ment.
January 1999	• Media management at Delhi level. • Organization of National Seminar on topic–Panchayat Election and Bihar. • Procurement of 50,000 signatures from 2,00,000 signatures from ISS a Delhi level organization and submission in the office of Honourable Chief Justice, Honurable Supreme Court in delegation.	• To raise at national level. • To widen the path of early election in Bihar. • To sensitize Judiciary regarding the issue for early formation of constitutional bench for early disposal of Panchayat election case.	• Contact and discussion with press correspondents and others. • Successful organization of programme on 19.01.99 at Gandhi Shanti Partisthan. • A delegation of five people submitted the signature in Honourable Supreme Court.

Contd......

Contd......Efforts in Panchayat Raj Advocacy Programme

1	2	3	4
February 1999	• Remained in regular contact with officials of Panchayati Raj department of Bihar Government other VO's and library of Bihar Vidhan Sabha.	• To procure copies of Government orders regarding PRI system. • To establish cordial coordination with Government officials for obtaining relevant documents for helping advocate.	• Copies of order were procured and co-ordination was established.
March 1999	• Visit of three Panchayat of Bihar. • To obtain signature by dispatching letters to Honourable President of India, and Honourable Members of Parliament. • Meeting and discussion with core team of Delhi, Ex-Justice Mr. V.M. Tarkunde and Advocate.	• To obtain documents of Judgment passed by old Gram Kachahari. • To obtain signature after sensitizing political leaders so that constitutional bench be formed early. • As above. • To give preference to case number for early hearing by mentioning it.	• Minute books of Gram Kachaharies of Mokama, Beldaur, and Saharasa Gram Panchayat were produced. • Draft of letter was prepared with consultation with core team and advocate. • Bundle of 50,000 signature was taken back from Honourable Supreme Court and News of constitution of constitutional bench camp. M.P.s signature campaign was postponed.

Contd.....

Contd......Efforts in Panchayat Raj Advocacy Programme

1	2	3	4
			• An application was filed on 23.09.99 for the case mention.
April 1999	• Contact with Rajyapal, Panchayat Minister and Government officials at State level. • Meeting and discussion with core committee, advocate and others. • Analysis of available data, documents and orders by core team.	• For doing advocacy for making the rules and regulations of Panchayati Raj enactment. • To search out the measures of early hearing of the case. • To help the Advocate	• Memorandum was submitted and assertion received. • Formation of new strategy on the order of Honourable Supreme Court. • Final copy of all available data and documents prepared.
May 1999	• To get the case mentioned before Supreme Court for early disposal of pending case. • To obtain the photo copy of order of Honourable Chief Justice of Supreme Court, given at the time of case mention.	• To provide priority to case of early Panchayat election in Bihar and for its early hearing. • To document the orders of Honourable Supreme Court. • To monitor and evaluate the endeavour undertaken	• The case was listed on 23.3.99 and 11.5.99 for mention and order of Honourable Chief Justice for listing the matter was given. • Efforts were made to procure the document from Supreme Court through contact person.

Contd.....

Contd......Efforts in Panchayat Raj Advocacy Programme

1	2	3	4
	• To contact and to solicit the cooperation of Bihar Raj Panchayat Parishad	regarding Panchayat at election in Bihar.	• To obtain guidance from Mr. B.B. Singh, Advocate, Government of Bihar and A.I.P.P. officials from time to time.
June 1999	• Contact with B.R.P.P. and suggestions. • Contact and lobbying with Welfare Department, Panchayati Raj Directorate, Village Development Department, Social Welfare Board of Government of Bihar and Voluntary organizations of rural level and their representatives and associates. • To evolve network of voluntary organization at regional level North Bihar. • To organize contact meeting with Sathi group VO's.	• To solicit suggestion and cooperation in the efforts of Research and Advocacy. • To chalk out activities of and hold discussion about people awareness regarding women participation in development programme, strengthening of Gram Sabha and Panchayat election at regional level. • To establish an organized structure of voluntary organizations in North Bihar for achieving goal. • To ensure strategy of making one day women conference, proposed by Social Welfare Board, a successful.	• Acquired adequate sugges-tion and cooperation. • Acceptance of time and date for holding one day women conference on the topic of participation of women of North Bihar in Panchayati Raj to be organized by Social Welfare Board. • Formation of regional network of 18 voluntary organizations in North Bihar, under Sathi. • To determine direction of programme after getting cooperation of Sathi.

Contd......

Contd......Efforts in Panchayat Raj Advocacy Programme

1	2	3	4
July 1999	• Organization of one day women met on 7.7.99 at Town hall Betiah. • Contact meeting and discussion with Bihar Rajya Panchayats Parishad. • Telephonic conversation with AIPP Delhi.	• To generate people awareness regarding decision making of women participation in Panchayati Raj activities. • To link Sathi network with Social Welfare Board. • Review of case work at Supreme Court level. • To make relevant present information available for planning future strategy.	• Dissemination of message of women participation in PRI activities among 5000 women who assembled at Town Hall Bettiah on 7.7.99 with the collaboration of Sathi network. • Proclamation regarding other programmes by chairpersons of both Central and State Welfare Boards and application from VOs were invited too. • Assurance from chairperson of these boards for securing full cooperation from Prime Minister and Law Minister at Centre for early disposal of cases of Bihar Panchayat election. • Telephonic dialogue with contact persons at Delhi and plan for Delhi visit for planning strategy.

Contd......

Contd......Efforts in Panchayat Raj Advocacy Programme

1	2	3	4
			• Possibility of hearing of Panchayati Raj election case of Bihar in Honourable Supreme Court on 22-23 July 99. • Departure to Delhi for ascertaining meaningful efforts.
August 1999	• Meeting with Mr. Ram Jethmalani, Law Minister, courtesy of Mrs. Mirdula Sinha, Chairperson, Central Welfare Board. • To discuss the present position of cases of Bihar Panchayat election with Advocate who is monitoring the case. • To meet with secretaries and officials of voluntary organizations of Delhi.	• To ensure help and lobbying from Attorney General at Supreme Court for providing priority of pending case in Supreme Court for its early disposal. • To solicit necessary instruction from State advocate Mr. B.B. Singh and Mr. Amarendra Sharan, Advocate of VOs for early disposal of case. • To have intensive discussion on the issue of Bihar Panchayat election and to decide future strategy.	• With the help and cooperation of Ms. Mirdula Sinha, Chairperson, it was possible to brief Law Minister with the facts relating to this case and assurance regarding intervention as per availability of Attorney General. • Mr. Amarendra Sharan is well prepared for early argument as he was provided with relevant and useful documents. • The same was also made available to Mr. B.B. Singh. State Advocate.

Contd......

Contd......Efforts in Panchayat Raj Advocacy Programme

1	2	3	4
		• To take initiative for impressing upon political parties for incorporating the issue of Panchayat in their election manifesto of 13th Parliamentary election.	• White paper as prepared by Mr. B.B. Singh; Advocate was submitted to Honourable Supreme Court as desired by it in its judgment of 11.5.99. It is being presumed that the case has been given priority and it might be possible for its hearing before constitutional bench during the month of September. • Advocacy was done through a committee of six members in the collaboration with AIPP with prominent political parties for incorporating the Panchayat issue in their election manifesto, which was preferred by their leaders.
September 1999	• Organization of block level meeting.	• To develop pressure group. • To collect information and	• Formation of regional organization.

Contd......

Bihar At A Glance

1. Area	9,94,163 Sq. K.M.
2. Population Total Male Female	8,28,78,796 4,31,53,964 3,97,24,832
3. Population Growth Rate (1999-2001) in %	28.43
4. Density	880 Sq. K.M.
5. Sex Ratio	921/1000 Men
6. Literacy Rate (%) Total Male Female	 47.53 60.32 33.57
7. Most Populous District	Patna (47,09,851 – population)
8. Lest Populous District	Shivahar (5,14,288 – population)
9. District with higher population growth rate	Shivahar 36.16%
10. District with least population growth rate	Nalanda (18.64%)
11. District with higher Density	Patna 1471 / Sq. K.M.
12. District with Least Density	Kaimur 382 / Sq. K.M.
13. District with high sex ratio	Siwan 1033/1000 Males
14. District with Least Sex Ratio	Patna 873 / 1000 Males
15. District with high literacy	63.52%
16. District with least literacy	31.02%
17. Number of Division in State	9
18. Number of Districts in State	38
19. Number of Sub Division in State	101
20. Number of CD Block in State	533
21. U.A. in State	9
22. Number of Town in State	130
23. Number of Revenue Villages	45,103
24. Average Population in District	22,39,967
25. Position of State in the Country from Population view point.	Third

Details of Elected Members at various tiers

Institution	Total Post	Scheduled Caste		Scheduled Tribe		Others		Total Elected		Total Elected	Vacant post
		Male	Female	Male	Female	Male	Female	Male	Female		
ZP	1192	120	73	02	08	622	318	744	399	1143	49
PS	11620	1237	795	48	55	6160	2915	7445	3765	11210	410
GP	116040	10824	8596	391	424	60274	28628	71489	37648	109137	6903
M	8471	134	02	49	01	7900	69	8083	72	8155	316
	137323	12315	9466	490	488	74956	31930	87761	41884	129645	7678

ZP : Zilla Parishad, PS : Panchayat Samiti,

GP : Gram Panchayat, M : Mukhiya

REFERENCES

Devolution to PRIS – Directorate of Panchayati Raj, Department of Rural Development, Government of Bihar, 2001.

"Legislative Statutes of Panchayat Raj in India"–S.S. Singh, Suresh Mishra and Sanjay Pratap-IIPA, New Delhi-1997

"Panchayati Raj in Bihar", Data At A Glance CENCORED, Patna 2001.

Role and responsibilities of Elected Members under Panchayat Raj System – UNICEF and CENCORED, Patna, 2001.

"State Panchayati Raj Act –A Critical Review" – Voluntary Action Network, India (VANI), New Delhi, 1995.

"Vision for Development of Bihar, An agenda for political parties for the 12th Assembly Election in Bihar," By ADRI, Patna, 1999–2000.

3

DEVOLUTION OF POWERS, FUNCTIONS AND FINANCES ON PANCHAYATI RAJ INSTITUTIONS IN MAHARASHTRA

C.S. SINGHAL

The Government of Maharashtra has been giving importance to the Panchayati Raj since its inauguration on 1st May, 1960. The three-tier Panchayati Raj set-up is functioning in the State on the basis of the following two State enactments passed in 1958 and 1961.

1. The Mumbai village Panchayat Act 1958.
2. The Maharashtra Zilla Parishad and Panchayat Samitis Act, 1961.

Thus, the Panchayati Raj set-up as envisaged in the 73rd Amendment of the Constitution was functioning in the State for over a period of about 30 years prior to the 73rd Constitution Amendment. The requisite changes as necessitated by the 73rd Constitutional Amendment were of minor in nature and the same were made applicable to the existing system by amendments in the State Legislation in April 1994.

The Amended Act followed the mandatory provisions of 73rd Constitutional Amendments like it has provision for :

(a) Gram Sabha;

(b) There are fixed terms of 5 years for the three-tier of PRIs;

(c) State election and Finance Commission is formulated;

(d) The reservation for scheduled castes, scheduled tribes and women in the PRIs in the state was already existing, the following specific provision have been stipulated for reservation of seats for members and chairpersons in the PRIs:

  (i) Reservation of SCs and STs is in proportion to their total population in the State. One-third of these seats shall be for women belonging to this group;

  (ii) One-third of the total number of seats (including the number of seats reserved for women belonging to SCs, STs and backward classes) to be filled in by direct election shall be reserved for women;

  (iii) 27 per cent of the seats shall be reserved for backward classes; One-third shall be for women from this category; and

  (iv) The reserved seats in PRIs will be allotted by rotation.

Innovative features of Panchayati Raj System in Maharashtra

(a) MLAs and MPs have no representation in the Zilla Parishad;

(b) District Collector has no role to play in the working of Zilla Parishad;

(c) The term of tenure of ZP Chairperson and Chairman of various subject Committees is two and a half year from March 2000.

(d) There is provision to replace chairpersons with two-third majority from March 2000.

PRIs at a glance in Maharashtra

As on 31st December 2000 there are 33 Zilla Parishad, 320 Panchayat Samitis and 28,711 Gram Panchayats in Maharashtra State. The election of all the three-tier is being held regularly since 1961. After 73rd Amendment the election of ZP and PS were held in March 1997 (as it was due on this date). The election of 14,000 Gram Panchayats were held in 1996 and for the remaining Gram Panchayats elections were held in June/October 2000.

The average size of Gram Panchayat is minimum 600 population in general area while in hill area minimum population cover is 300. The area of Gram Panchayat will be as per notification in the gazette. The size of Gram Sabha will be as per size of village Panchayat. It may cover both single village or group of villages.

Zilla Parishads in Thane district

1. The members not less than 50 and not more than 75 directly elected from the Zilla Parishad electoral division in the district by adult franchise. (64 in Thane District).
2. All the Chairman of Panchayat Samitis in the District are ex-officio Members (12 in Thane District).
3. Thirty three per cent reservation for women is there (number of women members in Thane District is 21). Out of the elected members, President is elected by ballot. Zilla Parishad also elects Vice President and four other Chairman of Subject Committees. The terms of office is two and a half years. Reservation has been ensured for the Scheduled Castes and Scheduled Tribes in Thane District. Out of 64 elected Councillors there are 2 SC and 23 ST in Thane District.

Committee System

In order to ensure on adequate *de facto* disposal of the democratic authority of Zilla Parishad even though ZP has an elected President and Vice President, the ZP works through a set of `10 subject committees in Thane district viz. 1. Standing, 2. Finance, 3. Works, 4. Agriculture, 5. Health, 6. Education, 7. Social, Welfare, 8. Animal Husbandry & Dairy, 9. Women & Child Welfare, and 10. Water Conservation and Drinking Water Supply Committee.

The composition formulation and power of these committees are given in detail in Chapter IV of Maharashtra Zilla Parishad and Panchayat Samitis Act 1961. The Standing Committee, the most powerful one is comprising eight councillors. Out of these not more than two seats are reserved for SC or ST or socially or educationally backwards councillor. The President shall be ex-officio, Chairman of the Standing Committee. The chairman of Subject Committee is the member. The Dy. Chief Executive Officer is the secretary, ex-officio, of the Standing Committee. The each committee are comprising minimum 5 to 10 elected councillors of ZP and two members having special knowledge or experience on the related subject. More than 70 per cent councillors shall be from amongst women in Women & Child Welfare Committee. Chairmen of W & C W Committee shall be from amongst the elected women councillors.

The Standing and Subject Committee must meet minimum once in each month. The Subject Committee in relation to subjects allotted to it shall be in charge of works and development schemes, ensure that the estimates of works and development schemes are prepared and sanctioned and supervise their execution. In addition to this, the Standing Committee shall supervise and the imposition and collection of taxes, rates, dues, fees, manage and regulate the investment of the district fund and examine and pass monthly accounts of receipts and expenditure of the ZP.

Section 106 of Maharashtra Zilla Parishad and Panchayat Samiti Act 1961 explain about power and function of Zilla Parishad. ZP may sanction works or development schemes within district (except block grants given to Panchayat Samitis), call for any proceedings of standing or any subject committee or any return, statement, account or report, exercise administrative control over officers under it, revise or modify decision of standing a subject committee, presiding authority or officer of or servant of the Zilla Parishad [as subject to certain direction or condition under sub - section (1) of section 261].

Section 108 of Maharashtra Zilla Parishad and Panchayat Samitis Act, 1961 explained about power and functions of Panchayat Samiti. As per this section every Panchayat Samitis shall (i) prepare an overall plan and development schemes to be undertaken in the block for for enabling the Zilla Parishad to prepare its development plans; (ii) prepare a plan/sanction, execute, supervise of works and development schemes to be undertaken from block grants; (iii) shall execute, maintain, supervise and administer the works and development schemes of Zilla Parishad; (iv) shall forward every quarter to Zilla Parishad a summary of proceedings of its meetings.

Administrative Structure of Zilla Parishad and Panchayat Samitis

The chief Executive Officer (CEO) drawn from Indian Administrative Services cadre is the head of the entire administrative organisation of Zilla Parishad, including the organisation of Panchayat Samiti Level. There is a Additional Chief Executive Officer from Maharashtra Development Service. There are two Deputy Chief Executive Officers (General and village Panchayat) following District Heads of Departments, under Zilla Parishad – District Education Officer, Agriculture Officer, Chief Accounts and Finance Officer, Executive Engineers (Irrigation and Water Supply), Animal Husbandry Officer, Project Officer ICDS, Social Welfare Officer.

CEO is vested with the executive authority for the purpose of carrying out the provision of the Act. He is a pivot in communication of various department and control different departments through inspection, day-to-day administration, review of works and controlling their finances. He also ensures coordination between Block Development Officers at Block level and various heads of departments. CEO is supposed to give his clear opinion to safeguard government policies on every decision and in case a Zilla Parishad or subject committee resolution is against government's directives, he can refer the matter to Commissioner and get it set aside.

At the Block level, Block Development Officer is the

Administrative head. He is assisted by Extension Officers of different departments. He is also the ex-officio Secretary of the Panchayat Samiti.

Village Panchayat

Village Panchayat consists of 7-17 elected members depending upon the population of the village Panchayat. 30 per cent seats are reserved for women and reservation is also given to Scheduled Castes and Scheduled Tribes according to 73rd Constitutional Amendment. The terms of village Panchayat is 5 years. The Bombay Village Panchayat Act, 1958 also provide for Gram Sabha, meetings to be held at least twice in a year.

Panchayat elects Sarpanch and Upa-Sarpanch. Powers and duties of Panchayat are prescribed in chapter III of Bombay Village Panchayat Act, 1958.

Under Section 62 of the Maharashtra Municipalities Act, 1965, the appointment of statutory committees is obligatory. This section enables a Panchayat to form one or more committees of its members and entrust to each committee certain duties. Panchayat has power to dissolve any such committee or withdraw powers and duties of any committee and entrust it to any other committee.

Under Section 124 of Bombay Village Panchayat Act, 1958 Panchayat can levy taxes on building, octroi (with previous sanction of State government), pilgrim, fairs, festival and entertainment, shop, hostel keeping, sanitary cess and water rate.

Besides, panchayat gets grants from land revenue, adivasi, stamp duty, education cess, royalti on minerals.

Devolution of Power and Functions

Out of 29 subjects under 11th Schedule of the 73rd Constitutional Amendment, nine subjects like road, non-conventional energy, cultural activities, health and sanitation, women and child development, social welfare maintenance of community assets are transferred fully to Panchayat. The other nine subjects like agriculture, minor irrigation, animal husbandry, minor forest produce, rural housing, Zilla Parishad, primary and secondary education, vocational education and markets are transferred to large extent and remaining eleven siubjects viz. land reforms, dairying, poultry, fisheries, social forestry, small scale industries, khadi and village industries, fuel and fodder, rural electrification, poverty alleviation, libraries and public distribution system are yet to be transferred to the Panchayati Raj *(see Annexure-I)*.

The Zilla Parishad president and councillors, Thane District were by and large satisfied with their power and schemes transferred under Schedule 11 of 73rd Constitutional Amendment. However, they wanted that DRDA should be made directly under the Zilla Parishad, libraries and public distribution system should be given to Panchayati Raj. They wanted all power related to secondary school education should be given to Zilla Parishad. About rural electrification (including distribution of electricity) which lies with State Government and Maharashtra State Electricity Board, they were of the view that Zilla Parishad may not be able to run.

In June 2000 Government of Maharashtra took decision to do away with the implementation of the schemes through parallel machinery which is at executive level in the district parallel to the ZP machinery. Accordingly, on 2nd October, 2000 Government transferred 123 schemes of eight development departments along with 34,881 employes and funds to Zilla Parishad (see Table 3.1). The different departments are in the process of issuing administrative order in this regard.

Tenth Finance Commission Grants

On the recommendations of Tenth Finance Commission, Government of India, approved and released Rs. 347.01 crore for four years (1996-2000). An amount of Rs. 86.75 crore released each year to Z.P. for three years (from 1996-97). During 1999-2000 an amount of Rs. 89.20 crore (including Rs.17.35 crore as matching share of State government) released to Z.P. These grants were utilized mainly for construction and maintenance of school building, maintenance of primary health centre, veterinary hospital, latrine, purchase of medicines and instruments for PHC, training for Village Panchayat members, tubewell, joint road, purchase of vehicle, construction of anganwadi centre, electrical poles in SC/ST locality and purchase of fogging machine.

Table 3.1 : Department-wise number of schemes and employees transferred to Zilla Parishad

S. No.	*Department*	*No. of Schemes transferred*	*No. of employees transferred*
1.	Agriculture	37	20501
2.	Publi Health	06	8672
3.	Social Welfare	39	1915
4.	Primary Education	04	1464
5.	Water supply & Sanitation	03	1262
6.	Animal Husbandry	07	1056
7.	Cultural Affairs & Sports	03	-
8.	Women & Child Development	10	-
	Total	123	34881

The Thane district got an amount of Rs. 3.33 crore each year (1996-2000) out of this grant.

Financial Devòlution of Power

The First Finance Commission were constituted on 23 April, 1994. It has given its recommendations on 31st January 1997. The most of the recommendations are accepted. The First Finance Commission recommended Rs. 72,864 lacs. The Maharashtra Government accepted the liability of Rs. 32,164 lacs. However, only Rs. 7,589 lacs were released by State Government due to financial constraints (during 1999-2001). The President, a councillor and officials of Thane district were not aware about this grant and informed that they have not received any grant as per recommendations of the First Finance Commission.

An additional grants of Rs. 3703 lacs (1999-2000) and Rs. 3886 lacs (2000-01) were given to all Z.P. in the State to take up different development schemes.

The Second State Finance Commission also constituted and gave its interim report in 1999. Its recommendations are under consideration.

Finances of Zilla Parishad can be best understood from the various kinds of development schemes they implement. Broadly, the schemes implemented by the Zilla Parishad fall in four categories viz. (I) schemes implemented by the Z.Ps. from their own resources; (ii) schemes transferred by Government to the ZPs for which ZPs enjoy substantial powers of granting various kinds of approvals to the transferred schemes like primary education, rural health, agricultural extension etc. About 300 schemes of various sectoral departments are being implemented by ZPs. About 123 more schemes of sectoral departments were handed over to ZP; (iii) Schemes entrusted by the Government to the ZPs on agency basis where ZPs act as mere agents of government and claim 3 per cent agency commission on such schemes like family welfare, bio-gas, Integrated Child Development schemes, school feeding programmes etc, ZPs enjoy limited power in respect of these schemes and are mainly under control of the government; (iv) Schemes implemented by the government by requisitioning the services of the ZPs employees. However the services of ZP are requisitioned only in rare cases e.g. implementation of schemes such as employment Guarantee Scheme.

The Maharashtra Zilla Parishad and Panchayat Samitis Act, 1961 provides for a number of avenues for raising resources for ZPs like:

(i) Government has levied a cess of 200 paise per rupee of land revenue and this amount is passed on to the ZPs by way of grants. Further, ZP are allowed to levey additional cess per rupee of land revenue upto a limit of 500 paise. To supplement the funds of ZPs in the matter of raising resources and to encourage them to levy more cess on the land revenue, there is a scheme of incentive grants to ZPs, and these grants are called as local cess matching grants.

(ii) Forest revenue collected by the government from the forestarea is handed to the ZP in the form of Forest Revenue Grants.

(iii) Government imposes additional one and a half per cent levy on the stamp duty and the amounts so collected are passed on to the ZPs by way of stamp duty grants.

(iv) The Zilla Parishad Act also provides for levy of 20 per cent cess on the water rates levied. These amounts are also fully passed on to the Zilla Parishads.

(v) In addition, the Maharashtra Zilla Parishads and Panchayat Samitis Act, 1961 allows the ZPs to levy a number of local taxes such as property tax, land tax, tax on fairs, markets and water tax on water supply for drinking purposes etc.

As per Maharashtra Zilla Parishad and Panchayat Samiti Account Code, 1999 the details of powers given to Zilla Parishad and Panchayat Samiti officials are given in Annexure - II.

District Rural Development Agency

DRDA is not merged with Zilla Parishad. It is an autonomous body under societies registration Act, 1960. The Chief Executive Officer of the Zilla Parishad is also the chairman of DRDA, and at times many programmes of DRDA are implemented at Block and Village level through the machinery of the ZP. Sometimes District level officials under ZP also coordinating the activities on the request of DRDA. The president and a councillor of Thane District wanted that DRDAs should be under ZPs. Since their staff is involved in implementation of the DRDA's programmes.

Strengthening Resource Base of Panchayati Raj Institutions

The main problem of Panchayati Raj Institution is inadequate resources. The P.B. Patil Committee had made a number of recommendations for improving resource-base of Panchayati Raj Institutions. The government has taken decision on a number of important recommendations. Important decisions in this regards are as (i) The Village Panchayat cess of 20 paise per one rupee of land revenue has been raised to 100 paise; (ii) The Zilla Parishad Cess of 20 paise per rupee of land revenue has been raised to 200 paise; (iii) The limit of additional cess leviable per rupee of land revenue has been raised from 180 to 500 paise; (iv) Forest Revenue Grants have been raised from 5 to 7 per cent of forest revenue; (v) stamp duty grant payable to Zilla Parishad and Village Panchayats has been doubled; and (vi) Formula for local cess matching grants (Incentive Grants to the ZPs and PSs) has been revised so as to ensure more incentive grants to ZPs for levying additional cess on land revenue.

District Planning Committee

District Planning Committee is constituted in the year 1999 in all the District as per Maharashtra Act No. XXIV of 1998. It consists of 30-50 members. The Minister-in-Charge of district shall be the chairperson of the district planning committee and the collector of the district shall be the member-secretary of DPC. There is provision of reservation of seats for SC/ST and women as per section 4 of the Act.

The main function (given in section 10) of DPC is to consider and consolidate District Annual Plan. Five Year Plan and Perspective plans prepared by the Panchayats, review and monitor the progress of District Annual Plan and suggest reappropriation of approved provision of District Annual Plan in accordance with the guidelines issued by the state government and to recommend approved draft development plan to the state government.

Panchayat in Scheduled Area

Maharashtra Government vide Maharashtra Act No. XLVI of 1997 amended their Panchayat act and gave power to Panchayati Raj under schedule area as per 73rd Constitutional Amendment. Only law relating to management of village market is yet to be amended, which is under consideration.

REFERENCES

Government of Maharashtra, The Maharashtra Zilla Parishads and Panchayat Samitis Act, 1961 (As modified upto the 18th October, 1996).

Government of Maharashtra, The Bombay Village Panchayats Act, 1958 (as modified upto the 14th September, 1994).

Government of Maharashtra, Planning Department, Maharashtra District Planning Committees (Constitution and Functions) Act, 1998 (Mah.XXIV of 1998).

Government of Maharashtra, Rural Development and Water Conservation Department, Maharashtra Zilla Parishads and Panchayat Samitis Account Code, 1999, Notification Dt. 5-8-1999.

Government of Maharashtra, Maharashtra endowing upon the Panchayats in the Scheduled Area the Power to Function as Self-Government (Amendment of certain State Laws) Act No. XLVI of 1997.

Government of Maharashtra, (1986), Panchayati Raj Evaluation Committee Report, P.B. Patil Committee, Bombay.

Rahim, C.A. Maharashtra, in Patterns of Decentralised Governance in Rural India by R.C. Choudhury & S.P. Jain, NIRD, Hyderabad.

ANNEXURE-1

Details of Subjects Transferred/not yet Transferred as per Schedule of 73rd Constitutional Amendments

Subject transferred fully	Subject transferred large extent	Subject not yet transferred
1. Road, culverts, bridges, ferries, waterways and other means of communications	1. Agriculture	1. Land improvement, Land reforms, Land consolidation and soil conservation
2. Non-conventional energy sources	2. Minor irrigation water management and watershed development	2. Dairying and poultry
3. Cultural activities	3. Animal husbandry	3. Fisheries
4. Health and sanitation including hospitals	4. Minor forest produce	4. Social Forestry and Farm Forestry
5. Family welfare	5. Rural Housing	5. Small Scale industries including Food Processing Industries
6. Women and child development	6. Zilla Parishad	6. Khadi Village Industries and Cottage Industries
7. Social welfare including Welfare of the handicapped and mentally retarded	7. Education including primary and secondary	7. Fuel and Fodder
8. Welfare of the weaker sections (SC/ST)	8. Technical training and vocational education	8. Rural electrification including distribution of electricity
9. Maintenance of community assets	9. Markets and Fairs	9. Poverty alleviation programme
		10. Libraries
		11. Public distribution system

ANNEXURE II

Devolution of Powers of Zilla Parishad/Panchayat Samitis

Sl.No.	Nature of power	Authority of which power is delegated	Extent of power			
			Estimated recurring expenditure (Rs. per annum)		Estimated non-recurring expenditure	
			Exceeding	But not exceeding	Exceeding	But not exceeding
1	2	3	4	5	6	7
	Part I	**Zilla Parishad**				
	Power to accord administrative approval in respect of works or development schemes	1. Deputy Engineer		20,000	20,000	50,000
		2. Executive Engineer	20,000	50,000	50,000	2,50,000
		3. Chief Executive Officer	50,000	1,00,000	2,50,000	6,00,000
		4. Chairman of Standing Committies or Subject Committee	1,00,000	2,00,000	6,00,000	8,00,000
		5. Subject Committee	2,00,000	3,00,000	8,00,000	10,00,000
		6. Standing Committee	3,00,000	5,00,000	10,00,000	20,00,000
		7. Zilla Parishad	Full Powers	Full Powers	Full Powers	Full Powers

1	2	3	4	5	6	7
		Panchayat Samiti				
		1. Block Development Officer		10,000		75,000
		2. Chairman of the Panchayat Samiti	10,000	50,000	75,000	3,00,000
		3. Panchayat Samiti	Full Powers	Full Powers	Full Powers	Full Powers
	Part II Power to accept a tender or contract for works of development schemes	**Zilla Parishad**				
		1. Deputy Engineer	—	—	—	50,000
		2. Executive Engineer	—		50,000	2,50,000
		3. Chief Executive Officer	—	—	2,50,000	6,00,000
		4. Chairman of Standing Committee or Subject Committiee	—	—	6,00,000	8,00,000
		5. Subject Committee	—	—	8,00,000	10,00,000
		6. Standing Committee	—	—	10,00,000	20,00,000
		7. Zilla Parishad	—	—	Full Powers	FullPowers
		Panchayat Samiti				
		1. Block Development Officer	—	—	—	75,000
		2. Chairman of the Panchayat Samiti	—	—	75,000	3,00,000
		3. Panchayat Samiti	—	—	Full Powers	Full Powers

Source: Maharashtra Zilla Parishads & Panchayat Samitis Accounts Act Code, 1999.

4

PANCHAYATI RAJ
Challenges Ahead

George Mathew

It is an honour to be here at the Gandhigram University to deliver the third Justice V.R. Krishna Iyer Endowment Lecture. This is one place in India where the great ideals of the Mahatma are alive and generations of young women and men get education in the ideal rural setting. The entire nation should be proud of this institution. I recall my association and friendship with Shri M. Aram and Shri Markandan, former Vice-Chancellors, who helped me immensely to understand the complexities of rural development and Panchayati Raj. The lecture in the name of Justice Krishna Iyer is of special significance to me personally as he has been my guide and philosopher. He is a powerful voice of the underprivileged.

In 1917, after 35 years of the Ripon Resolution, Shri C.P. Ramasamy Iyer addressed the Malabar district conference. Pointing to the not-so-satisfactory results of the first official attempt to set up institutions of self-governance in India following the Ripon Resolution, Dr. Iyer in his Presidential address had remarked, 'Unless the people are trusted to manage local affairs without official control from within, they will never learn adequately to discharge their functions' (Dharampal, *The Madras Panchayat System,* Vol. II, p. 6). By this he certainly did not mean that Indians were incapable of managing their affairs even at the local level. What he wanted to emphasize was the lack of trust between the people and their alien rulers. Here was a government whose head office was situated far away in London, whose executives could not communicate in the languages of the country where they had been dispatched to establish an imperial administration and who was trying to befriend the natives by involving them in the three-tier structure of local bodies.

Describing the positive outcome and drawbacks of the local self-government system, Dharampal in his classic work on *Panchayats in Tamil Nadu* writes,

> "In many areas the bodies grew in strength, did substantial amount of work in terms of construction and maintenance of roads, starting and maintenance of schools, hospitals, dispensaries, etc. Their total expenditure though not very large by present day quantitative standards, were substantial in comparison to the governmental expenditure in those days. Yet a deadlock began to develop in the functioning of these bodies either between the bodies and the presidency government or between their chairman who were officials and the general membership. In most places this led to people losing interest in the body, and in some the members trying to assert themselves. One way of such assertion which became somewhat common in the district boards was to reverse one or other decision of the Collector-president, particularly in regard to punishment meted out by him to any employee of the district board. This became irksome, if not quite intolerable, both to the Collector and to the government and in 1905 the government provided for an appeal by the Collector-president to the Governor-in-Council against the decisions of the district board. A real impasse in the structure was thus reached." (*The Madras Panchayat System,* Vol. II, p. 3)

Obviously, the government of the day did not trust the people who had been invited to share the responsibility of managing the roads, schools, dispensaries and the like in their villages, talukas and districts. As stated above, most often either the chairpersons of these local bodies, who were officials, did not agree with the majority of general members, many of whom had been drawn from the public; or if the whole board was unanimous, the presidency government had a different view. If making a provision for an appeal by the Collector himself against the majority decision of the District Board he had presided over became unavoidable, it is clear that the government was not trusting the machinery it had itself created.

Has the situation changed today? It is painful for me to state that although we have been breathing in a free and democratic country for the last fifty-four years, the lack of trust in the people's representatives at the village, block/taluka and district levels persists in no small measure. The Parliament is trusted to run the country. The Assembly is trusted to run a state. But a District Panchayat is not fit enough to administer to govern the district. It is no strange that the lower a house of representatives of the people is located on the democratic ladder, the weaker it is found to be. Consequently, the Village Panchayats, which represent the very foundation of this vast democratic edifice of one billion Indians, are the weakest democratic bodies with very little to spend and with minimum powers to decide how to spend the little it has. A Village Panchayat is required to depose trust in the highest Panchayat of the land, that is to say, Parliament and act accordingly, but the Parliament and the Assemblies feel no compulsion to trust the Village Panchayat–its wisdom, its competence and its eligibility to handle a small amount of power. What does it mean? The voters choose a wise M.P. or a competent M.L.A. but a good-for-nothing member to the village, union and district Panchayats!

It is often pointed out that members of the Village Panchayats are, in a large number of cases, illiterate or with insufficient education, and if they are not males, they have little understanding of the world outside because they have been confined within the four walls of their homes. Let me remind you that when the first Lok Sabha was elected through adult franchise, the literacy rate in India was merely 14 per cent. And yet, it was that Lok Sabha and the government that emerged from it which laid the foundation for the nation's giant leap towards progress. Voters may be uneducated but they are not ignorant. Women may have been behind doors but they know the true nature of the world outside, for they bear the brunt of everyday life. Only those who recognize this fact truly believe in democracy and institutions of self-governance. This release of mass energy, however, cannot be stopped in this age of emancipations. However, the self-centered leaders have managed to ensure the tenth year of the passage of the 73rd and 74th Constitution Amendments, we have powerless and ineffective local bodies in place of powerful local governments. It is the writ of the national capital and State capitals that runs in most villages even in the matter of opening a primary school or constructing a few kilometres of road. And yet, the complaint continues to be heard that villagers are not educated enough to handle power even at the local level. How can one learn to swim unless he/she be allowed to plunge into the river?

Lack of trust in people or their representatives at the ordinary level is not confined to the Panchayat issues alone. Take the case of the use of national flag by ordinary citizens. So far the flag had been treated by the political class and the bureaucrats jealously as the guarded emblem of the State. All arms of the State were allowed the automatic privilege of flaunting the flag but not the common people. As *Times of India* (18 January 2002) editorially puts it, even as India became a democratic Republic the State—politicians and bureaucrats—continued to threat the people's right to bear their national colour with suspicion. Under the pretext of preserving the honour and dignity of the flag the assumption was that the ordinary citizen could not be trusted to respect it.

However, lack of trust is not the only reason why true decentralization has been held up people at the top. Fear of the people is an equally important factor. May I submit that this fear is not born out of the democratic values or democratic nature of their work which keeps the elected rules in Parliament and State Assemblies as well as the bureaucrats always on their toes and prevents them from taking an anti-people measure. Success of democracy depends on the quantum of this healthy and constructive fear. However what we find in our country is the other kind of fear; the fear of people taking over democracy. This is perhaps the greatest challenge to the rapid growth of Panchayati Raj. Panchayats have been denied their legitimate share of power because the rules are afraid that the common people equipped with Panchayat power will not rest until they succeed in making the state accountable to the public. Once Panchayats begin to assert their powers, they will change the very nature of our polity or expose its fault lines which have not allowed the fruits of development to percolate to the common masses.

Take the case of proliferation of parallel bodies in almost all states, which have been set up to bypass the elected Panchayats and municipal corporations. The *Janmabhoomi* programme in Andhra Pradesh has earned the dubious distinction of being the most notorious of these parallel bodies. The *Janmabhoomi* Programme is the brainchild of Mr. Chandrababu Naidu, Chief Minister of A.P., who kept the Panchayat elections in abeyance for full one year and agreed to hold them only after the intervention of the Supreme Court of India. Under the provisions of this programme, the Gram Sabha, consisting of all adult voting population in a habitation, is supposed to be the basic unit. Habitation level Committee or People's Council is the institution through which the *Janmabhoomi* is implemented at the habitation level. This committee consists of group leaders of self-help groups, representatives of NGOs, members of weaker sections, women and ward members with the Sarpanch as the chairperson. This is the official position. What happens at the ground level has been documented by Anil Vaddiraju in a study conducted by PRIA, New Delhi. The report says:

"But in reality the participation of the Sarpanch and the ward members is only nominal and the entire show is carried on by the officials and the political executive who derive their constituency from beyond a particular habitation or village" (Participation and Governance, July 2001). According to Tirupati Reddy, Sarpanch of Maheshwaram village: "The Sarapanch sits in the Janmabhoomi Gram Sabha (or habitation Sabha) like a doll and the entire show is run by the nodal officer. In the *Janmabhoomi*, the Gram Sabha officials sanction government schemes to whosoever the local MLA wants them to sanction. There are instances when the local

MLA (the ruling Telugu Desam Party) openly had said that he gives preference to his own party people for sanction of the scheme" (*ibid.*). More importantly, "The *Janmabhoomi* programme takes up all the local issues related to the functioning of local institutions and implementation of government schemes into its purview and tries to substitute the Gram Panchayat. In the name of direct interface between people and administration the entire institutional relevance of Panchayati Raj Institution is undermined" (*ibid.*). In Tamil Nadu also, several schemes, programmes and projects are assuming the nature of parallel bodies. Mention may be made of the self-help groups, water user's associations, Parent-Teachers' associations, Sarva Siksha Abhiyan and so on. They are being strengthened at the expense of the Panchayats.

This is what one can call the policy of giving by the left hand and taking way by the right hand. In other words, what has been bestowed upon the local government institutions by the 73rd Constitution Amendment has been taken away by the State governments. Power still remains concentrated in the hands of the Union and State governments. The people are yet to take charge of their lives.

It takes me to the wider question of slow growth of what I call the Panchayat will. It is a well-recognized fact that from time immemorial our village people have been conducting their community life as they wished without any interference from outside. No emperor could force a village community to accept what it did not find worth accepting. From Marx to Weber to Gandhi, India has been hailed as a land of the little republics. This was as it should have been, for in the name of large empires the central authority dictated its decrees to far away places, whose needs and inspirations could not reach the capital in the absence of the requisite machinery. However, this was a mixed blessing, for in the long run it proved a device for cultural conservatism and not an instrument of change or renewal. Why? Mainly because these little republics had no representation of women and depressed classes. The power of knowledge remained monopolized by the twice-born castes, prohibiting the illiterate masses from probing and questioning. Lacking a national coordination, the parts failed to make a whole.

Today, the situation is totally different. We are an organized nation. We have a written republican constitution to run the country. In the place of local lordships, there are State government who have their powers and duties duly laid down in black and white. Panchayats of the day are perfectly democratic entities with mandatory representation of women and SCs/STs. About half of the executive posts of Sarpanches and Deputy Sarpanches have also been kept apart for these unprivileged classes. We can say that through social democratization of the local bodies serious inroads have been made into the caste system and male supremacy which are responsible for the tardy progress of country. The Gram Sabha is being strengthened in all respects, which has the potential of establishing direct democracy in our five lakh villages. Some States have provided the 'right to recall' to the electorate of the local bodies—a clear warning to the incumbents that they should be prepared to step down if they fail to deliver.

What prevents the people from having the final say at least in their local affairs? Why cannot they tell the politicians: 'You have failed to provide us with even the basic civic amenities. From this moment we are going to manage them on our own. If you want us to support you, let us take hold of our due share in all resources of the State'. There is no aggressiveness in such a democratic pronouncement. It is, in fact, a sacred democratic duty of the voter from whom this entire system derives its legitimacy and strength. It is the constitutional task of the system to provide a prided place to the citizenry. When the entire system is interested only in perpetuating its vested interests, it becomes the responsibility of the citizenry to assert for its legitimate rights. No democracy can be run from the above. Grass roots democratic bodies are needed to exert pressure on the government of the day to act responsibly. Fortunately, we have a countrywide network of Panchayati Raj Institution to fill this vacuum, which are peopled by the local leaders elected through adult franchise. These third-generation Panchayats enjoy a sound constitutional status and cannot be removed except by unconstitutional methods.

To me, this constitutes the most formidable challenge before the votaries and functionaries of Panchayati Raj. It is futile to blame the masses. They have been deprived of power for centuries. Most of them have not even been allowed to exercise their civil rights. The women, the *Dalits*, the backward castes, constitute majority of Indian society. These are the people who had no significant role in the regulation of our public life. Even places of God were not open to all. Even today, there still remains a large part of this ugly legacy with us.

It is a matter of concern that elections to four Panchayats in Tamil Nadu could not be held in October last year for the second consecutive term because of the refusal of the upper-caste people to work under a *dalit* Sarpanch. The ghastly murder of Leelavathy. The councillor from the weaver community elected to the Madurai Municipal Corporation, for bringing drinking water to her poor locality, defying the rich contractors cannot be erased from public memory. The dastardly killing of six citizens including the President and Vice-President of the Melavalavu village Panchayat in 1998 within six months of their election for the sin of being born in the Scheduled Caste community and contesting the elections, is the darkest chapter of our democracy. If these cruelest actions against democratic process could happen in a state which had a pioneering role in building up a glorious social movement for restoration of *swabhiman* (self-respect) to the low castes and which was the first State to give reservation in government jobs to the deprived classes, one can well imagine what must be happening to those parts of the country which are still suffering from the age-old prejudices of caste and gender.

We shall be *asking for the moon* if except that these down-trodden people will rise in revolt and fight for genuine decentralization of power. It does not mean that no such potential exists in our society. The potential is certainly there. For proof, I can cite any number of cases where Panchayat presidents and members of very humble origin have fought for dignity and have ultimately won. The story of poor *dalit* women President of Tikamgarh Panchayat in Madhya Pradesh, Gundiabai, is well-known. In1997, she was not allowed by the upper castes to hoist the national flag during the Independence Day celebrations in her tiny village. The sweets brought by her supporters for distribution on this occasion were thrown into the drain. The news created such a commotion and impact that in the next year's celebrations Gundiabai was the chief guest to hoist the flag with full police honours at the district headquarters. There was no protest. In the next Panchayat elections held in January 2000, the post of President of Tikamgarh village Panchayat was not reserved for SC women. And yet, Gundiabai got elected with a huge majority. It is no mean achievement of our democratic process that despite all hurdles brought about by social conservativeness and bureaucratic insensivity such significant incidents are regularly taking place.

The indication is clear; winds of change have begun to blow. My submission is that we should be thankful to experiment of the Panchayati Raj introduced by the Seventy-Third Amendment for this radical transformation of attitudes in our public life.

However, this is far from satisfactory. These achievements are only small beginnings. The big task lies ahead. That is, the countrywide structure of Panchayati Raj has to be invested with meaning. Unfortunately, the state governments have not taken these new generation of local governments—the Panchayats—with any degree of seriousness. Even the Union government has not been able to enforce the Constitutional provisions for regular elections to Panchayats, devolution of functions, powers and funds to the local bodies. Several States have not even constituted the District Planning Committees and yet no action is taken against them. Sometimes court cases have hindered the smooth functioning of the local government system. The media still treats the Panchayats as non-entities. The local bureaucracy is hostile to the Panchayat representatives for if the latter are given their due respect, the government officials will have to change their attitude and work style. The officials will have to work hard to maintain their accountability to the common people who are in touch with the ground reality daily. Today even a BDO behaves as if he is the master and the Panchayat presidents are minions. The state of Gram Sabha is pathetic. Crucial decisions are taken without taking the village into confidence. The veil of secrecy acts as the iron wall for bureaucrats at all levels. Some of the government reports have come out with shocking revelations. For instance, the Approach Paper to the Tenth Five Year Plan says that the Centrally

Sponsored Schemes (CSSs) today have reached a staggering number of more than 200 with the result that there is no correctness of data or facts; rampant overstatements of physical and financial performance; rampant misuse of funds provided for vulnerable sections; wanton abuse of the authority to misuse the funds provided for the victims of calamity and so on. Except in Kerala nowhere the CSSs are implemented by the Panchayats. Now there is a strong demand even in Kerala by the line departments that the CSSs should be taken out of the Panchayats and returned to them. *The Report of the Task Force on Devolution of Powers and Functions upon Panchayati Raj Institutions* (Krishi Bhavn, New Delhi August 2001) has stated that more than Rs. 40,000 crores of the total annual plan outlay of the State Plans, partly or wholly, related to the 29 subjects mentioned in the XI Schedule are implemented by the State governments at the state and district level. Consequently, rampant corruption has become the order of the day.

A Study Report on Fund Management by the DRDAs and Implementing Agencies for the year 1999-2000 has this to say: "Non-delivery of cheque to beneficiary for more than three months in DRDA, Rampur was noticed. It is shocking to find that people in Shahbad Block of Rampur approached central team that the money has not been given to them for construction of latrines. They made a complaint that 'cut is being demanded' for release of cheques. Whereas as per records, full payments were made to the beneficiaries." Take another case, National Family Benefit Scheme cheques amounting to Rs. 1,45,000 were not handed over to the beneficiaries in Bhagalpur district. This report by the Dy. Controller of Accounts, Ministry of Rural Development has innumerable cases of corruption by the rural development officials. A study conducted in Tamil Nadu by the Rajiv Gandhi Chair for Panchayati Raj Studies of the Gandhigram University about the problems faced by the elected leaders in the state found that the powers of the Block level Panchayat Samiti (Union) is unlimited and the engineer "is embodiment of corruption". He is more powerful than the BDO and "makes the Gram Panchayat president dance to his tune. The union of engineers demands 15 per cent commission for each and every work" (p. 7).

I am not saying that there is no corruption in the management of Panchayats by the elected members or presidents and vice-presidents. There are, of course, many cases of corruption in Panchayats as well. But this only reflects the sad fact that Panchayat bodies have not been allowed to function democratically. Transparency is the hallmark of democracy. Where the bureaucracy is extremely secretive, the Panchayats cannot be expected to be open. The chain of vested interests begins from the capital and reaches up to the local unit.

All this is only a reflection of how serious we lack the Panchayat will. Turning the tide is the primary task of the intellectuals, activists, political leaders and social workers. Only through their consistent intervention, an atmosphere favourable to the growth of institutions of self-government can be created. Many non-government organizations are doing extremely well in this respect. Some State governments have also shown interest in treating the Panchayats as instruments of distributive justice, although small events are being packaged under big labels. But, taking everything into consideration, it must be said that the driving forces of social and political change are not on the scene in enough numbers to create a deep impact.

This is the biggest challenge before the Panchayati Raj today. Other things are bound to follow at the government and political levels if the atmosphere is continuously charged with vibrations of social craving for power to the people. Here, everybody, I repeat, everybody, from the village graduate to the university professor and from a humble party worker to the leading intellectuals of the city, has some role to play. The future of this vast country now depends upon the success of the Panchayat experiment. Today, the people have hardly any expectation from the present political leaders. But which Sarpanch does not feel the pinching eyes of his neighbours—the eyes which are full of frustrations and complaints and yet, which radiate big hopes for small things—a pucca road, a school, a BPL card, some job under the EAS, a loan for erecting a house, electricity and perhaps the seed money for setting up a small business. These humble people need to be encouraged to look forward to bigger things. The number of people wresting with poverty, disease and lack of any future is far bigger than what the official files suggest. Let us dedicate ourselves to meet this challenge.

5

RURAL DEVELOPMENT AS A MECHANISM TO STRENGTHEN PANCHAYATI RAJ

S.S. MEENAKSHISUNDARAM

We, in India, always had a Panchayati Raj system. It was in vogue for several centuries. Jawaharlal Nehru in the *Discovery of India* points out that "the Village Panchayat or elected council had large powers both executive and judicial and its members were treated with the greatest of respect by the King's officers. Lands were distributed by this Panchayat which also collected taxes out of the produce and paid the government's share on behalf of the village. Over a number of these village councils there was a larger Panchayat or council to supervise and interfere if necessary". Sir Charles Metcalfe, a British Governor in India during the nineteenth century, called these panchayats "little republics" which "seem to last where nothing else lasts". The Panchayats gradually disappeared under the British rule possibly because of the compelling need of a foreign ruler to centralise. Though Lord Ripon, another British Viceroy, did take the initiative of establishing an alternative system of local self-government in India, the institutions that came into being then lacked in resources as well as autonomy. The Village Panchayats and the district boards that were established by Lord Ripon did not make much impact either in the polity or in the economy of the country.

It was Gandhiji who for the first time in the Twentieth century, openly articulated the need to revive the Panchayats with democratic bases of their own and invest them with adequate powers so that the villagers could have a real sense of *swaraj*. In his opinion, the village would be "a complete republic independent of its neighbours for its own vital wants and yet inter-dependent for many others in which dependence is a necessity. The government of the village will be conducted by the Panchayat of five persons annually elected by the adult villagers, male and female, possessing minimum prescribed qualifications. These will have all the authority and jurisdiction required. Since there will be no system of punishment in the accepted sense, the Panchayat will be the legislature, judiciary and executive combined to operate for its year of office. Here there is perfect democracy based upon individual freedom. The individual is the architect of his own government."

Despite the insistence of Gandhiji to recognise the Village Panchayat as the basic institution for Indian democracy, Dr. Ambedkar who made the most significant contribution to the drafting of the Indian Constitution did not share this view. He openly asked in the Constituent Assembly: "what is the village, but a sink of localism, a den of ignorance, narrow-mindedness and communalism." He genuinely believed that these village republics have been the ruination of India. The condition of the caste ridden Indian village then was such that one can easily understand why Dr. Ambedkar thought this way. His strong opposition to the concept of village as the basic unit of administration had resulted in the Panchayats not even finding a mention in the first draft of independent India's Constitution. However, as a compromise, the organisation of Village Panchayats ultimately found an entry through Article 40 of the Constitution under the Directive Principles of State Policy. This Article merely states that "the State shall take steps to organise village panchayats and endow them with such powers and authority as may be necessary to enable them to function as units of self-government." Since this left little obligation to introduce Panchayati Raj in India, there was no legislation at all to implement it until 1959.

The need to establish a Panchayati Raj system in India was highlighted by the Balwantrai Mehta Committee, which incidentally was appointed to study the Community Development Programme in India. This team was expected to review the economy and efficiency of the community development projects and national extension services and assess the extent to which the movement had succeeded in utilising local initiative and creating institutions to ensure continuity in the process of improving economic and social conditions in rural areas. In their report, the study team stated: "Admittedly one of the least successful aspects of community development and national extension service work is its attempt to evoke popular initiative. So long as we do not discover or create a representative and democratic institution which will supply the local interest, supervision and care necessary to ensure that expenditure of money upon local objects conforms with the needs and wishes of the locality, invest it with adequate power and assign to it appropriate finances, we will never be able to evoke local interest and excite local initiative in the field of development". Therefore, it recommended the establishment of a three-tier Panchayati Raj, the middle tier, namely, the Panchayat Samiti at the Block level playing the pivotal role in the scheme of decentralisation. The Samiti's jurisdiction was to be coterminous with that of the community development block, its members being directly elected.

Accepting the recommendations of the study team, the National Development Council directed the State governments to devise their own Panchayat systems that would suit their local conditions. By 1959, all the States had passed their Panchayat Acts and by mid-1960s Panchayats had reached all parts of the country. The purpose of my narrating this history of Panchayati Raj in India which, I am sure, most of you already know, is to make my first point here viz., Panchayati Raj in independent India came to be established only as a means to deliver the benefits of the Community Development Programme. But for the need to establish people's institutions to evoke popular initiative for the success of these rural development programmes, Panchayati Raj institutions might not have been established in India during the 1960s.

All of us are aware of the decline and fall of the Panchayati Raj system in India during the 1970s. With the passing away of the second Prime Minister of India, Lal Bahadur Sastri, the commitment to democratic values weakened. The flow of funds for Block development slowed down to a trickle, after the closure of the intensive stages of the Community Development Programme. Where the party in power apprehended that their performance in the polls to the PRIs might not be good, the tendency was to postpone elections indefinitely. The decline was conspicuous in every state except Maharashtra and Gujarat, where the primacy was with the top tier, namely, the Zilla Parishads (ZPs), which had considerable administrative powers. Even in these States, Ministers and Members of Legislative Assembly (MLAs) felt threatened by the rising political power and influence of the ZP Presidents and there was a kind of backlash. The Government of Maharashtra, for instance, set up separate District Planning Committees with the State Minister in charge of that district as Chairman; district planning which was a major function of the ZP was taken over by this committee and the stature of the ZP was deliberately curtailed. The same situation occurred in Gujarat also almost simultaneously.

Several factors contributed to this decline of the Panchayati Raj system. Firstly, the bureaucracy, local vested interests and the elected representatives in the State Legislature and in the Parliament did not take kindly to the PRIs, whose ascendancy they feared. Secondly, since the Panchayats were created more as vehicles for rural development rather than as units of self-government, they had no real autonomy and were entirely at the mercy of the State governments and their bureaucracy.

Thirdly, there was a strong tendency in India, as in several other parts of the world, to concentrate power at the Centre to an excessive degree. This resulted in the creation of parallel agencies to execute special development programmes and centrally sponsored schemes such as Drought Prone Area Programme, Intensive Tribal Development Project, Small Farmers Development Agency etc., which were kept outside the purview of the PRIs thereby weakening them even in the field of development. Fourthly, many state governments would not hold elections to the PRIs for years together under one pretext or the other. This lack of political will hastened the decline of the PRIs.

Fifthly, there was also a feeling that PRIs are dominated by economically or socially privileged sections of the society, yielding no benefit to the weaker sections. Finally, it must also be admitted that notwithstanding the unwillingness of the State level politicians to part with their power, even the local people themselves were not adequately educated to understand the role and the importance of the PRIs.

The revival of interest in the PRIs however came about with a change of government at the national level during 1977. A committee was then set up under the chairmanship of Ashok Mehta to take a fresh look at the Panchayati Raj system. This committee, while recommending a two-tier structure of decentralisation, preferred the ZP to be the first point for decentralisation below the State level and favoured the participation of political parties in all the Panchayat elections. Since the government that constituted this committee went out of office soon after the submission of the report of the committee, no serious action was taken by the Central Government on the recommendations of this committee. However the Ramakrishna Hegde Government that came to power in Karnataka during 1983 made use of this report to introduce a two-tier Panchayati Raj system in that State in 1987.

Admittedly, the Karnataka pattern carried the process of democratic decentralisation the farthest and had, therefore, evoked considerable interest nationwide. Almost simultaneously, the GVK Rao Committee appointed by the Planning Commission to review the existing administrative arrangements for rural development strongly recommended for the revival of PRIs all over the country, highlighting the inevitable need to transfer power of the State to democratic bodies at the local level. The Government of India then set up a committee in June 1986 headed by Dr. L.M. Singhvi to prepare a concept paper on the revitalisation of the PRIs. This Committee recommended that local self-governance should be constitutionally recognised, protected and preserved by the inclusion of a new chapter in the Constitution.

Accepting these recommendations of the Singhvi Committee, the Rajiv Gandhi Government in 1989 and the V.P. Singh Government in 1990 brought constitutional amendments providing the establishment of local self-governance throughout the country. Though both these amendments fell through for different reasons, most of the political parties in India had by then agreed in principle to the establishment of PRIs all over India, despite differences over details and procedures. The Narasimha Rao Government again introduced a comprehensive amendment bill in 1991, which after several deliberations was finally passed with near unanimity in the Parliament in December 1992.

The Constitution 73rd Amendment Act 1992 which was brought into effect from April 24, 1993 clearly envisages the establishment of Panchayats as units of local self-government. It empowers them to prepare plans for economic development and social justice and also implement schemes in these areas as may be entrusted to them by the respective State governments. The amendment thus gives the Panchayats a constitutional status as units of local governance and not mere vehicles for delivering development benefits. I find that Justice E.S. Venkataramaiah, while delivering the first lecture under this Endowment here had, after an analysis of the constitutional provisions on decentralisation, come to this conclusion:

> "Thus it is seen that the constitutional amendments made by the 73rd and 74th Amendments ensure the setting up of Local Bodies, such as Panchayats and municipalities throughout India and to keep them going and for entrusting to them powers to administer matters which are of local interest. These institutions have thus acquired permanency and are considered as the third level of government with responsibilities of decentralised governance and planning."

That takes me to my second point viz., the constitutionally recognised present day Panchayats have a larger space and responsibility in the field of governance and they are intended to achieve far beyond just evoking local initiative in the field of development. Article 243G of the Constitution, which visualises panchayats as institutions of self government however makes it clear that the primary role of the Panchayats will continue to be in the area of development. Planning and implementation of programmes of economic development and social justice will still be the main focus of their activities. The 11th Schedule to the Constitution in fact contains an impressive list of development activities, which could be entrusted to the Panchayats.

Ideally, as units of government, the Panchayats should have full autonomy in deciding their priorities and determining the allocations to different programmes. But, in reality, the system of centralised planning, which the country has followed for the last five decades, severely constrains local autonomy. When such constrains operate at the State level, it is not surprising that they should also be felt at the sub-State levels. This limited freedom that is available to the Panchayats in the existing system of planning is further compounded by the reluctancy on the part of several State governments to devolve adequate functions and powers to local bodies. Though the process of devolution has to be based on the cardinal principle that what can be undertaken by a particular tier should be got done by that tier only and not by a higher tier, this is not being followed in practice. Even though the 11th Schedule to the Constitution has envisaged the transfer of 29 items to the PRIs for implementation, neither the functions nor the functionaries nor the funds required to implement schemes relating to these items have been transferred to the PRIs in several States. The decentralised planning process with people's participation which is a pre-requisite for the effective implementation of development programmes by the Panchayats have also not been put in place in most parts of the country except a few progressive islands of hope like Kerala, West Bengal, Madhya Pradesh etc.

While in actual practice even the minimum functions indicated in the Constitution have not been actually transferred to the local government institutions in several States, some people feel that Article 243G should have specifically provided for the entrustment of the total range of government functions at the local levels to the PRIs instead of leaving it to the State governments to prescribe. Some others also feel that even law and order and other regulatory responsibilities must also have been given to the PRIs so as to strengthen their position as units of self-government. In my opinion, this may not be justified. At the present stage when institutions of local government have yet to take a firm root, it is important that they win the acceptability and confidence of the people through efficient implementation of development programmes, rather than be perceived as organs of State power. Also, the feeling that the rights of the underprivileged sections of society, including minorities and Scheduled Castes and Scheduled Tribes, are likely to be better safeguarded by structures of government which are not directly susceptible to local pressures and influences, is not entirely unfounded. Therefore, for the present, PRIs may better exclusively devote themselves to the task of development.

What is important is that in the areas assigned to them, the PRIs must enjoy as large a measure of autonomy as possible. They should be able to provide a responsive administration in these areas, which implies a degree of freedom to adjust programmes according to local needs without being hamstrung by detailed government directives. To the extent possible, they should mobilise local resources and augment the scale of development efforts. The third point I wish to make before this august gathering, therefore, is: If the PRIs have to make their mark in the field of governance and win the confidence of the people, they must start the process by effectively implementing their rural development functions.

That takes me to the main theme of my talk today viz., how to strengthen Panchayati Raj through rural development in the present context. Any textbook on decentralisation would say that local governments are the most efficient instruments for conveying benefits to the needy, with the least cost, in view of their closeness to the people. Accountability and transparency, the two cornerstones of decentralised governance should ensure minimisation of beneficiary misidentification, better asset acquisition, its retention and maintenance etc. Since local wisdom and local resources are readily available to local governments, local human, animal and physical resources can be effectively utilised, resulting in creation of employment opportunities and production of goods and services relevant to the needs of the people. Do these things really happen in the field? What is the experience of States, with a reasonably good record of decentralised governance?

To get an answer to these questions, I undertook a research study in the State of Karnataka a couple of years ago. Since panchayats are responsible for implementing poverty alleviation programmes in Karnataka, I picked up two programmes viz., Jawahar Rozgar Yojana (JRY) and the Drought Prone Area Programme (DPAP) for this study. As most of you know, JRY was essentially a programme for wage employment, to provide purchasing power to the rural poor. This programme incidentally results in creation of assets for the community. On the other hand, DPAP is primarily meant to create assets for developing core sectors of the economy, thereby improving the prospects of employment and income generation. Since these programmes in a way complement to each other, a study of these two programmes in the field, I thought, it would help me in understanding the performance levels of the delivery system. My study examined schemes implemented under JRY and DPAP during the ten-year period between 1987 and 1997 in three districts, nine blocks and twenty village panchayats of Karnataka. We interviewed 642 respondents during our study. Let me now briefly share with you, what we learnt through this study.

Broadly our study revealed two distinct advantages in utilising PRIs as delivery mechanism for rural development. First is the wide dissemination of knowledge about development schemes implemented by the Panchayats in the field. The second is the absence of complaints regarding misuse of public funds. Our respondents generally felt that PRIs are better suited for delivering development benefits as against the bureaucracy, especially in view of the better accountability of the PRIs to the people as against the bureaucrats. The areas where the PRIs had an edge over the all India pattern (in which mostly government agencies like the DRDA were responsible for the implementation of poverty alleviation programmes) are the type and quality of assets, employment generation and in terms of costs incurred by the beneficiaries for obtaining the benefits. Though there were some negative points viz., poor participation of women in JRY works, misidentification of beneficiaries, involvement of contractors in the execution of works and only a small percentage of beneficiaries getting substantial employment etc., these shortcomings have been noticed throughout the country. While some of them could have been rectified by the PRIs, some others are results of conceptual flaws in the very design of JRY.

Similarly, some of the shortfalls noticed in DPAP viz., the programmes not being implemented on watershed basis, local people not being involved in the process of planning and the core sector activity not being taken up in an integrated manner are common throughout the country. However the works executed under DPAP in Karnataka were comparatively more relevant from the point of view of land improvement, afforestation and pasture development. The benefits of the programme largely reached the people of the area and no wasteful expenditure was reported unlike in many other parts of the country.

However, we noticed two major shortcomings in the delivery of rural development by the PRIs in our study area. As all of us know, most of the schemes meant for rural development are centrally sponsored. The guidelines prescribed and the rigid norms insisted upon in the pattern of expenditure by the Central Government under these schemes do not provide any flexibility to the Panchayats. Lack of their own resources, very little untied funds and excessive dependence on centrally sponsored schemes for delivering developmental benefits have reduced the Panchayats to mere agencies of government rather than retaining their position as constitutional bodies for local governance. Secondly, we also noticed that the Gram Sabhas have not been meeting in most of the Panchayats and their role in development has been minimal. Unless these two shortcomings are rectified soon, the advantages PRIs have in delivering development benefits will be nullified.

That takes me to the concluding part of my lecture viz., what needs to be done to set right these shortcomings. I would rather start with the second point viz., the Gram Sabhas. Admittedly the Gram Sabhas constitute the bedrock of the Panchayati Raj system in India. While the Gram Panchayats, the intermediate Panchayats and the Zilla Panchayats are organs of representative democracy, it is only at the level of the Gram Sabha, we have a participative democracy. It is in the Gram Sabha that every voter has the right to participate. He or she can propose the right type of schemes required for the village. He or she can identify people within the village who deserve to be helped under a particular scheme. He or she can seek clarification and demand action from the representative he or she has chosen. Unless the Gram Sabhas meet regularly, we cannot ensure direct accountability of the elected representative to the electorate. Only through better accountability, the implementation of schemes by the PRIs will be effective. The question therefore is what should be done to ensure regular meetings, proper attendance and disposal of functions in the Gram Sabha.

This issue can be looked at from two different angles. One relates to the practical aspects of convening the Gram Sabha and the other relates to the legal and constitutional aspects. On the procedural side, it may be said that the date, time and location for the Gram Sabha meeting should be convenient for all the people to participate in the meeting. There should be enough publicity for the Gram Sabha meeting through the local media and local communication methods such as wall posters, handbills, tom-tom etc., must be freely deployed. The people who attend the Gram Sabha meetings should be encouraged to express their opinion freely, so that no single group dominates the proceedings. The non-governmental organisations active in the field of rural development must be encouraged to educate the people so that they could actively participate in the Gram Sabha meetings.

Of late, there is a tendency to establish parallel institutions at the village level to implement various development programmes. For instance, the watershed development committee constituted at the village level deals with issues relating to the watershed that may fall entirely within a Gram Panchayat. Similarly, the water supply and sanitation committees under the World Bank assisted water supply programme, the village education committees under the district primary education programme again assisted by the World Bank etc., have all ended up in creating parallel institutions at the village level to deal with certain aspects of development, which fall within the domain of the PRIs. Though these institutions may be unavoidable, as they deal with only specific subjects and many a time function within one or two villages of the Gram Panchayat only, it is necessary that all of them are made accountable to the respective Gram Sabhas. Each committee functioning within a village under any scheme must report to the Gram Sabha in their periodical meetings and explain their activities during the interregnum. This will certainly strengthen the role of PRIs in rural development.

All this, of course, requires a very strong political will at the local level. The chairperson and the secretary of the Gram Panchayat should take interest to convene the Gram Sabha meetings regularly. They must also frankly tell the people what is possible and what is not, particularly in the field of infrastructure development, so that the Gram Sabha can concentrate on its functions of reviewing and determining development programmes rather than becoming a forum for receiving complaints, petitions and even shopping lists. But, how do we institutionalise this?

That takes us to the next set of issues, which relate to the constitutional and legal structure of the Gram Sabha. According to Article 243 (b), Gram Sabha consists of all persons registered as voters in the electoral roll relating to the village comprised within the area of the Panchayat at the village level. Article 243(g) defines a village as one specified by the Governor by public notification to be a village for the purposes of the Act and includes a group of villages so specified. The Gram Sabha, under Article 243A, may exercise such powers and perform such functions at the village level as the Legislature of a State may, by law, provide.

Admittedly the Gram Sabha is the foundation of our Panchayati Raj. It is through the Gram Sabha that the elected representative is made accountable to the electorate. This requires two things. Firstly, if the participation in the Gram Sabha has to be meaningful the gathering should not be large. Secondly, the Gram Sabha should meet periodically and the subjects placed before it are such that they attract public attention. Only then, the electorate will have any interest to attend the Gram Sabha, foregoing their day's income. Unfortunately, the existing legislations do not appear to provide for both these requirements explicitly.

While in some States, the Gram Sabha meetings take place in every village whenever the Village Panchayat consists of several villages, in some other States only one composite Gram Sabha is convened for all the villages which constitute the Gram Panchayat. Since this composite Gram Sabha is usually held in the headquarters village of the Panchayat, citizens from the other villages either do not attend the Gram Sabha or are reluctant to articulate their needs. Unless we insist on each village having a Gram Sabha of its own, the purpose of accountability may not be served, especially when the Village Panchayat serves a population of a few thousands. Since even a single village Gram Sabha may not provide an adequate forum for propular participation, unless the population of the village is around a thousand or so, holding Gram Sabhas on constituency/ward basis has to be thought of.

It is pertinent to mention here that under the provisions of the Panchayats (Extension to Scheduled Areas) Act, 1996 extending the provisions of Part IX of the Constitution relating to the Panchayats to the Scheduled Areas of the country, the village and the Gram Sabha are better defined. Under this Act, "a village shall ordinarily consist of a habitation or a group of habitations or a hamlet or a group of hamlets comprising a community and managing its affairs in accordance with traditions and customs" and "every village shall have a Gram Sabha consisting of persons whose names are included in the electoral rolls for the Panchayat at the village level". It may perhaps be desirable to provide for similar definitions either in the constitution itself or in the State Legislations on Panchayats.

Secondly, by leaving the powers and functions of the Gram Sabha to be designed by the Legislature of the State, the Constitution has not really empowered the Gram Sabhas, to be meaningful and effective. It may, therefore, be necessary to specifically provide that the Gram Sabhas would have to meet at least twice a year, discuss and review all development problems/ programmes of the village, select beneficiaries for all beneficiary-oriented programmes transferred to the PRIs, plan for local improvement including minimum needs, welfare and production oriented programmes including the cropping pattern for the season for the village etc.

Here again, the provisions of the Panchayats (Extension to Schedule Areas) Act, 1996 spell out more clearly the role of the Gram Sabhas. Under this Act, "Every Gram Sabha shall be competent to safeguard and preserve the traditions and customs of the people, their cultural identity, community resources and the customary mode of dispute resolution; every Gram Sabha shall (i) approve the plans, programmes and projects for social and economic development before such plans, programmes and projects are taken up for implementation by the Panchayat at the village level, (ii) be responsible for the identification or selection of persons as beneficiaries under the poverty alleviation and other programmes," and "every Panchayat at the village level shall be required to obtain from the Gram Sabha a certificate of utilisation of funds by the Panchayat for the plans, programmes and projects". There is, therefore, a need to suitably amend the Constitution further, on similar lines, to provide for the twin purpose of ensuring a Gram Sabha for every village and prescribing a minimum agenda for discussions in the Gram Sabha meetings.

It may even be necessary to make a specific provision in the State legislations to the effect that it is the duty of the chairperson of the Gram Panchayat to convene these meetings without fail and in the event of his or her not complying with this provision for a period of one year or more, he or she should be disqualified from holding the post of the chairperson of the Panchayat. Similarly the chief executive officer of the Taluk Panchayat and/or his representatives must be directed to attend the Gram Sabha meetings without fail, if necessary through stringent administrative instructions.

Let us look at the other shortfall now. Our study revealed that the limited availability of untied funds and the restrictions imposed by the centrally sponsored schemes have made the PRIs agencies of the State government rather than independent units of local governance. To change this situation, the scope of earmarking by the Planning Commission should be reduced considerably so that the States can enable PRIs to have a substantial untied funds and some say in prioritisation. The need to reduce the ever-expanding number of centrally sponsored schemes is obvious. I understand that the Planning Commission has recently decided to prune the centrally sponsored schemes and it is proposed to bring down the number of these schemes to 117 from 256 at present. While this is a step in the right direction, further reduction of centrally sponsored schemes has to be undertaken and achieved as early as possible.

While the Zilla Panchayats can have the planning and coordinating roles, the intermediate panchayats can be the implementing agencies. The Gram Panchayats can, in a limited way, be involved in programme implementation. For instance, in Tamilnadu the selection of beneficiaries, identification of works, their supervision and execution can be assigned to the Gram Sabha/ Gram Panchayat. The Taluk Panchayat should be responsible for the implementation of the programmes and the Zilla Panchayat for the disbursal of funds and overall planning and supervision.

Any rural development programme to be successful has to be flexible so as to provide for local talents and innovations. They must essentially be people centered. The Panchayats must therefore be encouraged to use their discretion and involve the people more and more in the implementation of development programmes. To encourage innovative approaches by competent local bodies, a measure of fiscal independence may also be given to the PRIs by assigning part of tax revenue and increasing their per capita grants. The financial assistance to the Panchayats can be in two parts—one consisting of Block grants recommended by the State Finance Commission and the other linked to the resources mobilised by the panchayats themselves.

The practice of giving special grants to the Members of Parliament and State Legislatures for local area development should be done away with. Instead, such funds should be allotted to the Panchayats, which have been designated as governments responsible for local development. In view of the major role played by the bureaucracy in aiding and advising the elected representatives at the Panchayat level, there is also a need to bring down the attitudinal difference between the politicians and the bureaucrats. This can happen only over a period of time. Till then, programmes will have to be organised to train both of them independently and also jointly, with a view not only to equipping them for their tasks but also to coexist harmoniously.

Before I conclude, I must also mention as to what we all can do to ensure the success of PRIs in the field of rural development. As I mentioned earlier, the two crucial areas which require attention are: strengthening Gram Sabhas to provide accountability and delegation of adequate powers, functions and funds to the Panchayats to carry out their responsibilities, with some measure of fiscal independence. Unless genuine decentralisation takes place at the grass roots, the PRIs will most certainly degenerate into another set of government departments without fully performing their designated role in the field of rural development. As enlightened citizens of this country we may have to play a more than advocacy role. Persuading State and Central level politicians to recognize the utility of PRIs for rural development and to devolve on them more and more functions, funds and functionaries is no doubt important. But we can do much more. Perhaps, even an active participation, may be desirable. It is always felt that the educated middle class in our country does not participate in the electoral mechanisms. While contesting assembly and Parliamentary elections may be beyond the reach of most of us, it should be possible for us to take an active part at least in the Panchayat elections. If competent people do come to power in the Panchayats and demand their rights, I am sure the Panchayats can provide the right kind of lead to the nation as the strongest pillars of democracy.

REFERENCES

Constituent Assembly Debates. November 1948.

Gandhiji. (1942) My idea of village swaraj, *Harijan*.

Imperial Gazetteer of India, 1909, Vol. 4.

Jawaharlal Nehru. (1964). *The Discovery of India*. Signet Press, Calcutta.

Meenakshisundaram, S.S. (1999). Gram Sabha: Lessons from Karnataka. *Kurukshetra*, New Delhi.

Meenakshisundaram, S.S. (1994). *Decentralisation in Developing Countries*. Concept Publishing Company, New Delhi.

Report of the G.V.K. Rao Committee on Administrative Arrangements for Rural Development, (1985).

Report of the Team for the Study of Community Projects and National Extension Services, 1959.

Venkataramaiah., E.S. (1997). *Panchayati Raj Institutions in India*. V.R. Krishna Iyer Endowment Lecture. Delivered at Gandhigram Rural University, Dindigul.

6

DIMENSIONS OF DECENTRALIZATION

A View from States

P.R. Sharma and R.P. Joshi

Mahatma Gandhi said : "In a democracy, decentralization of political and economic power is essential, because a few centres of power cannot realize or fulfil the needs of vast multitudes of people. If India is to develop, the power and responsibilities must be shared by all."[1] When Panchayati Raj was initiated in India, the basic idea was to procure people's participation and people in the villages could be associated in plan formulation through Gram Sabha, plan execution through village Panchayats, monitoring by Block Panchayats and review for guidance by District Panchayats. It was also envisaged that there would be certain amount of democracy which would give people a sense of involvement. Basic object was to take democracy to masses and take decision making closer to the people. So far democracy had accorded voting rights to people at large. Administration and planning task carried out by bureaucracy only. There has been no involvement of people for whom the programmes are meant at any stage. It was felt that by providing power to people, bureaucracy would come under local popular control and the process of socio-economic development would get accelerated. Panchayati Raj Institutions, it was argued, would fulfil the long felt need of providing rural infrastructure for rural development of backward areas. This Chapter attempts to understand the various aspects of decentralization process in the context of Indian States.

Panchayati Raj in various States prior to 1993

A varied of Panchayati Raj was prevalent across States. Table 6.1 below elicits situation as it existed across States prior to 1993. In a large country like India, it is really difficult to have a uniform system of Panchayati Raj. Local circumstances differ from State to State. It is observed that there are certain basic features like tiers of structure, system of election, duration of Panchayati Raj Institutions, judicial functions which are uniform with minor differences reflecting the size of the State or nature of people residing there in having different cultural traditions as found in tribal areas or hill districts[2].

Structure

It is observed that it is the 3-tier structure that prevailed across States with the exception of Assam, Haryana, Manipur, Orissa and Sikkim where 2-tier was adopted. Assam, Haryana and Orissa did not provide for District Panchayat at all. The Panchayati Raj, therefore, was only at village and Block level in these States.

The small States like Goa, Kerala, Tripura and Jammu & Kashmir had Panchayats only at village level. Kerala is even now opposing the 3-tier system. The Sikkim's 2-tier system was distinct as it had a Panchayat at the village level and at the district level. However, all these institutions provide almost a similar set-up irrespective of the nomenclature. At village level it is normally Gaon Panchayat or Gram Panchayat. Block Panchayat is Mandal Praja Parishad, Mohkuma Parishad, Taluk Panchayat, Panchayat Samiti, Block Panchayat Board, Janpad Panchayat, Panchayat Union Council, Kshetra Samiti as people of the area could follow. At the district level it is generally called Zilla Parishad or Zilla Panchayat. It is known as District Development Council in Tamil Nadu. Tribal States like Maghalaya, Nagaland and Mizoram have the traditional councils of village elders.

To a very large extent, the geographical size and the administrative need of the State has been instrumental in deciding the structure of Panchayati Raj. Smaller States have a single tier system whereas larger states have three-tier system, keeping in view their requirements.

Table 6.1: Panchayati Raj in Various States Prior to 1993

S. No.	State	Adopted System	Mode of Election	Term of Office Years	Judicial Body
1	2	3	4	5	6
1.	Andhra Pradesh	1. Gram Panchayat 2. Mandal Panchayat 3. Zilla Praja Parishad	Direct Indirect	5 5	Nyay Panchayat
2.	Assam	1. Gaon Panchayat 2. Mohkuma Parishad	Direct Indirect	4 4	Panchayat Adalat
3.	Bihar	1. Gram Panchayat 2. Panchayat Samiti 3. Zilla Parishad	Direct Indirect Indirect	5 5 5	Gram Kutchery
4.	Goa	1. Panchayat	Direct	4	—
5.	Gujarat	1. Gram Panchayat 2. Nagar Panchayat 3. Taluka Panchayat 4. District Panchayat	Direct Indirect Indirect Indirect	5 5 5 5	Nyay Panchayat
6.	Haryana	1. Gram Panchayat 2. Panchayat Samiti	Direct Indirect	5 5	Adalati Panchayat
7.	H.P.	1. Gram Panchayat 2. Panchayat Samiti 3. Zilla Parishad	Direct Indirect Indirect	5 5 5	—

Contd.....

Table 6.1 *(Contd.)*

1	2	3	4	5	6
8.	Jammu & Kashmir	1. Village Panchayat 2. Block Panchayat Boards	Direct Indirect	4 4	Panchayat Adalat
9.	Karnataka	1. Mandal Panchayat 2. Taluk Panchayat 3. Zilla Parishad	Direct Direct Direct	5 5 5	Nyay Panchayat
10.	Kerala	1. Panchayat	Direct	5	—
11.	Madhya Pradesh	1. Gram Panchayat 2. Nagar Panchayat 3. Janpad Panchayat 4. Zilla Panchayat	Direct Direct Indirect Indirect	5 5 5 5	Conciliation Boar
12.	Maharashtra	1. Gram Panchayat 2. Panchayat Samiti 3. Zilla Parishad	Direct Indirect Indirect	5 5 5	Nyay Panchayat
13.	Manipur	1. Gram Panchayat 2. Panchayat Samiti 3. Zilla Parishad	Direct Indirect Indirect	5 5 5	—
14.	Orissa	1. Gram Panchayat 2. Panchayat Samiti	Direct Indirect	5 5	—
15.	Punjab	1. Gram Panchayat 2. Panchayat Samiti 3. Zilla Parishad	Direct Indirect Indirect	3 3 3	Adalati Panchayat

Contd......

Table 6.1 *(Contd.)*

1	2	3	4	5	6
16.	Rajasthan	1. Village Panchayat 2. Panchayat Samiti 3. Zilla Parishad	Direct Indirect Indirect	5 5 5	Nyay Panchayat
17.	Sikkim	1. Village Panchayat 2. Panchayat Samiti 3. Zilla Parishad	Direct Indirect Direct	5 5 5	
18.	Tamil Nadu	1. Village Panchayat 2. Zilla Panchayat	Direct Indirect	5 5	
19.	Tripura	1. Panchayat 2. Panchayat Union Council 3. District Development Council	Direct Indirect Indirect	5 5 5	Panchayat Secretary (one of elected member) empowered to settle disputes
20.	Uttar Pradesh	1. Gaon Panchayat 2. Kshetra Samiti 3. Zilla Parishad	Direct Indirect Indirect	5 5 5	Nyay Panchayat
21.	West Bengal	1. Gram Panchayat 2. Panchayat Samiti 3. Zilla Parishad	Direct Indirect Indirect	4 4 4	Nyay Panchayat

Contd......

Table 6.1 *(Contd.)*

1	2	3	4	5	6
22.	Manipur	Traditional Village	—	—	
23.	Mizoram	Council having Special powers	—	—	
24.	Nagaland	Powers are in operation in this state	—	—	

Source : Singh, S.S. and Suresh Mishra, *Legislative Framework of Panchayati Raj in India*, pp. *xv-xviii*.

Elections

There were some variations in election processes across the States. Direct elections were held at village Panchayat level. Block level bodies and Zilla Panchayat were constituted from amongst the chairpersons of Panchayati Raj Institution at next lower level, MLA, MP members co-opted from women, Scheduled Caste/Tribe etc. Karnataka State was an exception where direct election for members of Zilla Parishad as well as Mandal Panchayat was provided in act of 1983 whereas this provision was made compulsory in 1993 through Constitutional Amendment.

In Andhra Pradesh, the head of Panchayat at District level was directly elected while in Arunachal Pradesh, the Chairman was nominated. In Tamil Nadu and Nagaland, the Collector becomes the Chairman of the District Development Council. In all other States, the election of chairperson of Zilla Parishad was indirect. At the Block level, Gujarat, Madhya Pradesh, Manipur, Maharashtra, Arunachal Pradesh and West Bengal elected some members directly while in other States they were elected indirectly. Bulk of members in these States were ex-officio by virtue of their being Sarpanch/Pradhan of Gram Panchayats. In Andhra Pradesh and Tamil Nadu, the head of Block Panchayat was elected directly while in other States he was elected from amongst the ex-officio members were elected directly except in Bihar. In Bihar, four members were directly elected whereas other four were nominated by Mukhia, who was directly elected by the electorates. Madhya Pradesh, Andhra Pradesh and West Bengal allowed the political parties participation in elections to Panchayati Raj Institutions. Kerala allowed political parties to contest Gram Panchayat elections.

Powers and Functions

Powers and functions of Panchayats had variations across the states. The distribution of powers and functions among Panchayats at village, Block and district levels was quite clear. It was only in Gujarat that post of Talati for land revenue collections was transferred to Gram Panchayat. Most of the functions like agriculture, animal husbandry, co-operation women and child welfare, rural employment, poverty alleviation, primary education, village industries, handlooms, minor irrigation tanks, local development works had been entrusted to Panchayati Raj Institutions along with staff and budget. But gradually they were withdrawn and the departmental hold was tightened. In this process of bureaucratic control, District Rural Development Agencies were created in 1978 in every district for sanctioning all rural development works from Central Government budget. Zilla Panchayats remained only a titular institution. District Rural Development Agencies under the chairmanship of District Collector sanctioned and monitored all rural employment generation and poverty alleviation schemes, though Block Panchayats and Gram Panchayats continued to implement the programmes at lower levels as development agencies of District Rural Development Agencies.

Panchayati Raj Institutions at village and Mandal level in all the States were authorised to levy taxes or fees on sometimes like, house, water rate, profession, trade, market, meals, slaughter house, registration fee for cattle etc.

In States like Andhra Pradesh, Assam, Bihar, Haryana, Punjab, Tamil Nadu, Himachal Pradesh, Karnataka, Kerala and Madhya Pradesh imposition of taxes was compulsory by law.

Such taxes were mainly:

1. Housing tax or building tax (all the above States)
2. Trade and Callings or Profession Tax (Assam, Bihar, Punjab, Himachal Pradesh, Kerala, Madhya Pradesh)
3. Surcharge on Transfer of property (Kerala, Madhya Pradesh, Tamil Nadu and Haryana)
4. Advertisement Tax (Kerala)
5. Private latrines (Madhya Pradesh)
6. Light Tax (Madhya Pradesh)
7. Portion of Entertainment Tax (Tamil Nadu and Rajasthan)
8. Octroi on liquor (Rajasthan)

Despite these allotted functions, findings of numerous committees and finance commissions reveal that Panchaytai Raj Institutions failed to raise their own resources. It was mainly because of fear about unpopularity and did not want to take risk of losing votes in next elections. In States like Maharashtra, Gujarat, Orissa, Rajasthan, Uttar Pradesh, West Bengal, where imposition of taxes was left to the will of Panchayati Raj Institutions, hardly any taxes were imposed. They mostly depended on central or State government grants. There were few Panchayats which did raise their income through sale of natural produce, water bodies, education, income from cattle fairs and the like sources. There was a provision of matching share to be paid by State government equal to own income raised by Panchayats. This was availed by very few Panchayati Raj Institutions.

Government Control

Prior to 1993 acts, State government control existed in almost all the States. States enjoyed enormous powers and had the ultimate say in matters of Panchayati Raj Institutions. Panchayati Raj Institutions were really like any other government department with the only difference that delegated/decentralized powers were exercised by elected representative within the overall directives issued by the State or Central government. The government had the power to suspend, supersede or dissolve a Panchayat. It could cancel any resolution passed by Panchayati Raj Institutions. Even Collector could suspend a resolution on the basis of law and order or danger to person or property. State had the sole power to enact law and by-laws. It was only in Gujarat that the Panchayat Parishad–non-governmental apex body of the Panchayat–was taken into confidence if any change was to be brought about in any matter concerning the Panchayats. It was, however, only in Gujarat that District Collector did not exercise any power over Panchayati Raj Institutions in the State except that District Magistrate could suspend Sarpanch/Up-Sarpanch against whom criminal proceedings involving moral turpitude was instituted. In Orissa, the Collector could suspend a Sarpanch if he did not call a meeting for three months and disqualify Sarpanch for one year.

Even sub-divisional officer had powers to rescind/modify a resolution of Gram Panchayat in case it was in contravention of the act. In Punjab, the Director Panchayats could remove a Sarpanch. In Tamil Nadu, the Collector was himself Chairman District Development Council. States like Karnataka and West Bengal, where Panchayats had taken deep roots, did not give full freedom to the Panchayat. States controlled the Panchayats through their acts. Commissioner could remove the president for failure to discharge his duties in Karnataka.

In Maharashtra, Section 41 provided that the Collector may suspend any elected representative if a criminal case is pending against the member. In Panchayat Samiti and Zilla Parishad Act 1961, Section 39 empowers Zilla Parishad in Maharashtra to remove Sarpanch/Up-Sarpanch for misconduct or neglect of duty. Collector ws empowered to suspend any resolution of Panchayati Raj Institutions in Andhra Pradesh, Rajasthan and Assam. No post can be created in any Panchayati Raj Institution without previous approval of the State government. In Goa, even secretary of every Panchayat was appointed by the Lt. Governor.

Budget

Budget of every Gram Panchayat was generally approved by Block Panchayat and that of Block Panchayat was approved by Zilla Parishad. The budget of Zilla Parishad was approved by the State government. This meant that financial control was exercised by the upper tier of government at all levels.

Gram Sabha

Almost in all the State acts, there was a provision for holding at least two meetings of Gram Sabha or electors of a Panchayat every year. In case of Assam, Gram Sabha was to meet every three months. In case of Kerala, it was to meet once in a year, but in each constituency. Similarly, in case of Orissa, there was a provision of 'Palli Sabha' (Ward Sabha) for every village twice a year. Uttar Pradesh provided for two meetings, normally after Kharif and Rabi crop harvesting. A quorum of 1/10th voters was provided for Gram Sabha meeting in most of the States. However, it was one-fifth in Uttar Pradesh and Himachal Pradesh, one-fourth in West Bengal and one-third in Karnataka. Gram Sabhas were expected to perform wide range of functions of poverty alleviation, identification of beneficiaries, submission of budget, accounts and progress of development schemes.

Gram Sabha was really corner stone of the entire scheme of democratic decentralization. It was direct democracy at grass root level. Legal empowerment of Gram Sabha was done almost in all the State acts right from inception of Panchayati Raj. It was really a 'watch dog' of working of Panchayats if they understood and performed their actual role in practice. It was really the concept of Gandhiji's 'Swarajya'.... Democracy at the grass roots. Thus, Gram Sabha was really to develop into an institution capable of exerting effective influence on the village Panchayats. The greater the power of Gram Sabha, the better it is for the people also. In this context J.P. Narayan opined that "Let us not have only representative government from the village up to Delhi one place, at least let there be direct government, direct democracy...... the relationship between Panchayat and Gram Sabha should be that of cabinet and Assembly".[3] In practice, the situation was diametrically opposite. Gram Sabha remained only a formality. Sarpanch held the formal meetings because Block development office announced day-to-day programme and nominated officials to attend such Gram Sabhas. Publicity was not properly made. These meetings were sparely attended, and they too were people connected with the Sarpanch and influential Panchs. Attendance was hardly as per quorum prescribed for it—signatures were obtained later on from people's homes, if necessary, to complete the legal formality. People took interest of people also dwindled especially as their needs and aspirations were not fulfilled by the Panchayat for paucity of funds. Moreover, Gram Sabha was never treated as an assembly by Panchayat, at the most it was created as an advisory body. Gram Sabhas meetings slowly turned into a formality.

Even Jawaharlal Nehru, the first Prime Minister of India was of the opinion that "Local Self Government was and must be the basis of any true system of democracy. People had got into the habit of thinking of democracy at the top and not so much below. Democracy at the top could not be a success unless it was built on this foundation below"[4]. Almost every great leader who believed in democracy wanted it from below. When Panchayati Raj was inaugurated in 1959, the then Central Minister for Community Development, S.K. Dey also strongly felt that "Panchayati Raj as we now visualize will, therefore, mean progressive increase in competence from the ground upwards and corresponding transfer of responsibilities from the centre to ground. If one wishes to climb higher, one must reduce the burden of avoidable weight on his shoulders….. In order to function at the level, it should, our centre must be relieved likewise of responsibilities such as can be discharged by the Panchayati Raj Institutions along the line…. The Zilla Parishad, Block Panchayat Samiti, Panchayat, Associate Voluntary Institutions and the individual families. Panchayati Raj will grow thus to be a way of life and a new approach to government as against a unit of government. It will bring about a complete link up, of our people from the Gram Sabha to Lok Sabha"[5].

Diwakar Committee was appointed by the government of India to review the working of Gram Sabhas. While commenting on the working of Gram Sabha, it said, "though Gram Sabha should serve to strengthen Panchayati Raj, but it did not function effectively and has to be developed in the course of time" [6].

Satya Brata Sen (Kerala)[7] in his detailed report in 1997 to make Gram Sabhas effective recommended that (i) Gram Sabha should meet as frequently as possible not less than once in three months; (ii) There should be written invitation to every household to ensure 10 per cent quorum; and (iii) Every member should be given a copy of the government order mentioning detailed rights and responsibilities of Gram Sabhas with a covering letter by the Gram Panchayat president.

Iqbal Narain argued that "What is needed is an honest and sincere effort, first to make the institution of Gram Sabha a live institution in its present form and then let it grow to its full stature on the principle of gradualness and spontaneous and natural growth, not in isolation, but in organic unity with Panchayati Raj movement, not merely in the light of theoretical surmises but keeping in view the actualities of India's rural scene"[8]. Hence common people were to be brought in the fold of Gram Sabha especially because in spite of legal provisions affiliated groups and prominent persons in the village. The idea had not so far struck the roots in the minds of all classes of society.

No Confidence Motion

Normally Sarpanch of a Gram Panchayat is directly elected by the electorates and it should be only the voters who should be competent to remove him in case of no-confidence. In most of the State acts, there was a provision that Panchs by two-third majority could pass a vote of no-confidence and could be brought only once in five years in Andhra Pradesh and that too not in first-two years from the date of election. No such period was prescribed in Acts of Assam, Bihar, Gujarat, Himachal Pradesh, Karnạtaka, Maharashtra and West Bengal. In case of Punjab, no-confidence could be brought only after two years, after one year in Madhya Pradesh, Orissa, Rajasthan, Uttar Pradesh and after six months in Kerala. However, the only Haryana Act had provided that two-third majority in Gram Sabha could pass no-confidence motion against a Sarpanch of a Gram Panchayat.

Committee System

It was almost in all the States that working committees/standing committees have been formed for execution of different functions of Panchayati Raj Institutions. Though the number of such committees vary from State to State, the normal number ranged between three to seven, the average membership was three to five members. In some committees, women, Scheduled Caste, Scheduled Tribe member was also included specially in social justice/social welfare committee. These were generally at Block level and district level. In case of Rajasthan, Assam, Bihar, Gujarat, Kerala, Madhya Pradesh the committees were also formed at village Panchayat level. In Kerala, since Panchayats cover a large population, provision was also made for formation of Ward committees by Gram Panchayats though it was voluntary. The various committees formed for :

1. Planning, finance and budget.
2. Agriculture and allied schemes of production programmes like Animal Husbandry, Irrigation etc.
3. Education, Health and Sanitation.
4. Welfare of weaker sections or social justice including women and child welfare and social welfare.
5. Amenities/public works and communications.
6. General Administration, Policy Guidelines, Administration and Establishment.

Panchayat Development Service

Almost in all the States, officers of Panchayati Raj Institutions were placed on deputation from different line departments. Separate Panchayati Raj service was constituted only in Gujarat and Punjab. In Rajasthan separate service rules exist for officers and subordinate officers. Officers still come on deputation from other departments. In Karnataka and Tamil Nadu, presidents of Gram Panchayats, Taluka Panchayat and Zilla Panchayats acted as executing heads and bureaucracy paid only facilitative role. In Orissa, status of State minister was given to the president and that of Deputy State Minister to Deputy President and that of Deputy State Minister to Deputy President of Zilla Panchayat. In Tamil Nadu, District Collector was designated as 'Inspector of Panchayats'.

There was a general complaint regarding shortage of staff at Village Panchayat and Block Panchayat level looking to functions regarding execution of various development programmes. In many States every Gram Panchayat did not even get a single secretary to open the office regularly and conduct day-to-day business. Invariably, one Secretary was looking after two to four panchayats. In such cases how the concept of village government could have ever materialized. At Block level, there were hardly four extension officers and four to six clerical staff with one driver and two to three class IV employees. One Junior Engineer was looking after local development works to the extent of more than one crore rupees for which normally there were two executive engineers in government department. Education Extension Officers could not inspect the schools in required number and maintain the quality of education. They were merely pay masters and trouble shooters for teachers serving in Block Panchayat area.

Conditions of service applicable to all the persons on deputation are guided by conditions of their parent service. As such, Panchayat officials could take any disciplinary action against officials on deputation. At the most, they were transferred if no political interference comes in between. Moreover, persons on deputation invariably do not develop affinity to development and Panchayat department. Moreover, Panchayati Raj Department is considered as a department that absorbs surplus staff of other departments. This is more so in Rajasthan. Normally service conditions regarding leave, disciplinary action, retirement pension, gratuity etc., are same in Panchayat services and government service, though they are not inter-transferable. Within the State, officials can however be transferred on administrative grounds.

Agency of Development *Vs* Institution of Self-Government

Panchayati Raj Institutions were initiated to devolve powers of the State government to District, Block and Village levels so as to facilitate administration and to develop Gram Sabha as grass root democracy. It was also provided in section 40 of Directive Principles in Indian Constitution to develop Panchayats as institutions of self-government. In real life situation, Panchayati Raj Institutions only remained as agencies of development in rural areas and that too for implementation of employment generation and poverty alleviation programmes. Neither the Gram Sabha could take the shape of grass root democracy nor the Panchayats could assume the role of self-governing institutions. Panchayati Raj Institutions always suffered from shortage of staff, lack of financial resources as well as autonomy in decision making. Planning from below remained only in theory. Almost all the terms and conditions were decided at the Central or State government levels and all the funds were always tied to such schemes.

There was hardly any flexibility with Panchayati Raj Institutions to implement plans at their level, nor un-tied funds were allotted to such extent to utilize local resources or fulfil local needs and aspirations. Moreover, Panchayati Raj Institutions neither imposed taxes nor raised own income from other sources so as to become institutions of self-government. Panchayati Raj Institutions worked like other government departments. They got grant-in-aid from the State government for staff and other administrative expenses. They got development grants from Central and State governments tied to different plans, schemes and programmes. Terms and conditions were laid down. Panchayati Raj Institutions were expected to achieve such targets, spend the grants and send utilization certificates to become eligible for subsequent grants. Neither the object of decentralized planning was achieved, nor weaker sections of society were involved, nor democracy could develop at base level, nor socio-economic upliftment of masses could come to the expected levels. There was no change visible even the mental attitude of bureaucrats. Co-ordination in governance was almost like a dream, far from field reality. Panchayati Raj Institutions were at the most an agency for implementation of rural development programmes.

Panchayati Raj system was officially oriented rather than a people's programme. It was hardly development of the people, by the people and for the people. There was lack of political education decreased day by day treating all the development programmes as government programmes. *Shram Dan* or people's contribution which came in initial years was almost absent. Except voting, common people withdrew interest and enthusiasm in Panchayati Raj. It was a great challenge for the country that after 30 years working, the picture was hazy and people's involvement was not forth coming as expected staff and finance was common complaint of Panchayati Raj Institutions. State Ministers/Officials were jealous of Panchayati Raj Institutions and hesitated to devolve any powers to them. On the contrary, the powers given in initial years were withdrawn by different departments and agency of rural development at district level was created. Regular elections as provided in State acts were not held for years together. In some

States, even Panchayati Raj Institutions were superseded and administrators had been appointed at village, Block and district level.

Climate for New Panchayati Raj

It was at such a juncture that the then Prime Minister Rajiv Gandhi, held workshops of Collectors and elected representatives in various States. All advocated for strengthening and rejuvenation of local bodies because democracy at grass roots could be possible only through Panchayati Raj Institutions. Moreover, the poor and by-passed sections, who had so far remained beyond the fold of Panchayati Raj Institutions, should also get an opportunity to associate themselves in decision making at village level. The 64th Amendment bill was prepared in 1989 and introduced in Lok Sabha in July 1989 to confer constitutional status to Panchayati Raj Institutions. This was the first attempt by any government to do so after independence. Rajiv Gandhi while addressing conference of Chief Ministers in New Delhi on 5th May 1989, pronounced "we are on the threshold of a mighty revolution. It was revolution envisaged by Jawaharlal Nehru it is a resolution based on maximum democracy and maximum devolution"[9]. He stressed laudable objectives of Panchayati Raj i.e., 'Power to the People'. Grass root democracy which had so far remained populist slogans and paper revolutions. Devolution of authority and power as well as finances from Centre to the Panchayats was laid down as the objective. It seemed that the idea of decentralization of power had not struck the roots in the minds of people. Common people were to be brought into the fold of Panchayati Raj. Gram Sabha had reached only the elite people in the village. A revolutionary step was to be taken towards emancipation of the rural poor.

The Rural Development Ministry also stressed on decision making power to be given to Gram Sabha which had so far remained as consultative rather than executive body. Workable relation between Gram Sabha and Gram Panchayat was yet to emerge. It was said "It is Gram Sabha where rural poor, the women, Scheduled Caste, Scheduled Tribe get an opportunity to actively participate in decision making. It is Gram Sabha which ensures transparency and accountability in public life" [10]. Gram Sabha is the very bedrock of Panchayati Raj. It is through the Gram Sabha that the elected representative is made accountable to the electorates. But such role of Gram Sabha should be imbibed in the minds of people through intensive training and capacity building of elected representatives. However the bill could not become an Act as the ninth Lok Sabha was dissolved.

74th Constitution Amendment Bill 1990

After the defeat of the 64th Amendment bill on the floor of the Rajya Sabha due to serious apprehensions regarding the aiming and the intention of the bill, the national front government which came to power after the elections, introduced in the Lok Sabha in September 1990 a new Amendment Bill known as the 74th Amendment Bil 1990. However the 74th Amendment Bill also could not become an Act of Parliament as ninth Lok Sabha was dissolved. The Congress Government brought about the 72nd Amendment Bill to confer constitutional status to Panchayati Raj Institutions.

72nd Constitution Amendment Bill 1992

Within a span of three years, this was the second bill brought about by the Congress government, however, the two bills (64th and 72nd) differed greatly. Several objectionable and controversial provisions were removed and views of the opposition parties incorporated. It tried to balance between the 64th and 74th Amendment Bills. There is no doubt that according constitutional status to Panchayati Raj Institutions is a welcome move. It aimed at revitalizing these institutions and initiating a new phase in participatory democracy and rural development. But if all such measures are implemented in all sincerity, the Panchayats may be able to play an effective role. There has to be genuine commitment to decentralization and it is the political parties that have to ensure this. There are many provisions in the Constitution which do not have much value due to their non-implementation.

The fear that grows out of experience is that no matter what status is conferred to Panchayati Raj Institutions, the State governments may not allow them to function as institutions of self government at the local level. There is a nexus between the rural elites and the political leaders at the State level. Therefore, how and to what extent the move to accord constitutional status to Panchayati Raj Institutions will guarantee the survival, growth and development of these institutions and enhance their prestige as well as increase people's participation, which would enable them to function as true institutions of local self-government, is the question that needs to be ensured. In the light of the experience of Panchayati Raj Institutions in the last 40 years and in view of the shortcomings which have been observed, it was considered that there was an imperative need to enshrine in the Constitution certain basic and essential features of Panchayati Raj Institutions to impart certainty, continuity and strength to them.

72nd Amendment Bill was introduced in September 1991 which was subsequently referred to joint Select Committee of the Parliament in December 1991 for detailed examination. Amendment was passed with near unanimity in Lok Sabha on December 22, 1992 and the Rajya Sabha on December 23, 1992. Thus, 72nd Constitutional Amendment Bill 1992 was passed by the parliament. It got the assent of majority States as well as the President on 20.4.1993. Thereafter it was known as 73rd Constitution Amendment Act 1993 which came into effect from 24th April 1993.

73rd Constitution Amendment Act 1993

The Amendment provides for certain reaching steps to strengthen Panchayats. Article 243(G) thus recognizes Panchayats as 'institutions of self-government' with prime responsibilities of promoting economic development and ensuring social justice. Panchayats have come to stay as integral part of our constitutional polity. The Amendment envisages the establishment of uniform three-tier system of strong, viable and responsive Panchayats at village, Block and district levels. The Amendment has also laid down necessary guidelines for the structure of Panchayats. compositions, powers, functions, devolution of finances, regular holding of elections, reservation of seats for the weaker groups including women and authority positions in favour of weaker sections an attempt at expanding the social base of the Panchayats.

The objective of 73rd Constitution Amendment was the successful establishment of the third tier of governance at the district level and below. It aims to bring democracy to the door step of the rural poor who had no opportunity to share power thus far. There was constitutional compulsion to get the State governments committed to share their powers and resources with Panchayats so that they might fulfil the mandate as institutions of self-government. The integrity and stability of democracy really depend on the empowerment of Panchayats at the level of cluster of villages, Block and Zilla levels and that the emancipation of the oppressed, dispossessed and marginalised segments of the rural society can be achieved by appropriately strengthening of these institutions of self-government. Amendment was hailed as a revolutionary step towards establishing grassroots democracy specially because it gave constitutional guarantee for people's participation and self-governance. In order to translate the above, into a reality, the State governments were given necessary freedom to feed 'flesh and blood' to the framework provided by the amendment.

Salient Features of the 73rd Amendment Act

There shall be a Gram Sabha comprising all the registered voters of that Panchayat circle in which Gram Panchayat exercising such powers and performing such functions at the village level as the legislature of a State may provide by law. A three-tier system of Panchayati Raj has to be constituted from village to Block and to district levels in a State, but the State with the population of less than 20 lakhs may not have the intermediate tier if it likes. The provision for the composition of the Panchayat at each level is to be made statutory by the State legislature. Seats in the Panchayats at each level are to be filled by direct elections. The State legislature, however, may provide for ex-officio membership in the district level and intermediate level Panchayats for Chairpersons of the Panchayats located at the level below.

Reservation of seats for Scheduled Castes and Scheduled Tribes has been provided in proportion to their population at each level. Not less than one-third of the total membership has been reserved for women and these shall be allotted by rotation to different constituencies in a Panchayat. Similarly, reservation has also been made in respect of office of the Chairperson for Women, S.C. and S.T. though reservation for O.B.C. was left to the discretion of the States.

A uniform term of five years has been provided for the Panchayati Raj Institutions and in the event of supersessions, elections to constitute the body should be completed before the expiry of six months from the date of supersession.

The State Legislatures have been given the power to authorize Panchayats to levy, collect and appropriate suitable local taxes and also provide for making grants-in-aid to Panchayats from the consolidated fund of the concerned State. A finance commission has to be constituted once in every five years to review the financial position of the Panchayats and to make suitable recommendations to the State on the distribution of funds between the State and local bodies.

With a view to ensuring continuity, it has been provided in the Act that all the Panchayats existing immediately before the commencement of the Act will continue till the expiry of their duration unless dissolved by a resolution to that effect passed by the State legislature concerned. The State Legislatures should bring in necessary amendments to their Panchayats acts within a maximum period of one year from the commencement of the 73rd Amendment Act so as to conform to the provisions contained in the Constitution.

Measures Taken

As per provisions of the new Act, a three-tier system of Panchayati Raj, consisting of Zilla Parishad at the district level, Panchayat Samiti at the intermediate level and Gram Panchayat at the village level, has been constituted in different States. According to the new act, a Gram Sabha has also been constituted which has a dual role as a watchdog of the working of the Gram Panchayat and as a group assisting the Panchayat in matters in which public involvement and participation is necessary.

State-wise Panchayati Raj Acts passed in conformity with the 73rd Amendment[11]

S.No.	Name of the State	Year	Name of the State Act
1	2	3	4
1.	Andhra Pradesh	1993	The Andhra Pradesh Panchayati Raj Act, 1993
2.	Bihar	1993	The Bihar Panchayati Raj Act, 1993
3.	Gujarat	1993	The Gujarat Panchayat Act
4.	Himachal Pradesh	1994	The Himachal Pradesh Panchayati Raj Act, 1994
5.	Karnataka	1993	The Karnataka Panchayati Raj Act, 1993
6.	Kerala	1994	The Kerala Panchayati Raj Act, 1993
7.	Madhya Pradesh	1994	The Madhya Pradesh Panchayat Act, 1994
8.	Maharashtra	1994	The Bombay Village Panchayats and the Maharashtra Zilla Parishad and Panchayat Samities (Amendment) Act, 1994
9.	North East		
	i. Assam	1994	The Assam Panchayat Act, 1994
	ii. Tripura	1993	The Tripura Panchayat Act, 1993
	iii. Manipur	1994	The Manipur Panchayat Raj Act, 1994
	iv. Arunachal Pradesh	1994	The Arunachal Pradesh Panchayati Raj Ordinance, 1994
10.	Orissa	1993	The Orissa Gram Panchayats, Taluk Panchayat, Zilla Parishads (Amendment) Act, 1993
11.	Punjab	1994	The Punjab Panchayati Raj Act, 1994

Contd......

Contd...... State-wise Panchayati Raj Acts

1	2	3	4
12.	Rajasthan	1994	The Rajasthan Panchayati Raj Act, 1994
13.	Tamil Nadu	1994	The Tamil Nadu Panchayati Raj Act, 1994
14.	Uttar Pradesh	1994	The Uttar Pradesh Panchayat (Amendment) Act, 1994
15.	West Bengal	1994	The West Bengal Panchayat (Amendment) Act, 1994

The State Governments were expected to bring their acts on conformity with the 73rd Constitution Amendment Act 19963 within a period of one year upto 24.4.1994. Only 15 States passed their Acts/Amendments within such prescribed time limit.

Post Amendment Phase

Task force on Panchayati Raj, Rajiv Gandhi Foundation New Delhi had been in the fore front in putting into effect the mission of restoring 'power to where it belongs'. Since its inception in 1993, Task force organized three national seminars, six Regional Workshops, forty-five sub-regional seminars and four interface workshops with three set of active players.... The elected Panchayat functionaries, members of bureaucracy and MLAs/MPs. In all these activities the task force associated like minded panchayat friendly NGOs and academic, research and training institutions. In a way, it was the most extensive and massive exercise undertaken by any single organization in the country to find out and enlighten from the raw experience of life, the road-blocks and potholes in the path towards successful establishment of the third tier of governance at the district level and below as mandated by the Constitution of India.

The Task Force received different suggestions and recommendations, found hope and despair, happiness and anguish, fear and courage, administrative lacunae and legislative deficiencies, generosity and sectional narrowness as revealed by and emerged from the participation of stake holders in this gigantic effort to bring democracy to the door step of rural masses.

Parliament also enacted a law "The Panchayat (extension to the Scheduled Areas) Act in 1996"[12]. Through this act, extensive power were given to the Gram Sabhas in tribal areas. Corresponding changes were to be brought about by respective States by 1997. There is lurking suspicion where traditional leaders would be able to settle disputes as per customary mode, exercise control over money lenders, land alienation and land acquisition, manage water bodies and minor forest produce and regulate mining leases and licenses as desired by the amendment act of 1996. Not only elected tribal Panchayat functionaries but the bureaucracy and intelligentia were largely ignorant of the existence of these laws and their implication.

Legislation

During post-amendment phase, there was a positive response from the States since almost all the States had passed legislation in conformity with the provisions of the amendment, to establish Panchayats at village, Block and district levels. For the first time in the history of Panchayati Raj Act, a high degree uniformity has been conferred on Panchyati Raj.

Except for Maharashtra, Orissa, Uttar Pradesh and West Bengal States who passes amendment acts, all other State laws are newly enacted. Some States like Tamil Nadu, Andhra Pradesh, Karnataka, Orissa, Madhya Pradesh and Rajasthan even after passing their new acts, have gone in for amendments to further strengthen their Panchayat acts or to bring them in line with the 73rd Amendment for instance, the Karnataka Panchayati Raj Act of 1993 has given executive power to presidents of both Zilla Panchayats and Taluk Panchayats and dissolution powers now rest with the higher level Panchayat bodies rather than the individual officers. Recent amendments in Orissa have given the status of Minister for State and Deputy Minister to the Chairman and Vice-Chairman of Zilla Panchayat. Paradoxically, amendments have been made not only to strengthen aspects of Panchayat administration but also to tighten the hold of the State government. In a majority of State acts, the State government is enabled to exercise decisive powers. Many State governments have retained both regularity, supervisory and more importantly, powers of dissolution. Such a situation raises the fundamental question how Panchayats can remain self governing institutions? Can they remain autonomous?

Elections

Elections were held for all the three-tiers. Impact of direct election of the Chairperson of the Gram Panchayat was good. Such Chairman is strong executive head and at the same time directly accountable to people. In States like Karnataka, the president is elected from among the elected members of the Gram Panchayat. The argument put forth is that there is possibility of the president turning dictatorial taking unilateral decisions and becoming partisan to a particular group or a community. But field experiences from Andhra Pradesh and other States reveal that the direct election of the Sarpanch of the Gram Panchayat tends to promote the emergence of the people not only for his actions but also for performance of the Gram Panchayat as a whole.

It is only in West Bengal and Kerela that election to Panchayats at all levels were fought on party basis. They are also working successfully where in all other States, Chairpersons of Panchayat Samiti and Zilla Parishads fought indirect election on party basis. Though in Uttar Pradesh, Karnataka and other States, Gram Panchayat elections were contested on non-party basis, how can we expect the Gram Panchayat to present an example of party less democracy? In real field situation, party politics played a decisive role not only in selection of candidates but also in managing the election campaign during Gram Panchayat elections in all the States. Those who were nearer to party bosses got tickets. Study of Uttar Pradesh and Karnataka showed that seats reserved for women were secured by sisters, wives and daughters, daughter-in-law of those in power. We are living in a fool's paradise that Panchayat elections take place on non-party basis. When every thing is being dictated today by party politics, Panchayats cannot remain an exception. Either the whole system should be freed from party politics, or Gram Panchayat should also be allowed to have a taste of it openly. Conscience should be clear in this respect of holding elections on party basis.

In almost all the States, there is a provision for constituting State Election Commission. It has also been constituted and elections also held as per schedule in most of the States. Bihar is, however an exception in this regard where neither the commission has been constituted nor Panchayat elections held for the last 22 years, though election notification for April 2001 has been issued but that too without providing for reservation of seats for women, SC and ST. Even where there was difference of opinion regarding timely elections between Election Commission and the State governments, the parties went to the courts who gave the direction to hold the Panchayat election on schedule dates. In case of Andhra Pradesh Supreme Court held the ordinance staying elections as illegal elections have not been held but they were due in July 2000. As regards Assam, Gauhati High Court has ordered on 12.10.2000 for holding long due elections which were held on 18, 22, 27, November 2000. Bihar High Court did not give stay on Panchayat elections, though case is still pending in Supreme Court regarding certain reservations in Panchayats. In Gujarat elections were held on 24th September 2000 but only for Panchayat Samitis and Zilla Parishads only. Village Panchayat elections are yet to be held.

Venkaiah Naidu, Rural Development Minister, observed on 16th October, 2000 that going to courts does not help the States when there is clear provision in Article 243(B) and Article 243(E)(1) of the Constitution for holding elections every five years. He said, "Union Government may move a constitution amendment bill to make it mandatory to hold Panchayat elections under 73rd Constitutional Amendment Act". Constitutional mandate is a clear as daylight. Action can be taken against the States under Article 355 and 356 of the Constitution and President can even dissolve State legislature for such constitutional failure. Article 355 enjoins the union government to 'ensure that the government of every State is carried on in accordance with the provisions of this constitution'. Article 356 empower the President to dissolve a State government, if it is found that 'a situation has arisen in which the government of the State cannot be carried on in accordance with the provisions of this constitution. Obviously, non-holding of

Panchayat elections in a State violates the spirit as well as the letter of the Constitution. But no staff has been warned that this may lead to action under Articles 355 and 356.

In Haryana also, no Panchayats are in existence though the term is over. State government has decided to bypass panchayats and decided to constitute village level committees to undertake development works costing upto Rs. 50 lakhs. It has been done in view of complaints of mis-utilization of funds by the Panchayats[13].

Punjab and Haryana High Court dismissed on 21st January 2000, review petition filed by State government against court order dated 27.12.1999 directing the State government and State election commission to hold elections to Panchayati Raj institutions positively by end of February 2000 and maintain the poll schedule.

In Himachal Pradesh also, elections were due in December 2000. They have decided not to contest Panchayat elections on party lines.

Madhya Pradesh held the election in January-February 2000 though they were to be held in May 1999 as per schedule. Madhya Pradesh Panchayati Raj Act, 1993 was challenged but was held valid by MP High Court. Hence election was delayed after removal of legal hurdles.

In Karnataka, elections due in December 1998 were ultimately held in February 2000. Writ petitions challenging excessive reservation beyond 50 per cent of total seats were filed in High Court which had reserved its judgement on the issue. Karnataka had passed on ordinance for reducing the term of president of Zilla and Taluk Pancayats from 5 years to 20 months. Elections had been postponed on the pretext of restructuring the Gram Panchayats as they were too large for effective supervision. Act was amended in 1999. Rotation of seats was deleted. Other amendments were regarding giving status of State Minister and Deputy Minister to Zilla Panchayat President and Vice President, disciplinary powers to the Executive Heads, Constitution of Nyaya Panchayats with police powers, mechanism to demarcate powers and functions between the Panchayats and executive functionaries, merging in all standing committees. Candidate for panchayat election must have a sanitary latrine in his should, otherwise they will take oath to construct it within one year from the date of election. Toilet Rule[14] as per notification dated 29.10.1997 was challenged in Karnataka High Court which relaxed the rule converting it into an undertaking to construct within six months of being elected. On a reducing period from five years to 20 months also, Zilla Parishad office bearers demanded its extension so as to give them sufficient time to implement on-going development programmes. On the whole, amendments in the act restored certain powers to the government which had been entrusted to the State election commission by Janata Dal in 1997 e.g. reservation of seats and delimitnation of constituencies. Autonomy of State Election Commission was thereby affected.

West Bengal Anti-Defection Act, 2000 according to which any elected member of Panchayati Raj Institutions who changes political party within six months of election, such person shall lose the seat. But if one-third members of a political party join another party, they would not lose seats.

In Jammu and Kashmir, elections were last held in 1977, Panchayats elections were in suspense since May 1999. Chief Minister announced probable date of 5th January 2001 in State Assembly and ultimately they were held.

In Kerala, Panchayat elections took place from 25th to 27th September 2000. Polling was 72 per cent main issue was "people's plan campaign". No elected body was replaced by administrator according to M.S. Joseph, State Election Commissioner. There were less than 150 defections during last five years, hence pessimists who predicted large scale floor crossing and resultant collapse of local democracy, did not come true. The election were fought on political party basis. "Party politics ideology was the most dominant single factor which influenced the voting behaviour. Even before the emergence of Kerala, political parties were firmly rooted in the rural politics of the State"[15] (MRK BAIJU). By amendment on 2nd August 1995, MP/MLA were excluded from membership of Panchayati Raj Institutions. All voting powers regarding election and no-confidence was with the elected members only. Chairpersons in lower Panchayati Raj Institutions were members in higher tier and this organic linkages exist among all Panchayati Raj Institutions tiers.

In West Bengal, elections are being held every five years since 1978 on party basis. Elections were held in 1978, 1983, 1993 and 1998. Next election of Panchayati Raj Institutions is due only in 2003.

Wherever the State level rulers are afraid of the emerging Panchayat power, they are hesitant. Example of BJP government in Gujarat is there where Congress captured 21 out of 23 Zilla Parishads and 152 out of 210 taluk panchayats in elections held during September 2000. In Uttar Pradesh also where BJP Government is the ruling party other parties captured Kshetra Panchayats and Zilla Panchayats during Panchayat elections 2000 which were being delayed beyond the scheduled date.

Reservation of Seats

The provision of reservation of seats both for ordinary membership as well as to offices of Chairpersons has been hailed as a radical step. Through this constitutional guarantee, person belonging to SC/ST, Backward Classes and women have adequate opportunity to fight elections. The access of weaker sections to rural poor structure has been ensured. Legally thereby enlarging the social base of the system. Members of the weaker sections and women hardly made any dent into the power structure in spite of amendments as shown by experience. The present policy of reservation has empowered them as a group to all their grievances and get them cleared through process of participatory decision making process. In fact reservation has made Panchayats more representative of the village community.

Though there have been allegations of lack of education, experience and knowledge among such reserved categories but intensive training and some educational qualification can remove this weakness. Special measures are needed for upgrading their skills and building their capacity.

Role of Gram Sabha

The Gram Sabha has been regarded as the 'soul' of Panchayati Raj. Constitutional status was given to Gram Sabha for the first time in 1993. Gram Sabha have given a political forum for the people to ensure transparency and accountability in the system. All State Panchayat acts have provided for Constitution of Gram Sabhas and for them to meet at least once in six months. But unfortunately the scenario that emerges from the reports does not make a strong case for sustaining these institutions in the system. Field based reports reveal that these bodies are not taken seriously by the functionaries of Panchayats and by the people themselves. This is mainly because Gram Sabhas are treated more as recommendatory and advisory or suggestive bodies. In most of the Acts, decisions of Gram Sabha are not binding on Gram Panchayats. Gram Sabhas are mostly involved in identification of beneficiaries for loans, Indira Avas and other beneficiary schemes. Panchayat Accounts and Audit objections are hardly discussed. Progress reports are placed in haphazard manner. Like Scheduled Areas Act, Gram Sabha can be made more effective body by investing such powers to Gram Sabha.

West Bengal government provided for 2-tier structure for facilitating direct democracy. Ward based bodies are named as Gram Sansad. Two meetings of Ward Sansad are compulsory in May and November. Gram Sansad guides and advises Gram Panchayats in regard to schemes for economic development, identify beneficiaries for poverty alleviation programmes, give suggestions regarding budget, audit report, yearly, administration report and record objections regarding failure to implement development schemes.

Rajasthan State also amended its act in January 2000 providing for Ward Sabhas to be held in each village under Chairmanship of Ward Panch. They would not only prepare annual plan but also identify beneficiaries, issue utilization certificates for building works and keep control over working as well as officials of social service institutions in the village. one-tenth quorum of women, SC, ST, OBC is also compulsory in such Ward Sabha and Gram Sabha. Proposals of Ward Sabhas would be considered in Gram Sabhas. During January 2001, Ward Sabhas were held from 1st January to 25th January whereas all Gram Sabhas at Panchayat headquarters were held on 26th January 2001.

In Orissa also, there is provision of Palli Sabha which consists of all adult persons in ward, hamlet or *basti* of a given revenue village. Palli Sabha meets once a year in February. Ward member presides. No quorum is prescribed. Proposals are passed by simple majority. It is democracy at grass root level.

In Kerala it was a novel experience. Key to success of Panchayati Raj Institutions is Gram Sabha. Considering high density of population, every ward in the village Panchayat constitute a Gram Sabha. Gram Sabha/Ward Sabha has to meet once in three months. Quorum is 10 per cent of total member. It discusses Panchayat progress report, budget and item-wise expenditure incurred within such area. Gram Sabha can set up sub-committees to oversee any kind of work. It functions as watchdog against corruption and monitors the performance at the implementation stage. The Kerala model of decentralization aims at empowerment of the people particularly the common man. It envisages power flowing to the people through the Panchayati Raj Institutions, which are to serve as a vehicle for participation. The policy aims at giving not only voice to the people but the power of choice as well. It has made a bold attempt to induce people's participation by creating a fourth tier in the form of Gram Sabhas equated with the electoral constituency of a village Panchayat member, as all the electors of the ward are members of the Gram Sabha. The experience of "people's plan" through Gram Sabha infused enthusiasm among people who have been taking very active part in Gram Sabhas specially because plan funds to the tune of 40-55 lakhs were placed at the disposal of every Panchayat to sanction need based proposals given by Gram Sabha whereby the aspirations of local people were fulfilled.

In Tamil Nadu Gram Sabha would meet thrice a year. If village panchayat failed to convene it, the Inspector of Panchayats (Collector) was authorized to do so. Quorum is also one-third as against 1/10th or 1/5th in other States. In Tamil Nadu it is important instrument of decision making.

In Punjab and Haryana, Gram Sabha approves the annual budget and the plan of development programmes and annual statement of accounts of Gram Panchayat. Gram Sabha oversees the functioning of Gram Panchayat and the Sarpanch and Panchas have been made accountable to the village assembly.

In Maharashtra, Gram Sabha did not exist in original village Panchayat act. They were not effective in practice. Gram Sabha had no control over Panchayat. After 1993, it is mandatory for Gram Sabha to hold two meetings in April and October every year. Meetings are now held on 15th August and 26th January. Now worthy feature is that if for no valid reason, Sarpanch or Up-Sarpanch fails to hold any meeting without sufficient cause, he shall be disqualified as per section 7(1). But even then one does not notice any remarkable impact of the provision of Gram Sabha on the overall governance of rural Maharashtra.

In Madhya Pradesh also, failure of Sarpanch to call Gram Sabha would disqualify him for the post of Sarpanch. Dates of meetings are fixed 26th January, 14th April, 20th June and 2nd October thus giving them a ritual, or ceremonial flavour. 1/10th of members forms quorum. Experience showed that 22 per cent male Panchas and Sarpanch were present in Gram Sabha meetings. There was no quorum in six out of 11 Gram Sabha visited by study team. Madhya Pradesh has recently empowered Gram Sabha by declaring 'Gram Swaraj' from 26th January, 2001 which became, the historic day in the history of democratic decentralization of India and Panchayati Raj in Madhya Pradesh when Governor Bhai Mahavir announced the beginning of 'Gram Swaraj' in the State from that day.

Gram Swaraj in M.P.[16]

The objective of the State's Panchayati Raj Amendment Act is to introduce direct democracy in the villages and empower Gram Sabhas with a view to ensuring holistic development of villages through decentralization. Following are the outstanding features of Gram Swaraj.

1. There shall be a Gram Sabha for every village. It will be headed by the Sarpanch. There shall be a joint Gram Sabha for matters having a bearing on more than one Gram Sabha of a Panchayat. The Gram Panchayat Secretary of the Gram Sabha.

2. The Gram Sabha will meet at least once a month. No less than 20 per cent of its members will form quorum for the meeting. Of this, one-third must be women in addition to a proportionate number of persons belonging to Scheduled Castes and Tribes. Generally, decisions will be taken unanimously by a Gram Sabha. If there is a lack of unanimity, discussion can be continued at the next meeting. After two deferments, secret ballot could be used to decide the matter.
3. There shall be a village development committee comprising of nine members. The Sarpanch and Up-Sarpanch will be its chairperson and deputy chairperson, respectively. There will also be eight outstanding committees dealing with public assets, agriculture, health, education, village development, village defence, infrastructure and social justice. More communities may be set up if a Gram Sabha finds it necessary but no person can be a member of more than one committee.
4. In certain matters, the Gram Sabha will act as an agency of the Zilla Panchayat, Janpad Panchayat and State Government. These matters include preparing schemes for basic services and their management, selection of beneficiaries, regulating available water for irrigation purposes etc.
5. There will be a Gram Kosh (village fund) for every Gram Sabha, comprising Anna Kosh, Shram Kosh, Vastu Kosh and Nagad Kosh. Public donations, Gram Panchayat funds, land revenue, grazing charges, education cess, taxes imposed by the Gram Sabha and funds devolved by the union and the State governments will be deposited into the Gram Kosh. There shall be a treasurer of the Gram Kosh.
6. Audit will be done by external agencies. In the case of an embezzlement of funds, the Gram Sabha will have the right to curtail the tenure of any member of any committee.

7. State government employees, who are posted in villages and whose jurisdiction is limited within a Gram Sabha, will work under the control of the Gram Sabha which will have the powers for payment of salaries, withholding of salaries, sanctioning leave, inspecting and supervising work and making recommendations for their punishment.
8. The provisions of the Amendment Act will not be applicable to the Scheduled areas.

Only future will tell the success of the democratic decentralization upto Gram Sabha really as fourth tier of the government in Madhya Pradesh.

Even in Karnataka, field data indicates that attempts have been made by the Gram Panchayat to identify felt needs and aspirations of the people by holding Gram Sabha meetings. These meetings have been called by giving enough publicity by distributing pamphlets and by beating the drum. As regards participation in Gram Sabha meetings, on an average 25-30 electorates have been participating in the meetings. There is strong feeling among the electorates that both the officials and the non-official members are found to be in the fore front as far as initiating the projects and taking final decisions, which smacks of the requirement of people's participation in decision making process. Common man is hardly consulted and participation is restricted to elite persons only.

In Himachal Pradesh, Gram Sabha has also been given power to form vigilance committees consisting of persons from the Sabha, other than the elected members, to supervise and put up reports on the work being done by the Gram Panchayat. Quorum is one-fifth of the total voters. It was noted that roughly 75 per cent of the Gram Panchayats were not able to hold a proper Gram Sabha meeting due to low turnout in the Gram Sabha meetings. There was complete absence of women in the meetings.

In Bihar also, legal provision exists. Annual Accounts, annual administration report, budget, beneficiary identification are to be placed before Gram Sabha. Gram Sabha may also form vigilance committees consisting of persons who are not the members of Gram Panchayat to supervise Gram vigilance committee shall be placed before next Gram Sabha meeting.

In Andhra Pradesh, similar provision does exist but ground reality is different. The Gram Sabha meetings are not convened regularly in majority of cases. The meeting are manipulated in the villages where group politics are active. Resolutions of such unheld meetings are passed by getting signatures of the members of the Sarpanch's group.

On the whole, the pattern of attendance of Gram Sabha meetings presents a dismal picture. Quorum requirement is hardly fulfilled though some women do attend meetings where there are women Sarpanchs. Villagers in the age group 40-60 and above participate in greater number than those in the younger age groups. Only men and women come to attend Gram Sabha meetings in the hope of getting facilities like Indira Avas. Old age widow pension etc. Relatively better off people do not attend it. They are indifferent to Gram Sabha meetings. Other reasons for non-attendance are long distances between village hamlets and the meeting place, inconvenient timings and fear of losing their daily wages.

Satya Brat Sen Committee (Kerala) gave detailed report to activise Gram Sabha. It recommended that (i) Gram Sabha should meet as frequently as possible not less than once in three months; (ii) there should be written invitations to every household to ensure 10 per cent quorum; (iii) Every member should be given a copy of Government order mentioning detailed rights and responsibilities of Gram Sabhas with a covering letter by the Gram Panchayat President; and (iv) Gram Sabha has right to know action plan for next three months, detailed estimates to proposed works, details of expenditure incurred in Gram Sabha area, rationale of every decision of Panchayat of that area, officials responsible for work during next three months, priorities for five year and annual plan, norms and criteria for selection of beneficiaries and then selected below poverty line families, form sub-committees to oversee items of works as per rights and responsibilities of Gram Sabha. In a democracy the decision makers should account for the use of their powers and that their powers should be used as for as possible with the consent and understanding of all concerned.

The inter-State workshop on Gram Sabha Empowerment in Rajasthan also identified four significant areas of focus for further action. These are:

1. Social Audit, its mechanism and implementation within the Ward Sabha. Social Audit should be mandatory. Conclusions of the Ward Sabha must be treated like an Audit Para. Corrective means should be adopted rather than punitive action because of limitations of criminal justice.
2. Monitoring and control of the Panchayat/Ward Sabha/ Gram Sabha over government functionaries. Gram Sabha/ Ward Sabha has been given control but how to exercise it effectively. Action on the recommendation of these bodies should be made mandatory. Government functionaries should be given the right to appeal to the collector to save them from political victimisation.
3. Ownership and control over natural resources like minor forest produce, minor minerals and water bodies should vest with the Ward/Gram Sabha.
4. The need for untied funds being made available to the Ward Sabha/Gram Sabha and the process of people's planning necessary within the Ward/Gram Sabha for use of those funds. Drawing lesson from Kerala, significant portion of plan expenditure of the State government must be made available directly for use by self-government bodies. This must be accompanied by a simultaneous process of planning in Ward/Gram Sabhas all over the State for ensuring optimum utilization of allotted funds. The State government should announce its commitment to devolution of funds and fixed time-bound schedule for planning process.

Decentralized Planning and Implementation

The success and failure of Panchayats depend on planning and implementation, Article 243G of the Constitution Amendment recognizes Panchayats as 'Institutions of Self Government' and has entrusted to them the responsibilities of preparing plans for promoting economic development and social justice. The State Panchayat acts have, at least formally, given necessary powers and functions to Panchayats to formulate plans. However, the State reports do not record much in this regard except for Kerala, Karnataka and Tamil Nadu. Kerala has gone much ahead in carrying out decentralized planning process or 'planning from below'. Its much acclaimed "people's campaign for Ninth Plan"[17] has provided many vistas of people's planning. Under this, Panchayats have been able to prepare and prioritise projects in an integrated and a scientific manner. Maximum participation at every stage of the planning process from proposals to implementation has been ensured.

Decentralised local level planning has been used as the engine for harnessing public action in favour of decentralization. In order to shake the system and force the process, a campaign approach has been followed in Kerala. The effort in Kerala is not to legislative decentralization into existence, but to realise it through a mass movement which is merely backed by legislation, as remarked by C.P. Chandrasekar. This not only ensures that decentralization does not remain in paper or amounts to merely administrative decentralization, but is a genuinely participative exercise.

The State Planning Board meeting resolved on 14th July 1996 to decentralize the planning process in Kerala and to organise a "people's campaign for the Ninth Plan". Around 35-40 per cent of Ninth Plan has been envisaged to consist of schemes formulated and implemented by local bodies within respective areas of responsibilities. The primary objective of people's campaign for ninth Plan is "to ensure that the Panchayat/Municipal bodies prepare and prioritise of shelf of integrated schemes in a scientific manner"[18]. Maximum people's participation at every stage of planning proposals from proposals to implementation has been ensured. People's participation in local level development has been exercised through formulation of Panchayat level development plan, project formulation, project appraisal and project co-ordination at intermediate and district levels of Panchayats. President of India, K.R. Narayanan, while appreciating Kerala people's plan, gave his message on the eve of Independence day on 14th August 2000 regarding decentralized planning "this decentralization and devolution of funds have given economic power to people at the grass root level, aroused their enthusiasm for developmental work and enabled them to work together for their own advancement in their respective areas"[19]. Gram Panchayats received 35 to 44 lakhs in the beginning every year as its share in people's plan. Outlay was raised to 77 lakhs for best Panchayat. Thirumarady which got 'swaraj' trophy 1999.

The plan campaign has six district phases as elicited below:

Phase I—Gram Sabha/Ward Committees (August-October 1996)

Identify local level needs, group-wise discussions in each Gram Sabha according to various development sectors, giving training to about one lakh resource persons at the local level at act as facilitators in the discussion groups. Around 650 key resource persons at the State level, 12,000 resource persons at district level and more than one lakh persons at local level facilitated structured discussions. People were encouraged not to limit themselves to listing of developmental problems, but to search for their causes and remedies, drawing from past experiences of their own. Through wide publicity and propoganda, using not only the print media but also music and folk arts, every effort was made to increase participation of the people in Gram Sabhas. It is estimated that nearly 30 lakh persons participated in these meetings — a fifth of them being women to the extent of 6 lakhs. At least one representative from one-fourth households in Kerala must have participated as reported by Thomas Issac, member, Kerala State Planning Board to *India Today* in June 2000. The success of Gram Sabhas created general awareness among the people about the decentralized programme and local level developmental needs were systematically listed.

The groups are : (1) Agriculture and irrigation, (2) Fisheries and Animal Husbandry, (3) Education, (4) Transport energy and markets, (5) Industry, (6) Housing and Social Welfare, (7) Public

Health and Drinking Water, (8) Culture, (9) Women's welfare, (10) Cooperatives, (11) Welfare of Scheduled Castes and Scheduled Tribes, and (12) Resource Mobilization. Aim was to collect quantitative information with respect to such development sectors in the Ward, development problems and their prioritisation and suggest solutions after analysis. From each group, one or two representatives were selected for participating in the development seminars in whole local body.

Phase II—Developmental Seminars (October–December 1996)

After the identification of felt needs in the Gram Sabhas, the next step in the planning process was to make an objective assessment of the natural and human resources of the locality. Collection of secondary data, study of local geography and natural resources, review of ongoing schemes, survey of local history, Consolidation of Gram Sabha reports were subsequent steps.

Phase III—Task Forces (December 1996–March 1997)

On an average, 12 task forces were constituted in each local body to cover various development sectors. As many as 12,000 task forces were trained at the village level along with a participation of at least 1.2 lakh persons. The task forces prepared around one lakh projects for consideration of the task force was an elected representative, an officer from the concerned line department was made its convenor.

Phase IV—Annual Plan Finalization (March–May 1997)

With the presentation of the annual State budget by the end of the March, the Plan allocation to each local body was announced. Out of a total State plan outlay of Rs. 28,550 million for 1996-97, Rs. 10,250 million (nearly 236 per cent) was earmarked for the local bodies. This allocation had two components: (1) State-sponsored schemes costing a total of Rs. 2,760 million i.e. schemes which are prepared by the departments but implemented through the local bodies and (2) Grant-in-aid of Rs.749 crore. The grant-in-aid had three parts—(a) Rs. 39 crore for tribal sub-plan,

(b) Rs. 194 crore for special component plan for scheduled castes, and (c) Rs. 516 crore for general sectors.

Plan funds under each of the above heads were devolved between urban and rural local bodies on the basis of population. As for the rural local bodies, the total general sector allocation was distributed between Gram Panchayats and District Panchayats in the ratio of 70:15:15.

Forty to fifty per cent of the plan allocation to the rural local bodies was to be invested in productive sectors and 30 to 40 per cent in the social sectors. A maximum of 30 per cent of the plan allocation might be spent on roads and other public works including energy. In the fourth phase, projects prepared by the Task Forces were prioritised and incorporated into the plan documents of the Panchayats and municipalities.

Phase V—Annual Plan of Higher Tiers (April–September 1997)

After Gram Panchayats had drafted their plans, Block and District Panchayats started preparing their annual plans. This sequential ordering of the processes was made in order to ensure that plans of various tiers were integrated and plans of the higher tiers did not duplicate, but complement those of lower tiers.

The plan proposals were consolidated at the district level and integrated with municipal plans. Broad strategy for district level development has been evolved by the task force constituted by the District Planning Committee for the purpose. At present, the rules favour the implementation of planned activities by District Panchayats. District Planning Committee forwards the integrated development plan for rural and urban areas of the district to the State. The State planning board is the State level co-ordinating agency for planning.

Phase VI—Plan Appraisal

The sixth phase of the plan campaign was for the appraisal of technical feasibility and financial viability of the projects and plans. Since district planning committees did not have sufficient technical expertise, voluntary technical corps were formed requesting retired technical experts and professionals to enroll themselves as volunteer to appraise the projects and plans of local bodies in order to rectify the weakness in technical aspects and financial analysis. It is important to note that the expert committees have no right whatsoever to change the priorities set by local bodies. Extensive training and orientation programme of various functionaries and volunteers was important component of the programme.

Main reason for people's participation on large scale was 35-40 per cent financial backing and sanction of need based prioritised demands of respective Wards. The process of democratic decentralization and decentralized planning — in Kerala has been attracting attention from all over the world. World Bank said "the decentralized planning process is largest of its kind in the world"[20].

The most noteworthy feature of the decentralized planning process is the freedom to the plan and prepare projects according to local priorities for which a huge grant-in-aid, practically united, is evolved to Panchayati Raj Institutions. The only restriction on the Panchayati Raj Institutions is that they have to spend at least 40 per cent on the productive sector and not more than 30 per cent on infrastructure. 10 per cent of the funds to be spent on women development, is the general stipulation. Thus one-third of development schemes in the State are conceptualised, formulated and implemented by local governments.

A remarkable feature of the people's planning campaign has been the effective capacity building efforts take up at various levels. 600 key resource persons (KRPs) at State level, 10,000 District Resource Persons (DRPs) and 100,000 Local Resource Persons (LRPs) were selected from government officials, professional and activists. The massive training programme was ensured at all levels.

In Kerala, Gram Panchayat prepares an annual action plan based on the works suggested by Gram Sabha. Village plans are consolidated at Block and District level and sanctioned accordingly. The implementation of the programmes like Jawahar Rozgar Yojana (Now Gram Smridhi) and Employment Assurance Scheme provided employment, income generation and meeting the basic needs of people. Quite a good number of beneficiaries could improve their living standards though there were some irregularities in the programme implementation of JRY, IRDP and housing.

In Tamil Nadu also, every village Panchayat has to prepare its annual action plan and submit to Panchayat union, Panchayat unions consolidate village plans and send to district where integration is done and annual plan is prepared. Very little planning is really done in the real democratic sense at village and Block levels. District plan is nothing but only synthesis of village plans. Out of local funds allocated to the district, 60 per cent is reserved for rural areas and 40 per cent for urban areas. Plans are prepared based on the criteria of 50 per cent for population and 50 per cent for backwardness. District Planning Committees have not become functional in Tamil Nadu. DPC consists of 120 to 190 members. Hence it is unwisely. Collector continues as Chairman of DPC hence questions are raised as regards to its democratic character.

In Rajasthan, Annual Action Plan is prepared at Ward Sabha and Gram Sabha level. District Rural Development Agency sanctions only such works as are included in Annual Action Plan. No work is sanctioned throughout the year unless it is included in Annual Action Plan prepared by Gram Sabha. Such instructions have been issued by the Government of India for all the schemes of rural employment and poverty alleviation as well as individual beneficiary programmes. It is for the State Governments to follow them in letter and spirit. However, no plan funds are allotted to the districts except some untied grants to the extent of about one crore per year per district to sanction works as per local needs. Panchayat Samitis and Zilla Parishads are generally like post offices to despatch plans to the State government. They are hardly included in the State plan since for the last two years, the District Plans were received so late that they could not be included in the State Plan. It would be proper to prepare Annual Plans in the Gram Sabha to be held in the month of May so that after approval of Panchayat Samiti and Zilla Parishad, it reaches the State by the end of August. Consultative and participatory planning like Kerala is almost missing in all other States. There is no orientation or training regarding plan formulation though true potentiality is at the grass roots.

District Planning Committee have been formed in seven States[21],—Gujarat, Karnataka, Kerala, Madhya Pradesh, Rajasthan, Tamil Nadu, West Bengal. Other States have yet to take steps for its formation. Even in States where DPC is formed, they are more on paper or in the staute book. Except Kerala, real decentralized planning is missing in the States. In Rajasthan, recommendations have been made to allot united fund to the extent of 2 crore to each district for implementing district plan proposals, but funds are yet to be transferred.

To evolve a meaningful implemental strategy of decentralized planning, following suggestions are offered:

1. There is a need for devolution of resources to each tier of Panchayati Raj Institutions. The criteria for devolution of resources to Panchayati Raj Institutions from State funds should be objective and unambiguous.

2. Panchayati Raj Institutions should be given full freedom to utilize these resources according to the priorities identified by them i.e., funds provided to them should be untied.

3. Panchayati Raj Institutions should also mobilise resources from other sources for the development activities for their areas as prioritised by them at the local level.

4. The job of prioritising development initiatives at the local level should be unambiguously assigned to Panchayati Raj Institutions.

5. There is need for demarcation of activities for which planning is to be done at the level of Panchayati Raj Institutions. Provision of drinking water, elementary, education, primary health care and link roads should necessarily be in the arena of Panchayati Raj Institutions.

6. Capacity for planning at each tier of Panchayati Raj Institutions should be built up by training and technical support from higher levels. A mechanism should be evolved to use the services of knowledgeable persons like lawyers, teachers and scientists residing in the area

in planning and implementation of the programmes at the local levels.

7. The linkages between Panchayati Raj Institutions at all levels and between District Planning Committee and Panchayati Raj Institutions in planning and implementation should be clearly spelt out. Some guidelines should be formulated in establishing these linkages. The norms that are specified should, however, be flexible.

8. Before undertaking planning and prioritisation exercises at the local level, existing status of development, infrastructure and capabilities should be assessed by Panchayati Raj Institutions at each local level.

9. The process of consultation with people should be institutionalised. Also, accountability of Panchayati Raj Institutions to the people should be built into the system.

10. Monitoring and evaluation, being indispensable parts of planing, should be assigned also to Panchayati Raj Institutions in respect of those activities for which Panchayati Raj Institutions are made responsible.

Role of Bureaucracy in Panchayati Raj

The effective functioning of Panchayats depend on facilitative functional relationship in terms of co-ordination, co-operation between the elected and official functionaries. Further, it is a prerequisite of democracy that administrative wing should function under deliberative wing, that is, bureaucracy should be answerable and accountable to the elected political leadership. But the information provided in the reports indicates disturbing trends. In most States, the bureaucracy is found to be in a prime position over the elected leadership. The State acts have given ample scope for the State governments, through bureaucracy to exercise control, supervision, powers of dissolution and of annulling resolutions. However, in States like Karnataka, such powers are vested with higher level Panchayats. As per section 152 and 193 of Karnataka Panchayati Raj Act, presidents of Zilla Panchayats and Taluk

Panchayats have been recognized as 'Executive Heads' of respective Panchayats giving them powers of superintendence and control over the staff. Orissa has given the status of Minister of State and Deputy Minister to president and vice-president of Zilla Panchayat. Karnataka Act of 1983 had provision for similar status which was subsequently dropped.

In Andhra Pradesh and Assam, Collector can suspend the resolutions of Panchayati Raj Institutions. Only in Gujarat, there is no controlling power with the Collector and there is separate Panchayat and Development service including Panchayati Raj Service Commission. Officers are mostly on deputation from various services and they are transferred by the government. It is only in Maharashtra, that elected members can get Chief Executive Officer withdrawn from Zilla Panchayat, In Tamil Nadu, district Collector is himself Chairman of District Development Council in which elected representatives are also members. Thus, bureaucrats feel themselves superior to elected leaders who are temporary and may get changed early.

Such provisions reflect problems like recurring confrontation figuring between District Panchayat leadership and administrative leadership. This is mainly due to the absence of a clear cut demarcation of powers, functions, responsibilities between Panchayat functionaries, particularly between the presidents and Chief Executive Officers of the Panchayats. Many State governments have constituted 'High Power Committees' for making recommendations to reallocate responsibilities, duties and functions between Panchayats and bureaucracy and amongst the three tiers. Notwithstanding the confusion, on paper the prevailing situation in most of the States, except in few States like Karnataka, Kerala and West Bengal, bureaucracy is found to be a dominant partner in decentralized governance. Though Panchayats have vertical organizational and functional linkages between them and the functionaries, there appear to be gaps in role perception, role appreciation and role performance.

It makes out a case for establishing a separate 'Panchayati Raj Service' as in Gujarat and Punjab.This may solve many of the organisational, functional and personnel problems which confront the Panchayati Raj administration. Also there is need to follow certain principles like the "principle of subsidiarity" as done in Kerala, transferring all the line departments functions of Panchayats. Principle followed in Karnataka is to allocate functions between the Panchayats while overlapping of functions between the Panchayats while providing for demarcation of functions and responsibilities between the non-official and official functionaries of the Panchayats.

Rajasthan Government had appointed a committee for study of Panchayati Raj under Chairmanship of Sadiq Ali, Member of Parliament which submitted its report in 1964. He had remarked "Right of officers is to offer their advice on policy. It was well within rights of elected representatives to reject their advice"[22]. To maintain harmonious relations between non-officials and bureaucrats, Sadiq Ali gave following recommendations.

1. Officials and elected representatives should be got acquainted with the principles regarding their functions e.g. non-official's function to decide policy and give directions for its implementation. Officials should be responsible to translate policy into practice. Officials should be encouraged to give impartial advice fearlessly. Such advice should be based on laws, rules and experience.

2. There should be clarity about powers and functions between officials and people's representatives. Chances of misunderstanding and differences are more when such clarity does not exist.

3. As soon as information about dispute or difference at any stage is received, efforts should be made to remove it effectively. This function can be done by higher level officials and public representatives.

4. Bureaucrats and non-officials should not only be acquainted with their powers and responsibilities, but also each other's problems, difficulties and responsibilities. Mutual understanding and respect are useful for good

relations between them. Both should not consider each other as competitors but as complementary

5. Public representatives should know that officials have the right to give advice and accordingly it is also expected from them. Officials should also understand that elected representatives have the right to disagree with the advice of officials.

6. Officials as well as public representatives both should rise above personal interests and fulfil their duties in the interest of public welfare.

7. Such short term training camps should be organized where officials and public representatives both should be explained the importance of harmonious and co-operative relations between them.

Iqbal Narain, in his seminal work *Panchayati Raj Administration*[23] suggested that –

1. This principle should be clear that elected representatives from the policy and executives implement it.

2. Chief Executive will work in subordination to elected representative.

3. Chief Executive shall exercise full control over all the employees working in Panchayat.

4. Security of conditions of service of Administrative Officer should be ensured so that he may be able to function independently and fearlessly.

Officials and people's representatives are like two wheels of strong democracy. Elected representatives can get full cooperation provided they have faith in officials. Success of Panchayati Raj definitely depends on harmonious relations between the two. In case differences are settled between them in mutual faith and good will, a transparency and strong democracy in Panchayati Raj is expected.

Devolution of Powers

Keeping in view the spirit of the Eleventh Schedule of the Constitution 73rd Amendment, almost all State acts have devolved some powers and functions to the Panchayats. Kerala has given more powers, functions and schemes with necessary assets and staff to Gram Panchayats, whereas at intermediate level Panchayats have fewer functions. The District Panchayats are given second priority in the scheme of devolution.

Function of Panchayats have been grouped under obligatory, discretionary and functions entrusted by the Government in several States like Tamil Nadu, Andhra Pradesh, West Bengal and Karnataka. While mandatory and entrusted functions are binding, subject to availability of funds, the discretionary functions can be undertaken by the Panchayats at their option.

One of the common anomalies found in the devolution of powers and functions is that there is always a gap between the powers given and powers exercised and between functions as enlisted in the schedules and as they are carried out. This is more noticeable at the Gram Panchayat level. In most of the State Panchayat Acts, the Gram Panchayats have been entrusted about 30-35 functions, but in practice they are hardly carried out.

However, one positive feature with regard to devolution has been that the State governments have initiated efforts to democratic functions between the Panchayats by adding or deleting certain activities, programmes and schemes to schedules so as to streamline the allocation of functions. But the State governments have retained many regulatory supervising controlling powers which make for centralized process under a professed system of decentralized governance. In most of the State acts, it is in the hands of the State government. As a result, line departments are still independent of Panchayats although they come under Panchayat's administration. Only they had discretionary powers to write confidential reports of senior district level officer including the Chief Secretary of the Zilla Panchayat.

Almost in all the States, rural employment generation and poverty alleviation programmes are with Panchayati Raj Institutions. Provision of basic services and amenities, building rural infrastructure, primary education, hand pump maintenance, rural sanitation etc., are entrusted to Panchayati Raj Institutions. They co-ordinate rural development activities. They have basically functioned as an agency of the government for implementation of development programmes.

In Orissa, cabinet has agreed on principle to empower Zilla Parishad and accordingly decided to devolve 19 key departments of the government to Zilla Parishad. In Assam and Gujarat, all the 29 items as per Eleventh Schedule stand transferred to Panchayati Raj Institutions. In Rajasthan also, 16 functions transferred to Panchayati Raj Institutions in January 2000.

Maharashtra Zilla Parishad and Panchayat Samiti Act, 1961, Section 100 enumerates 129 subjects which fall within the purview of Zilla Parishad as per Schedule I. Section 101 for functions of Panchayat Samitis as per Schedule II. State Government also transferred many more subjects and schemes to Zilla Parishads under Section 102 and 103 of the Act. Section 45 of the Village Panchayat Act enlists 82 subjects within the purview of the Gram Panchayat in Schedule I of the Act. DRDA has also been transferred to Zilla Parishad. The State government withdrew 24 items in 1973 and 1975 thereby indicating trend towards centralization rather than decentralization and devolution. Almost all the development schemes are managed by the State government. Programmes to be handed over to Zilla Parishad on agency basis are also decided by State government. Though it provides funds for the purpose, but total monitoring of programmes is done by the State government and its bureaucracy leading to establishment of a parallel machinery.

In Madhya Pradesh, the experience has shown that the general tendency is to appear generous by listing a series of subjects, but the extremely tight fisted in spirit of the constitutional amendment. Section 53 of the act states that preparation of plans and implementation of schemes for economic development and social justice including those in relation to the Schedule XI may be entrusted to the Panchayats by State government through a general or special order. As per section 53(2), State government has retained the powers not only to add to the functions but also to withdraw the entrusted functions and duties when it decides to undertake their execution itself. This makes it to decide to undertake their execution itself. This makes every thing relating to functions of Panchayats subject to the executive discretion from time to time. Further the functions and duties of Gram Panchayat are only so far as the funds allow. Only in case of Zilla Panchayat, the duties are subject to the act and rules. Zila Panchayat shall control and supervise the administration of District Rural Development Agency which will implement the State government's schemes under its direction and control. This Zilla Parishad/District Rural Development Agency will work as per guidelines of State government. District Rural Development Agency and Zilla Parishad were merged in 1997. No evidence of fresh thinking on the function of Panchayati Raj Institutions is visible in the State in view of State executive control as provided in Section 53. Madhya Pradesh has publicized its scheme of 'District Government' since April 1999 but Minister in charge of the District has been made chairman of District Planning Committee which indicates increased State control rather than devolution of powers of Panchayati Raj Institutions.

Karnataka Governor Khurshid Alam Khan in an address to the Joint Session of Karnataka Assembly remarked on 27th October 1999 "Democracy has to be reinformed by devolving powers, resources and responsibilities to decentralized bodies. We do not want people to travel long distances and come to Vidhan Sabha for solving their problems which can be done at local level institutions. Panchayati Raj Institutions at the village, taluk and district levels should be empowered to take decisions on matters that directly affect people's lives. Thus our aim is to strengthen local administration and governance by the people for their own benefit. Local decentralized governance will have the advantage of involving citizens of every creed and class in this common venture and will promote greater harmony among different communities"[24]. Panchayati Raj as development mechanism primarily rests on power mechanism. Power to people for true democracy and development is real objective which needs to be fulfilled through devolution of powers and finances to Panchayati

Raj Institutions. Only then people of all classes can participate in democracy in an effective manner. Rural people will get opportunity to plan and administer their own affairs.

Union Finance Minister, Yashwant Sinha also stressed recently to increase decentralization by maximizing the functions of Panchayati Raj Institutions. He said "There is no alternative to devolving powers and functions and finance to Panchayats if we are serious about the development of India"[25].

As such, all such laudable observations have yet to be translated into practice in letter and spirit if we really intend to make Panchayati Raj Institutions real institutions of self government and bring democracy to the grass roots in rural areas.

Finances

K.R. Narayanan, President of India, in his address to the Nation on the eve of Independence Day on 14th August 2000 advocated for fiscal federation, saying "for Panchayats to grow as genuine units of self government, it is essential that they have a sound financial base of their own"[26]. That is why 73rd Constitution Amendment Act, 1993 had provided in Article 243 (I) that the Governor of a State shall, as soon as may be, within one year from the commencement of this act and thereafter at the expiration of every fifth year, constitute a finance commission to review the financial position of the Panchayats and make recommendations to the Governor as to the principles which should govern the distribution between the State and Panchayats of the net proceeds of taxes, duties, tolls and fees leviable by the State, which may be divided between them and the allocation between Panchayats at all levels, of their respective share of recommendation made by the commission and the action taken on to be laid before the legislature of the State.

In accordance with the above provisions of the Constitution, every State was to constitute first finance commission before September 1994 and second finance commission after 5 years.

Thus, it will be observed that Assam, Goa, Gujarat, Delhi and Chandigarh have not taken any action so far though the reports of State Finance Commission were submitted as back as 3-4 years.

In case of States of Haryana, Punjab, Sikkim, Andaman and Niocobar, Dadra and Nagar Haveli, Daman, Dieu and Lakshadweep, report is still pending for consideration for 1-3 years. It is only in case of States of Kerala, Rajasthan, Himachal Pradesh and West Bengal that the report was accepted *in toto*.

Andhra Pradesh, Karnataka, Madhya Pradesh, Maharashtra, Manipur, Orissa, Tamil Nadu, Tripura and Uttar Pradesh accepted State Finance Commission's recommendations with some modifications.

The notable recommendations[27] came in from Kerala, West Bengal and Karnataka. In Kerala, the Panchayats get around 35 to 40 per cent of the total plan expenditure in the form of grant-in-aid and untied fund. General category fund is divided among the Gram, Taluk and Zilla Panchayats in ratio of 70:15:15 respectively. In East Bengal, it is in the ratio of 50:20:30 and 16 per cent of net proceeds of all taxes collected by the State government is transferred to local bodies. Funds are transferred on the basis of backwardness and population. All the funds go in untied form so that local bodies can spend the funds as per local needs and aspirations. This amount is over and above the support for payment of salaries of staff.

In Karnataka, it is the opposite. Gram Panchayat received annual grant of Rs. one lakh for meeting electricity charges, maintenance of water supply, sanitation and other welfare activities. Taluk Panchayat get stamp duty to the tune of 4-5 lakhs per year. Plan and non-plan sector-wise allocation of resources are transferred to Zilla Panchayats in 45 major heads of accounts. 36 per cent of government's non-loan grants on revenue receipts are transferred to Village, Taluk and Zilla Panchayats in the ratio 25:33:40. Out of total allocation of 36 per cent revenues, Panchayati Raj Institutions get 85 per cent and 15 per cent goes to urban local bodies. The basis of allotment is population (33.33%), illiteracy rate (11.11%) and road length (11.12%). All individual beneficiary oriented schemes that came under either State sector or centrally sponsored sectors should be entrusted to Gram Panchayats for implementation and they should receive 25 per cent of the total devolution of funds.

One of the weakest links of Panchayat finances is the poor mobilization of tax, revenues even in the States where compulsory taxes have been provided for in the State acts of Andhra Pradesh, Assam, Bihar, Haryana, Punjab, Tamil Nadu, Himachal Pradesh, Karnataka, Kerala and Madhya Pradesh. Position is still worse in remaining States where imposition of taxes has been left to the discretion of Panchayati Raj Institutions. In fact this has been seen as a negative implication of decentralization of powers. Close access of people to these institutions has hindered the process of mobilization. In order to encourage Panchayats, some States including Tamil Nadu provided for matching share from the State equal to own resources raised by Panchayati Raj Institutions. Incentive scheme in Tamil Nadu was called 'equalization and incentive fund' which is shared between rural and urban local bodies at the ratio of 60:40. This fund is being used to give incentives for reasonable mobilization through own resources by the local bodies and to bridge the resource and infrastructural gap existing between the local bodies. The Tenth Finance Commission also earmarked funds for giving such matching grants to Panchayati Raj Institutions who raised additional resources. Such funds had also to be allotted without such parameters. The Rajasthan State Finance Commission has strongly favoured establishing a system of matching grants to Panchayati Raj Institutions who raised additional resources. Such funds had also to be allotted without such parameters. The Rajasthan State Finance Commission has strongly favoured establishing a system of matching grants, the State government should provide 50 per cent matching grant. A more important recommendation from this Commission was to set up a 'Finance Corporation' in rural and urban areas in order to facilitate investment in Panchayat and urban bodies, though it is yet to be started. NABARD has also sanctioned schemes to advance loans to Panchayati Raj Institutions for infrastructural development, Panchayats were to be awarded prizes for Best Panchayats and raising additional resources was important criteria but to no effect.

A question that often arises in the above context is the 'political will' and 'wisdom' of the government in power to honour some of the above recommendations. If the response is positive,

Panchayats would certainly have same financial autonomy to undertake developmental activity.

After extensive consultation with the Central and State governments, representatives of Panchayati Raj Institutions and various other organizations and on the basis of a study conducted by National Institute of Rural Development Hyderabad, the XI Finance Commission came to the conclusion that the 73rd Constitution Amendment has not significantly altered the functional domain of the Panchayats at various tiers. One of the serious concerns of the commission is that the Panchayats have been marginalised by the union and the States through sponsored schemes for rural areas without associating these bodies in their planning and implementation. The centrally sponsored schemes of the State level schemes for provision and improvement of civic services have not been transferred to the local bodies for grass root level planning and implementation. It is for the first time that key constitutional authority has come down heavily on the working of the Panchayats. It is also for the first time that a correct perspective about the role of local bodies in accordance with the Constitution of India is categorically emphasized in such a report. The commission has underlined the fact that the States now owe greater responsibility to develop local bodies as institutions of self-government a point which advocates of decentralization have been harping on but the politicians and bureaucrats refuse to accept.

Finance commissions in various States disappointed the Eleventh Finance Commission[28]. They found various anomalies:

Lack of synchronization of period of State Finance Commission with those of finance commissions,

Several State Finance Commissions had not done their work within the parameters listed in article 243(I),

There was no time limit for submission of 'Action taken Reports',

Even where the recommendations had been accepted, the implementation was tardy,

Wherever reports were available, they were not of much use because of there heterogeneity in approach, contents and period covered.

Many States had not adhered to the basic qualifications required for SFC members. In some States, serving government officers were appointed as chairpersons and members of SFCs and that too in ex-officio capacities. This puts limitation on the ability of SFC to act as an autonomous body to make recommendations in a free and independent manner as was envisioned in the Constitution.

The Commissior. recommended that every State mist have a legislation to ensure that the chair-persons and members of SFCs must be from amongst experts in specific disciplines, such as economics , law, public administration and public finance. Several states have not taken SFC reports seriously. Only 4 States—Himachal Pradesh, Kerala, Rajasthan and West Bengal—have fully accepted the recommendations of SFC, 3 States—Assam, Goa and Gujarat–have not taken any action.

Reiterating that the people are at the centre of the governance and development, the commission has given 40 per cent weightage for population, 20 per cent weightage to index of decentralization, 20 per cent weightage to distance from highest per capita income, 10 per cent weightage to revenue effort and 10 per cent weightage to geographical area.

Index of Decentralization

Index of decentralization, as given by Eleventh Finance Commission constitutes 10 parameters.[29]

1. Enactment of State Panchayat legislation in conformity with 73rd Constitution Amendment Act.
2. Intervention/restriction in the functioning of Panchayats
3. Assignment of functions to Panchayats in the State Panchayat legislation *vis-à-vis* the Eleventh Schedule.
4. Transfer of functions to Panchayats by way of rules/notifications/orders of State governments.
5. Assignment of Taxation Powers to village Panchayats as per the State Panchayat Act.
6. Levy of taxes by the Village Panchayats.

7. Constitution of State Finance Commissions and submission of Action Taken Reports.
8. Action taken on the major recommendations of SFC.
9. Elections to Panchayats.
10. Constitution of District Planning Committee.

Broadening the Resource Base

One of the important recommendations of Eleventh Finance Commission[29] is enhancing revenue through imposition of property tax and house tax, octroi/entry tax and user charges. House taxes should be periodically revised which is not done. Octroi is a contentious issue but there is a need for 'a suitable tax' that is buoyant and can be collected by local bodies. The local bodies have been shying away from raising resources because of the fear of being unpopular. But the Institute of Social Sciences Studies have shown that if people feel that they are getting the value for their money, they pay taxes willingly and revenue of the Panchayat goes up substantially.

Nine Commandments[30]

The Commission, in a futuristic perspective, has given considerable attention to the constitutional, legislative and administrative changes required to strengthen the Panchayats in the following areas.

(1) The schemes relating to subjects in the Eleventh Schedule have not been fully transferred to Panchayats by States. The funds and functionaries relating to these schemes continue to remain under the control of the State departments. Wherever the programmes have been entrusted to Panchayats, it is as an agency function—Panchayats having no role in planning and implementation. Therefore, the transfer of subjects, funds and functionaries as per the Eleventh Schedule must be made mandatory.

(2) Since the role of the three tiers of Panchayats have not

been clearly delineated, the executive decisions are creating a chaotic situation. Only a clear legislation on the subject can improve the position.

(3) The Ministry of Rural Development must take steps to clear the impediments—like the creation of parallel structures for implementing central schemes (e.g. DRDAs)—in the way of the local bodies functioning as institutions of self-government.

(4) The rigid uniformity of the three tiers envisages in the Constitution must be made flexible through a constitutional amendment.

(5) The extension of the 74th Amendment to the Fifth Schedule areas and application of the 73rd and 74th Amendments to the Sixth Schedule areas need to be speeded up.

(6) The Village Councils in Meghalaya, Mizoram and Nagaland must be recognized as Panchayats as defined in the 73rd Amendment by a legislative measure, or the respective States must extend the amendment to these areas.

(7) The hill areas of Manipur do not come under the 73rd Amendment. There are no enabling provisions in the Constitution for making the 73rd Amendment applicable to these areas. It is necessary to take necessary constitutional steps so that these areas get the benefit of the 73rd Amendment.

(8) Wide variations in the areas and populations of Panchayats are making them non-viable units in certain cases. An administrative reorganisation is called for to rectify the situation.

(9) The District Planning Committees have not been constituted in all States and some States have violated the constitutional provisions by making them executive bodies. This anomaly needs immediate correction.

The above nine 'commandments' of the Eleventh Finance Commission must be taken seriously by all concerned. They must become the subject of a national debate and legislative and administrative action. The Eleventh Finance Commission had done what it could with a clear perception and vision. Now it is left to the State governments as well as the Union to build on it. Panchayat representatives and civil society must put pressure on the States, for without that nothing will move.

Functioning of Panchayats

The overall functioning of Panchayats reveals both positive and negative trends. Panchayats, by and large, have been able to maintain the periodicity while calling their general body and standing committee meetings. However, this is somewhat better at the Zilla Panchayat and Taluk Panchayat levels, rather than at Gram Panchayat level. Lack of awareness, knowledge and experience have become obstacles to their effective functioning. The elected representatives faced various kinds of opposition, obstruction and functional difficulty such as gender, caste, family in nature. Villagers generally approached the representatives of their own caste.

Wherever Panchayat meetings are held, attendance of women is meagre. Even when they participate, they hardly participate in decision making. They put their signature or thumb impression, take sitting fees money and depart. Discussions and decisions are also not free from party interventions. The village unity, cohesion, community spirit and the village life are in most cases disintegrated owing to political party interventions in Village Panchayat elections. Instances may be few but they do affect the harmonious and cordial relations of the people at village level. In Orissa, however caste/ communal and other social tensions are almost non-existent not only due to simplicity of the people but also due to varied socio-economic as well a cultural factors.

Another factor observed in functioning of Panchayats is that though provisions for decisions by majority exist in the acts, it has been observed that influential group in the village dominates the decision making process. Due to reservations also tensions and frictions have been reported.

Kerala is an exception in functioning of Panchayats. Discussions in the Panchayat meetings are very live and help generate opinion of all the members of the Panchayat . In general, people's will for development is reflected in the discussion of the Panchayat members. Majority opinion is the rule in decision making in the Panchayats. Party politics does play a major role and hence decision making is not always free from bias. Party politics dominates because elections are also held on party basis.

In Kerala Panchayat meetings can also be attended by public. There is transparency in the proceedings of Panchayats. The public is allowed to observe all proceedings, discussion and decision making of Panchayats. Even president of Panchayat can avoid the presence of public by recording reasons in writing. Chapter XXVA introduced by 1999 'Right to know' seeks to increase transparency in the functioning of Panchayati Raj Institutions. The right to information includes the right for taking extracts and obtaining certified copies of documents of any material or information contained in a document relating to the administrative, developmental or regulatory functions of a Panchayat and includes any document or record relating to the affairs of the Panchayat. Kerala, Rajasthan and Andhra Pradesh governments have incorporated radical provision of "Right to information" in their rules.

The "Right to information" Legislation gained momentum at national level to such a great extent that various States passed acts as under[31].

(1) The Goa Right to Information Act, 1997 which received the assent of the Governor on 29.10.1997.

(2) The Tamil Nadu Right to Information Act, 1997 which received the assent of the Governor on 4th May 1997.

(3) Madhya Pradesh Right to Information Bill, 1998 (not in force).

(4) Rajasthan Right to Information Act, 2000 which received

the assent of the Governor on the 11th day of May, 2000.

(5) Maharashtra Right to Information Act, 2000 which was passed by the Legislative Assembly on the 18th July 2000.

(6) The Karnataka Right to Information Ordinance, 2000 on 25th August 2000.

(7) The Freedom of Information Bill, 2000 which will extend to whole of India except the State of Jammu and Kashmir.

The exceptions vary from 6 (Goa) to 22 (Tamil Nadu), 11 (Madhya Pradesh), 10 (Rajasthan), 22 (Maharashtra), 8 (Karnataka) and 7 in All India Bill 2000. Time limit in all States is 30 days for grant of copies which should not exceed 7 days normally. There is no provision in any State for urgent copy like other rules. Normally penalty for disciplinary action only is provided except in Karnataka where a penalty upto Rs. 2000 can be imposed for delay without reasonable cause or supplying wrong information. In none of the States, there is any provision for publicity of the Act or training and orientation of government functionaries.

Provision of Social Audit also exists in these States. Notice boards are painted outside Panchayat offices indicating year-wise works undertaken during last 10 years under various programmes/ schemes and amount spent. Details of village wise, scheme-wise, year-wise works with expenditure incurred are available in computers of District Rural Development Agencies in Rajasthan and detailed lists are available in every Block Panchayat also.

In Andhra Pradesh, Gram Panchayats are empowered to execute works by awarding contracts whereas in other States there is ban on contracts. According to rules, Gram Panchayat can sanction works upto one lakh in case of minor Gram Panchayat and upto two lakhs in major Panchayats. However, in case of Janma Bhoomi Programme, State Government is awarding contracts directly without the concern of Gram Panchayats. Andhra Pradesh Act is not specific about the supervisory role of higher tier of Panchayats over the lower tiers. Community assets including water sources, lands, forests and other properties are maintained by Panchayats though with lack of adequate staff and resources of their own, they are not able to manage them effectively. Unauthorized occupation of community lands is common.

Committee System is prevalent generally at Block Panchayat and District Panchayat level. They are meeting regularly also. At Gram Panchayat level, committee system is either non-existent or practically working rarely. Membership varies from 5 to 17. It ensures increased participation of members in decision making process.

One of the imperatives of decentralization is that it would ensure 'cost effectiveness' in implementing development programmes, because they do not incur costs on supervision and contractor profit and can save other over heads. Moreover due to active participation of elected members, local organization and people, the process of implementation will be cost effective and benefits should be optional. Sen Committee in Kerala suggested 'ombudsman' but perhaps effective Gram Sabha monitor and check corruption as well as complaints and ensure quality of work. Gram Sabha is the best social auditor.

Role of District Rural Development Agency

Sunderlal Patwa, Union Rural Development Minister wrote a letter to Chief Ministers of States in 1999 to take immediate steps to improve the effectiveness of DRDA. Independent existence of DRDA is highly desirable. Chief ministers should see that DRDAs do not become agencies to implement the programme by themselves. They should instead oversee the implementation and other agencies.

Government of India also issued directives to the State governments that Chairman of Zilla Parishad should be made chair-person of the governing council of DRDA also. Consequently many States including Rajasthan, Tamil Nadu and Madhya Pradesh nominated president of Zilla Parishad as chairman of DRDA also. Collector became Executive Director instead of Chair-person, though executive powers still rest with the Executive Director. Necessary amendments were carried out in the byelaws of these agencies in 1999.

The District Rural Development Agencies (DRDAs) cam into being in the year 1980 when the Integrated Rural Development Programme (IRDP) was extended to all the Blocks in the country. DRDA is a registered society under the societies registration Act. It has a governing body for approval of Annual Plan, expenditure and for giving policy direction. Though the inception of DRDA coincided with the introduction of the IRDP in October 1980, a number of other rural development programmes were entrusted to it over the years. DRDA was the principal organ at the district level to oversee the implementation of different rural development programmes, more particularly the anti-poverty programmes of the Ministry of Rural Development in 1993 when 73rd Constitution Amendment Act came into force.

Amendment Act of 1993 provided that all schemes of economic development and social justice would be planned and executed by Panchayati Raj Institutions. Hence, it was presumed that DRDA would automatically merge into Zilla Parishad, the Panchayat at the district level. Maharashtra and Gujarat were the States where District Development Officer is Chair-person of DRDA.

Shankar Committee made one of the recommendations in 1999 that DRDA must emerge as specialized Agency capable of managing the anti-poverty programmes. Role of DRDA is and must remain distinct from that of Zilla Parishad. At the same time it recommended that in respect of such States where DRDA does not have a separate identity, a separate cell should be created in Zilla Parishad which maintains a separate identity and separate accounts so that the accounts arc capable of being audited separately. In such States, where Chief Executive of Zilla Parishad is the Chairman of the governing body of DRDA, the CEO of the Zilla Parishad could be designated as the Project Director of the DRDA, which goes against the recommendations of the Shankar Committee as well as the letter and spirit of 73rd Constitution Amendment Act 1993. Government of Rajasthan had also appointed a committee in the year 1993, Commissioner, Arun Kumar, to recommend various powers to be given to Panchayati Raj Institutions consequent upon Constitutional Amendment Act. This committee had recommended that DRDA should be merged into the Zilla Parishad which should be only body at the district level to execute all the rural development programmes in the district.

In Kerala, DRDA was merged with District Panchayat in October 1999, though Project Director is responsible for distribution of funds of District Panchayats. But in West Bengal where decentralized planning is in vogue, DRDA is working as separate entity through Sabha Adhipati, Zilla Panchayat is Chairman of DRDA also. Collector acts as Vice Chairman. Karnataka was the first State to merge DRDA into Zilla Parishad as early as 1987 and gave more financial and functional autonomy to it.

Madhya Pradesh also merged DRDA into Zilla Parishad with effect from 2nd October 1997. In April 1999 Rajasthan made Pramukh Zilla Parishad as ex-officio Chairman of DRDA which maintains its separate entity as yet. In Himachal Pradesh also, Chairman of Zilla Panchayat is Chairman of DRDA also. In Uttar Pradesh, the resistance of State level bureaucracy is still continuing though in May 1999 DRDA has been transferred to Zilla Parishad in all the 83 districts. Orders have been issued that government staff working therein will also be administered by Zilla Parishad concerned. In Haryana though letter was received on 06.11.1995 from Government of India for re-structuring DRDA and place it under Zilla Parishad, merger is still under consideration. Till then, Zilla Parishad chair-persons preside over the meetings of governing council but executive powers are still with the District Commissioner as chairman to look after poverty alleviation programmes. Additional District Magistrate works as chairman of Zilla Parishad. There is no non-official elected representative as chairman in Panchayati Raj Institution at district level. In Tripura also, DRDA is headed by District Magistrate. In Goa, merger of DRDA is still awaited.

In Manipur, DRDA was reconstituted on 30.08.1997 when Adhyaksha of Zilla Parishad was made Chair-person of governing body of DRDA though executive powers continue with Chief Executive Officer. In Tamil Nadu, DRDA still works as separate entity, Collector continues as Chairman of DRDA on the pattern of Gujarat and Maharashtra. He is also Chairman of District

Planning Committee.

Thus, in most of the States, there are two separate bodies for rural development programmes at the district level, though in some States, Chairman of Zilla Parishad acts as ex-officio Chairman of governing council of DRDA also. In other States like Tamil Nadu, Gujarat and Maharashtra, Collector himself is Chair-person. But in all the States, executive powers vest in the District Magistrate or District Development Officer who is a bureaucrat.

State Control

Development of a nation of the size of India is not possible unless the millions of its citizens actively involve themselves both in the preparation and implementation of plans and schemes meant for their welfare and progress. But in all the State acts, there is provision for control of the State Government in following forms[32]:

(1) Supervision and control through application of laws;

(2) Control through local functionaries,

   (a) In form of disciplinary powers with the government;

   (b) Higher level officials are all government servants on deputation and on whom Panchayati Raj Institutions have limited control which is limited to remarks in their annual performance appraisal;

   (c) Control over decisions of Panchayati Raj Institutions by way of suspending resolutions through sub-divisional or district magistrate or cancelling resolutions at the State level;

   (d) Control of administrative activities through submission of periodic progress reports, inspections, enquiries, investigation of complaints through officers, power of appeal, review, revision to the government, administrative and technical sanctions, appointment of committee for execution of works if elected representatives fail to execute Panchayat development works;

(e) Control over finances in the form of sanction of budget, grant-in-aid, loans, matching grants, taxation and audit of accounts of Panchayati Raj Institutions.

In Tamil Nadu, bureaucracy exercises enormous control over Panchayati Raj Institutions. There it is legacy of the past since colonial masters, when government officials were made ex-officio members of the local bodies. Because of superior role assigned to bureaucracy, cordiality in the relationship between officials and elected representatives is missing. Organization of the Panchayat administration does not allow much functional autonomy to the elected representatives. Although at the village level, the village Panchayat president has its executive authority, the District Collector has the overall controlling authority as the 'Inspector of Panchayats' for all the 3-tiers. Bureaucracy has armed itself with arbitrary powers such as dissolution of Panchayats .

Punjab Panchayat Samiti and Zilla Parishad Act, Section 103, empowers the government to supersede Panchayat. Section 97 empowers Deputy Commissioner or Sub-Divisional Officer to suspend execution of any resolution or order of Panchayat. In Haryana, Sections 64 and 160 empower the Director of Panchayats to suspend chairperson/vice chairperson/members if criminal offence is established against them. All the powers of taxation are vested in the State government. Section 167 provides that the government shall advise, supervise and co-ordinate the functions of Panchayat Samiti if it is illegal or not in public interest. There is chance of misuse of power on political grounds. Government and Bureaucracy want to have a say at all levels. In Himachal Pradesh, real powers vest in the District Collectors, Sub-Divisional Magistrates and District Panchayat Officers. Collector is vested with the powers of the State government and can suspend a Panch or resolution of Panchayat. In Maharashtra, Chief Executive Officer of Zilla Parishad is an I.A.S. officer who is also chairman of DRDA and executes the programmes through Panchayati Raj Institutions. Decision of Collector is final.

In Orissa, State exercises control over Panchayati Raj Institutions through Collector and Director of Panchayats. State government retains absolute control and powers to negate its democratic process and working. Sub-Divisional Officer and Block Development Officer have been given all the financial powers. Chairpersons is merely a figure head. Threat of suspension, removal and supersession always hangs over the elected Chairpersons since such powers are used more for political purpose rather than administrative convenience. Collector can direct the B.D.O. to pay money for execution of works. Pramukh Zilla Praishad has to apply for leave also to Zilla Parishad only through the Collector, though in May 1999 he was also given status of State Minister.

In Uttar Pradesh, Zilla Parishads stood superseded for 15 years and Collector was Chairman Zilla Parishad. State can cancel and suspend any resolution passed by Panchayati Raj Institutions and issue directions, inspect, enquire into affairs of Panchayati Raj Institutions through its officers. State exercise administrative, technical and financial controls. Even in Madhya Pradesh where decentralization is progressive and 'Gram Sarkar' and 'District Government' is in operation, State Government has assumed over riding powers to suspend and remove office bearers, dissolve Panchayats and suspend the execution of resolutions or orders of Panchayati Raj Institutions. Andhra Pradesh State Government has started curbing Panchayat powers in 1999. It not only took away the power of Panchayats to draw cheques but also vested District Collectors and other officials with most other executive powers bypassing the elected representatives of Panchayati Raj Institutions. In West Bengal also where all the 29 functions stand transferred to Panchayati Raj Institutions. District Magistrate acts as executive officer 'to exercise general control over all officers and other employees of Zilla Parishad'. Additional District Magistrate is full time Secretary of Zilla Parishad. Chief Executive or Additional Chief Executive are not under administrative control of Sabhadhipati. Additional confidential report of Zilla Parishad staff is written by District Magistrate/Chief Executive Officer.

Thus in all the States, State governments have been exercising administrative, technical, financial controls over Panchayati Raj Institutions so that they fulfil their functions within the given parameters as per the broad guidelines of State policy.

Madhya Pradesh has adopted the scheme of 'Gram Sarkar' and 'District Government'. The State government had constituted a task force on 26th January 2000 to evolve a framework for village level government so as to empower villagers to take decisions on matters concerning them and making bureaucracy answerable to the villagers. Such twin objective is intended to be fulfilled through 'Gram Sarkar'. On 26th January 2001, 'Gram Sarkar' has been declared as 'Gram Swarajya' but the picture will be clear only when 'Gram Swaraj' works successfully in the years to come.

The concept of 'District Government' has been already introduced in Madhya Pradesh on 1st April 1999. Minister incharge has been made Chairman of District Planning Committee sanctions works in the district looking to local resources and local aspirations of people in the district.

Madhya Pradesh Amendment Section 21(A) giving 'Right to recall' Panch/Sarpanch by more than 50 per cent members of Gram Sabha after they completed two and a half years from the date of election. This clause was also upheld by Madhya Pradesh High Court in December 1999. Decision would be taken by way of secret ballot. There is also a provision of appeal to Collector who would take decision within 30 days. It is for the first time in the history of the country that Chairman of Nagar Panchayat Anoop Pur, District Shahdol (Madhya Pradesh) Smt. Pallavika was removed from her post through the process of recall after secret ballot in Gram Sabha. More than 3000 voters voted against her whereas more than 1500 voted in her favour, as reported in *'Rajasthan Patrika'*, daily dated 11 April, 2001.

The Panchayati Raj system built with the support of the provisions of the 73rd Constitution Amendment is only a necessary condition for the sound growth of the decentralized governance system. Its sustainability and legitimacy, however, depends to a great extent on the availability of the right kind of functionaries both official and people's representatives. And this is possible only when State governments initiate supportive measures such as regular training to upgrade skills, particularly in leadership and planning. Training had become essential specially for the women and members belonging to the weaker sections.

In order to strengthen the Panchayati Raj system, the State government should develop a positive attitude and consider the Panchayats as 'partners' in the development process. In majority of States, bureaucracy has been given the upper hand over the elected representatives. Through this institution, State governments are exercising overall control over the Panchayats. This is negation of the principle of democratic decentralization. As observed in Karnataka context by P.R. Nayak Committee, "in any democratic form of government, bureaucracy should always function under democratically elected body and the role of government officials should be facilitative and executive rather than an authoritative one"[33].

Thus, even after 73rd Amendment in the Constitution, Panchayati Raj Institutions are still lacking in administrative, financial and political autonomy. But even then, Constitution has reposed strong faith in the State governments which are supposed to play a progressive role with regard to devolution of powers, functions, staff and resources, so that Panchayati Raj Institutions really fulfil their role as institutions of self government as envisaged in the Constitution.

NOTES

1. N.K. Bose, *Studies in Gandhism,* Navjeevan, Ahmedabad, 1962, p. 202.
2. S.S. Singh and Suresh Mishra, *Legislative Framework of Panchayati Raj in India,* pp. XV-XVIII.
3. Dr. Mahipal, "Effectiveness of Gram Sabha", *National Herald,* New Delhi, 6th April, 2000.
4. S.P. Jain. *The Gram Sabha* : *Gateway to Grassroots Democracy*, NIRD, Hyderabad Journal, pp. 566-67.
5. Gram Sabha - 1999-2000, The Year of Gram Sabha, *Kurukshetra,* October 1999, p. 22.
6. George, Mathew *Kurukshetra*, October 1999, pp. 26-28.
7. *Kurukshetra*, October 1999, p. 42.

8. Gram Sabha - 1999-2000, The Year of Gram Sabha, *Kurukshetra*, October 1999, p. 22.
9. Gram Sabha - 1999-2000, The Year of Gram Sabha, *Kurukshetra,* October 1999.
10. Gram Sabha - 1999-2000, The Year of Gram Sabha, *Kurukshetra,* October 1999.
11. Panchayati Raj in India - Status Report 1999, Rajiv Gandhi Foundation, p. 263.
12. The Panchayat (Extension to the Scheduled Areas) Act, 1996, Gazette Extraordinary.
13. *Panchayati Raj Update,* February, 2000.
14. *Panchayati Raj Update,* February, 2000.
15. *Panchayati Raj Update,* March, 2000.
16. *Panchayati Raj Update,* January, 2000.
17. *Panchayati Raj Update,* August, 2000.
18. International Conference on Democratic Decentralization, Kerala, May 2000.
19. Thomas Issac, Member State Planning Board, *Panchayati Raj Update,* June 2000, pp. 6-7.
20. International Conference on Democratic Decentralization, May 2000.
21. Rajiv Gandhi Foundation, Status Report 1999.
22. Study Report, 1964, Government of Rajasthan, Department of Panchayati Raj.
23. Narain, Iqbal, Panchayati Raj Administration in India, *Indian Journal of Political Science*, April-June 1960, p. 61.
24. Khurshid Alam Khan, Governor of Karnataka, *Panchayati Raj Update*, November, 1999, p. 4.
25. Yaswhant Sinha, Finance Minister, *Panchayati Raj Update,* September 2000, p. 8.
26. *Panchayati Raj Update,* August 2000.
27. *Panchayati Raj Update,* July 2000, p. 7.
28. *Panchayati Raj Update,* July 2000, pp. 6-7.
29. Eleventh Finance Commission, *Panchayati Raj Update,* August 2000.

30. Eleventh Finance Commission, *Panchayati Raj Update,* August 2000, p. 8.

31. Right to Information, State legislations and central bill, National Campaign for People's Right to Information.

32. Prof. S.P. Ranga Rao, *Kurukshetra,* April 1998.

33. *Panchayati Raj Update*, June 2000, pp. 7.

7

E-GOVERNANCE STRATEGY IN INDIA

An Urgent Need for Re-orientation towards Local E-Governance

V. VENKATAKRISHNAN

India is ranked very high in the global list of countries, which have a substantial number of government websites, and it represents one of the leading advocates of E-governance in the developing world (Haque). However, as per the recent assessment of 144 UN Member States for their e-government capacity made by the United Nations and American Society for Public Administration based on web presence measure, telecommunications infrastructure measure and human capital measure, India is finding a place among countries with minimal E-government capacity and its e-government index has been a mere 1.29 which is very low compared to its commitment to e-governance.

As per this assessment, the web presence measure captures a country's online stage of development such as emerging presence, enhanced presence, interactive presence, transactional presence and seamless or full integrated. Emerging stage represents when a limited web presence is established though a few independent government websites which provide static information. Enhanced presence means a situation when the online presence of government increases and the content will be more of dynamic nature. When the country's presence on the web increased dramatically with access to a wide range of government institutions an services, the interactive presence stage is created. As and when complete and secure transactions like obtaining passports, birth and death records, online payment for services, etc., take place transactional stage would have been achieved. When services are clustered along common needs and ministerial/departmental/agency lines of demarcation are removed in cyberspace or fully integrated stage of web presence would have arrived.

The telecommunication infrastructure measure compares six primary indicators such as PCs per 100 individuals, Internet hosts per 10,000 individuals, percentage of a nation's population online, telephone lines per 100 individuals and televisions per 1000. Human capital measure consists of UNDP Human Development Index, Information Access Index and Urban/Rural population ratio (Ronaghan). The following Table 7.1 shows India's position among the countries of Asia/Oceania on these measures. In terms of web presence, only four countries of this region i.e. Australia, New Zealand, Singapore and South Korea are better than India. Japan, Mongolia, Malaysia and Brunei are on par with India on this count. However in terms of e-government index it ranks as low as 15 among 31 countries for which such index is available. It might be noted that in many ICT measures as well as human capital measures, India is lagging behind. Very high levels of rural population (71.9%), a majority of which may not be having access to information and communication technology might be one of the major reasons for such an abysmally low e-government index for India. This is not surprising in view of the fact that the e-governance efforts so far in India have been targetted towards Central Government organisations and State Government organisations, which are headquartered in national capital or State capitals thus providing enough scope to term e-governance efforts of India as lopsided. Contrarily, USA and Korea have e-government measures in these countries indicates development of e-governance across all the levels of government.

Table 7.1: E-Government index of countries in Asia/Oceania

Country	Web pre-sence measure	ICT infrastructure measure						Human capital measure			E-Gov. Index
		PCs/ 100	Int Hosts 10000	% of Pop online	Tele Lines/ 100	Mobile phones/ 100	TVs/ 1000	Human Dev. Index	Info Access Index	Urban pop	
1	2	3	4	5	6	7	8	9	10	11	12
Australia	4	46.46	843.52	52.5	52.41	44.63	639	0.936	0.999	84.7	2.60
New Zealand	4	36.02	900.87	46.1	49.57	40.25	501	0.913	0.999	85.7	2.59
Singapore	4	48.31	437.56	49.3	48.45	68.38	348	0.876	0.333	100.0	2.58
Rep. of Korea	4	19.03	84.10	46.4	46.37	56.69	346	0.875	0.833	81.1	2.30
Japan	3	31.52	365.66	37.2	58.58	47.30	799	0.928	0.916	78.6	2.12
Mongolia	3	0.92	0.64	1.3	4.97	4.04	63	0.569	0.750	63.0	1.64
Malaysia	3	9.45	29.33	17.0	19.93	21.32	166	0.774	0.333	56.7	1.63
Brunei	2	6.22	141.21	1.2	24.59	20.52	638	0.857	0.167	71.3	1.59
Armenia	2.5	0.57	7.57	1.1	15.53	0.23	217	0.743	0.500	69.7	1.59
Philippines	2.5	1.93	2.54	3.0	3.92	8.24	108	0.747	0.750	57.7	1.44
Georgia	2	0.31	3.17	1.1	12.31	1.88	472	0.742	0.500	60.2	1.39
Region	2.46	7.07	96.77	8.89	14.55	11.10	227.9	0.709	0.446	47.37	1.37
Indonesia	2.75	0.99	1.26	1.2	3.14	1.73	136	0.677	0.583	39.8	1.34

Contd......

Table 7.1 *(Contd.)*

1	2	3	4	5	6	7	8	9	10	11	12
Iran	2	5.58	0.27	0.8	14.90	1.51	157	0.714	0.167	61.1	1.31
Azerbajan	2	0.45	1.99	0.7	10.36	5.56	254	0.738	0.250	56.9	1.30
India	3	0.45	0.35	1.2	3.20	0.35	69	0.571	0.750	28.1	1.29
Kazakhistan	2	0.30	4.55	1.1	10.82	0.30	234	0.742	0.250	56.4	1.28
Tukmenistan	2	0.46	2.76	1.0	8.19	0.09	201	0.730	0.001	44.7	1.15
Vietnam	2	0.89	0.02	1.0	3.19	0.99	180	0.682	0.083	39.8	1.10
Uzbekistan	2	0.29	0.11	1.0	6.58	0.22	273	0.698	0.083	37.2	1.10
West Samoa	2.5	0.56	1.14	0.6	4.06	2.38	92	0.735	0.583	23.3	0.92
Pakistan	2	0.43	0.46	0.9	2.22	0.25	88	0.498	0.250	36.5	1.04
China	2	1.59	0.54	2.1	11.12	6.58	272	0.714	0.083	31.6	1.04
Kyrgyzstan	2	0.43	8.76	1.1	8.00	0.19	44	0.707	0.250	33.6	1.01
Tajikistan	2	0.28	0.44	0.2	3.53	0.01	285	0.660	0.167	27.5	1.00
Thailand	2	2.43	10.47	2.5	8.70	4.39	236	0.757	0.750	21.2	0.94
Nepal	2.5	0.27	0.48	0.3	1.16	0.04	4	0.480	0.583	11.6	0.94
Maldives	2	1.89	9.85	2.1	9.08	2.85	39	0.739	0.250	26.1	0.93
Sri Lanka	2	0.56	1.14	0.6	4.06	2.38	92	0.735	0.583	23.3	0.92
Bangladesh	2	0.10	0.25	0.8	0.34	0.12	7	0.470	0.583	23.9	0.90
Laos	2	0.23	0.01	0.7	0.75	0.23	4	0.476	0.083	22.9	0.88
Cambodia	1.5	0.11	0.37	0.1	0.26	1.00	123	0.541	0.167	15.6	0.67

Source : Ronaghan (2002).

Local Government websites in United States

In USA, even though the Local Governments have been a little slower than the State and Federal level governments in developing e-government, both Local and State Governments are erasing the early lead of Federal government quickly. This is based on a survey conducted for the Council for Excellence in Government, covering various respondents including 200 decision makers at the federal level, 100 in State Government and 100 in local governments at the city or country level. The results are shown in the Table 7.2 above. It could be seen that substantial changes have taken place in the State and Local Government online facilities such as documents, feedback mechanism and search engine between 2000 and 2001. The survey conducted in 1999 has also found out that there was more trust on local E-governance (35% had great deal of confidence) compared to Federal E-governance (21% had great deal of confidence) (commonwealth Centre for Electronic Governance, 2002). Another study, which surveyed 1,471 cities in USA, has found out that around 86 per cent of these cities have

Table 7.2: Development of online services by State/Local Governments and Federal Governments in the United States

Online Services	State/Local Governments in the Year			Federal Government in the Year		
	2000*	2001	Difference	2000	2001	Difference
Documents	70	89	+19	96	93	-3
Links to other Govt sites	—	89	—	—	82	—
Feedback mechanism	58	83	+25	69	76	+7
Calendar/ Event Info	69	77	+8	75	78	+3
Search Engine	45	69	+24	69	78	+9
Constituent services	70	77	+7	63	66	+3
Web-based service apps	—	53	—	—	50	—
+75 State and local government officials were interviewed in the August 2000 study						

Source : Hart-Teeter (2002).

websites. These cities had been across all ranges of population and it could be seen that in case of cities over 1,000,000 population six out of six cities surveyed had websites. Even in case of cities, which fall in the lowest range of 10,000-24,999 population size, 612 out of 779 surveyed (79 per cent) had websites (Moon, 2002).

Local Government Websites in Republic of Korea

In Korea also there is very little that separates Central and Local Governments in terms of their web presence. In fact, Metropolitan Governments have been well ahead of the Central Government in this regard even in the year 1998 wherein 100 per cent of the former governments had websites. It might be noted that the pace of Central Government and basic local governments in having the websites is more or less similar from 1998 to 2000. All these facts are presented in the Table 7.3.

Table 7.3 : Number of Websites year-wise

Category of Government Agency	Number of websites by year		
	1998	1999	2000
Central Government Strategy	69% (35/51)	86% (44/51)	96% (49/51)
Metropolitan Government*	100%(16/16)	100% (16/16)	100% (16/16)
Basic Local Government**	62% (146/234)	84% (195/232)	97% (225/232)

* Includes metro political cities and provinces;

** Includes cities, counties and district autonomous units

Source : Sin-Yong Moon (2001)

It has been further found out that service provision using the website is also very high in case of local governments in Korea. While the following Table 7.4 delineates this fact, receipt of payment (tax, fines, etc.) was still on a tribal basis in these governments.

Before proceeding further to find out the e-government efforts of local level governments in India, it might be relevant to have a look at the e-governance policies of the Government of India and a few leading State governments such as Andhra Pradesh and Karnataka.

Table 7.4 : Category of the Public Services in Local Government on Internet in Korea

Category of Service	Level of the use*
Information retrieval service	100%
Communication with citizen (Consultation, Opinion etc.)	100%
Agency information and News	100%
Information about the procedure of civil service application	89%
Applying for Insurance of Certificate, Permit or Approval	72%
Request for Public Access to Specific Government Information	34%
Request for Petition Appeal	21%
Policy Proposals or Response to the Activities of Government	59%
Receipt of Payment (Tax, Fines etc.)	Testing on a trial basis

* Based on review of 218 official websites of basic local governments.
Source : Sing-Yong Moon (2001).

E-governance policy of Government of India

The Government of India has approved the policy of allocation of two to three per cent of budget for Information Technology. It has been decided in view of limitation of resources, those services that have a direct interface with the public should be taken up for computerization on a priority basis. Various services in this regard had already been identified. It has been suggested that in five years time, majority of the transactional services would be provided by way of Internet. Sub-components of this policy such as engaging consultants, leasing of computers, use of local languages, spreading awareness, issuing indicative guidelines, preparation of a handbook to integrate key project findings, information kiosks, cyberlaws and internet servers have been delineated in this policy *(http://egov.mit.gov.in/backgound l.htm)*. Though services such as pension for aged, widows, birth certificate, death certificate, domicile certificate, utility payments/billing related to water supply, payment of house tax, property tax, octroi and road tax which are dealt by local governments have been identified among services with maximum citizen interface, it might be surprising to note that there is no explicit mention about the e-governance efforts to be made by the local governments in this regard. A centre for e-governance has also been set up in the premises of the Department of Information Technology in New Delhi to showcase successful e-governance applications in various States. Karnataka is one of the frontrunners of e-governance in India. Its e-governance policy, Mahiti, outlines the important initiatives in the e-governance such as Mukhya Vahini of development of comprehensive data base for a sophisticated decision support, *Bhoomi* relating to computerization of land records of all the villages in the State, *Nandani* for making land registration simple and easy for the citizens, *Khajhane* which involves computerization of treasuries all over the State, *Therige* which is related to computerization of commercial taxes department and *Reshme* covering online transactions in the silk market. In addition to these and many such efforts in various other sectors, information has been provided about efforts for computerization of Bangalore, Mangalore, Mysore, Belgaum, Hubli-Dharwad and Gulbarga Municipal corporations. It might be surprising to note that even though Karnataka has been considered as a pioneer in terms of local government reforms and e-governance efforts, there is no mention of e-governance about many important local governments such as municipal councils, nagar panchayats and rural local government institutions such as Zilla Parishads, Taluk Panchayati Samitis and Village Panchayats. The Government of India's website directory lists websites of just three Zilla Parishads i.e., Bellary, Raichur and Shimoga of this State. The following section shows the e-government efforts on one of these Zilla Parishads and a village Panchayat.

E-Local Governments in Karnataka

Shimoga Zilla Panchayat's efforts in having it sown website have to be lauded. This website consists of information on various of its governance like political structure, administration, annual budget, departments under its control, development schemes undertaken by it and the role of Taluka and Gram Panchyats in the Zilla Panchayat *(www.kar.nic.in/zpshimoga)*. The e-mail of the Chief Executive Officer of this Zilla Panchayat has been provided in this website for making any suggestion or comment. Efforts have been made to provide history, census details *(albeit, 1991)*, higher educational facilities, industries and tourism related to this district. The information provided on higher education in this website have been quite elaborate and links have been provided to the websites of a few academic institutions like Kuvempu University, Jawaharlal Nehru College of Engineering and National Education Society. Similarly specification of the list of financial institutions, backward classes hostels, social welfare hostels, and primary health institutions, in the district is also very systematic. A list of e-mails, telephone numbers of various government and non-government institutions is also an attractive feature of this website. The information provided can be termed as exhaustive. At the same time, it has to be noted that as on April 29, 2002 there were only 2967 visitors to this website and it has reached just 3999 as on August 24, 2002. It seems that this website has not been updated for long period and even on August 27, 2002 the Plan budget for the year 2001-2002 only was available and there was no information about budget for the years 2001-2002 or 2002-2003. It is seen that this website was last updated on January 21, 2002. Though having a website provides information to its citizens and others, it is a mere first step in e-governance as only one-way communication has been established to a large extent.

Belandur Village Panchayat near Bangalore is an example of successful e-governance at the local level in Karnataka. This Panchayat in collaboration with Comusol, an IBM and Microsoft joint venture company, has computerized the functions of property details, tax collection and data management. It is reported that the software used by the Panchayat has changed its way of functioning. This resulted in cutting the costs and removing corruption in the process. Improved tax collection has enabled the Panchayat to allot more funds for the development work. Buoyed by the success of the e-governance attempts, this Panchayat has even attempted to adopt certain methods of e-democracy also. Very recently, as per the report made by the Star TV News, it has made efforts to telecast the proceedings of the Panchayat meetings live through the local cable network.

E-governance policy of Andhra Pradesh State

Andhra Pradesh is one of the leading States in India in terms of its efforts towards digital governance. Apart from making use of information technology in various services provided by the State Government like filing First Information Report (FIR) while lodging complaints in police stations, land/property registration and delivering statutory certificates specifying the caste, place and date of birth by the local revenue administrative units as Mandals, laudable efforts have been made by a few LGIs such as Municipal Corporation of Hyderabad, Visakhapatnam, Guntur and Vijayawada.

In its vision of e-government (April 2002), Andhra Pradesh Government has clearly stated the objectives, approach and the essential framework for e-government. E-government roadmap survey of 50 departments is being taken up to identify services/ applications that have e-government opportunities. It has further listed 22 core e-government initiatives undertaken so far in this State. Among these, e-seva (electronic services to citizens acting as a single window), which has already been implemented in the State capital of Hyderabad is related to local governments. It has been proposed to extend this to 50 other towns in due course of time. Similarly the planning to provide access points for rural locations by way of kiosks in rural areas on private-public partnership model can also be related to local governments. 'The Big Picture' of e-governance drawn by this government includes municipal governments also. However, there is no mention about rural local governments where the population is more reliant on public services.

E-Local governments in Andhra Pradesh

The following section describes the successful efforts made by a few local governments in implementing e-governance in Andhra

Pradesh. It might be noted that compared to the total number of urban local governments such as Municipal Corporations and Municipal Councils and rural local government such as District Panchayats, Panchayat Samitis and Village Panchayats,the e-governance efforts are negligible.

Hyderabad Municipal Corporation

Hyderabad Municipal Corporation is another notable example of successful adoption of digital governance by the LGIs. The website *(www.ourmch.com)* of the capital city of Andhra Pradesh has provision for downloading forms and applications used to avail the services of the corporation like, birth certificate, death certificate, self assessment of property tax, self building application form, transfer of property, license for advertisement, etc., among other things. Online payment of property tax to this corporation has been made possible in collaboration with a website called *www.billjunction.com* under the category 'payees' wherein the service providers do not present the bills through the billjunction website. One can pay for the paper bills sent by the service providers by logging on to the website *www.billjunction.com.* It might be interesting to note that in case of Mumbai, Thane and New Mumbai Municipal Corporations, in addition to delivery of paper bills, details of bills for property tax can be seen electronically and payments are also accepted electronically.

Details about other payment channels like citizens service centers, e-seva and online payments have been provided in the Hyderabad's website. Opinion polls are also conducted through this website to learn about citizens' points of view. Moreover, procedures to seek building permission are also provided. The status of the building permission application can also be seen online. Property tax dues of an individual can be ascertained either by locality or circle. There are many other positive features of this website like engineering works search. Based on this search one can learn about details of work in various circles, assembly constituencies, wards and localities. The records to be displayed based on this search will show the name of the work, estimated cost, sanction date, stage of the work and the expenditure incurred.

All these features can be appreciated in view of the fact that they ensure transparency in undertaking various functions of the local governments. It seems that the attempts at e-governance at Hyderabad Municipal Corporation are much more carefully planned and useful to the citizens than that of many other municipal corporations in the country. It could be noticed that there were 38,723 hits to this website as on July 14, 2002 which has gone up to 70,454 as on October 6, 2002. It could be seen that this website is more dynamic in providing updated information and new information.

Visakhapatnam Municipal Corporation

Visakhapatnam's (known as Vizag) e-governance efforts revolve around its website based services delivery. The website is part of project Saukaryam (meaning facility or convenience in Telugu, local language) which is a joint venture between Net Savant and Vizag Municipal Corporation (VMC). While websites of many other city governments of India are designed and hosted by the National Informatics Centre (NIC) of the Government of India, VMC's website is designed, hosted and maintained by Net Savant. In this sense it can be called as a private-public cooperation in electronic delivery of municipal services, first of its kind in India. VMC has collaborated with many banks for online payment of taxes by citizens in addition to its own civic centres where such payment can be made. The following figure depicts the outline of e-governance in Vizag.

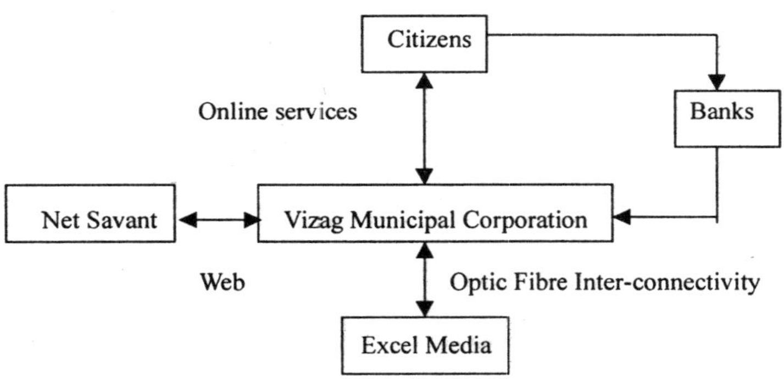

Online Services

The services, which are provided through internet or intranet, are called online services. Generally services, which are fully executed through these media, can be termed as online services. For instance, if a citizen can get any certificate from the municipal corporation by making necessary entries in the website of the local body concerned, it is known as fully executable service. In case, he/she has to visit the local body's office to collect the certificate after making an application either online or using the formal downloaded from the website, it cannot be termed as fully executable service. However, considering the nature of services provided by the local bodies such as VMC in India, their online services have been classified as informal, interactive, transactional and promotional services for this study.

Informational Services

In a country like India where a large number of governments (national, provincial and local) are operating, availability of right information itself can be a boon to citizens, a sizeable of whom are illiterate. For instance, in its website VMC provides details such as procedure for obtaining building permit, time limit for grant or refusal of building application, site and buildings requirements, factory/industrial building requirement, educational buildings, institutional and public office complexes, commercial/ mercantile buildings, residential buildings, security deposits lighting and ventilation requirements of buildings, mandatory inspections and issue of fit-for occupation certificate by local authorities and such other things as outlined in the Andhra Pradesh Government Order No. 423 dated July 31, 1998. These rules which are very much relevant for any proprietor of an existing building or a one who propose to construct a new building have been arranged in a sequential order in the website and it makes it easier to navigate. As these rules are uniformly applicable across the State of Andhra Pradesh, provision of this information in the website might be useful to the entire population across the State. This is all the more important in view of the fact that sanction of building permission happens to be an area where many citizens have been facing innumerable problems from the street-level bureaucracy of the local governments across the country.

Secondly, once an application has been submitted for building permission in the relevant counter, a number is allotted to the application. Using this number, any applicant can log into the website and check the status of the application. Probably this might reduce the number of trips one has to make to the local bodies office to get the permission for building construction. It might be noted that in the year 2001, there were 2,446 applications for such permission. In case of 2002, as on September 20, 2002, there were 1,774 such applications to VMC. A summary of pending building plan proposals can also be obtained through this website and this information can be used by any one, especially the elected representatives to make the officials of the local government more accountable by raising the issue in the meetings of the council.

Similarly, around 120,000 property and water tax assessment in the city have been computerized to a large extent and stored in a server at the VMC office. Using internet, connectivity has been provided between this server and the computer nodes available in various collection centres (civic centres) and a host of online banks. A fibre optic broadband network laid by a private partner in the city is used in this context. If any citizen wishes to know the calculations made by the VMC to arrive at the property and water tax dues to be paid by him, he can visit the website and get the details by entering the relevant unique assessment number. This reduces the many trips made by the citizens to the VMC to learn about the tax dues, remitting them and clarification regarding them.

With regard to taxation, procedure for valuation of property tax on buildings and lands has been prominently provided in the website. Many subjects related to this topic such as prevailing rates of taxation, calculation methodology, examples, etc., have been linked to this page of the website making the information much more easy to obtain. This also reduces the scope of manipulation by the lower level bureaucracy who otherwise might harass the citizens for pecuniary benefits.

Similarly information regarding officers who are connected with various functions with their contact details has been provided.

This will help the citizens of Vizag in contacting the concerned officer directly to get any service provided by the VMC. List of online banks for payment of tax dues, their addresses, timings and phone numbers has also been provided in the website.

Information about water supply, an important service provided by the local governments in this part of the world, are also available in the website. This includes the most important aspects such as status of water supply, water supply distribution timings in various locations in the 50 wards of the city and list of names of persons concerned with water supply in VMC.

General information such as weather forecast, local news, tourist places in and around Vizag, today's engagements, Vizag diary giving a list of events that will take place in the locality, city bus routes, flight, train and bus timings have been provided by linking with another website called *vizagcityonline.com* designed and hosted by Net Savant, a private service supplier.

Tender notices issued by the VMC are also available in the VMC website, department-wise (civil, electrical, health etc.) and class-wise. By including details such as name, value and time for completion of the work, efforts have been made to procure the services needed by the VMC. Similarly, an effort has been made to make the service procurement of the corporation more transparent by displaying details such as estimated cost, sanction date, contractor name and stage of work for various works awarded by the VMC. The search facilities available in the website would enable anyone to find out the works in various wards by different departments of the city government.

Interactive Services

There are various sections of the website which provide facility to contact the Commissioner (CEO of the Corporation), Mayor on any subject related to the corporation and provide feedback. In addition to that a page on citizen forum helps any citizen in posting a message about any aspect of the city. If anyone wishes to respond to the message, suitable facilities for reply to the person who posted the message are also available. A cursory glance of this section shows that various messages as stray dogs, violation of building rules by a citizen and conditions of roads have been posted in recent days. Provisions for civic polls on various issues of urban governance are also available and so far five polls have been conducted. Chat facilities are also made available for enabling interaction among various segment of the society.

Transactional Services

Transactions that can be completed through the website or through the nodes available in the civic service centres or at the banks connected with the server of VMC can be termed as transactional services. In case of VMC, online payment of property tax, water tax, online registration of birth and death by individuals and hospitals and online registration of complaints/suggestions can be considered as the major transactional services. In case of online payment at the counters of various banks, any citizen can pay by presenting his assessment number. Immediately all relevant information such as updated dues and arrears if any with interest would be available. Once payment is made by the concerned in the bank connected to the main server at VMC, necessary updating is carried out automatically at the main server. The bank would give an acknowledgement to the payee in turn immediately showing the details of payment made. In addition to the 18 collaborating banks in the city, there are bill junction counters directly operated by VMC in Suryabagh for this purpose. In addition to that online payments can be made using the credit cards of various banks such as HDFC Bank, IDBI Bank and ICICI Bank. To make this mode of payment through credit card attractive, possibilities of winning a free gift has also been introduced for those who use this facility. However, such facility is extended to the registered users only with a view to serve the genuine users. To become a registered users of some of the online services, a form available in the website has to be filled online by providing various details. On submission of the form there might be a telephone call or a physical verification on behalf of the VMC to get assured about the genuineness of the data. Such registration is necessary for birth and death registrations and for home delivery of birth and death certificates. With regard to online complaints, the information would be forwarded to the concerned officer for immediate attention and it would also reach the database for monitoring the grievances settlement.

Promotional Services

In addition to the above services, VMC is promoting issues such as rain water harvesting, public participation in city sanitation, greening the city, calling for adopting of various projects such as eco-friendly projects, beatification projects and community projects and save water campaign. Thus the website has been effectively used for campaigning civic issues also.

Other Features

Facilities to access Telugu (local language) version of the website are also in-built in VMC website. Links to websites of various other organizations such as *vizagcityonline.com* (a private website) and Visakhapatnam Urban Development Authority, Government of Andhra Pradesh, E-Seva, Railways and Andhra Pradesh Info-Tech have been provided in the VMC website. Links to various programmes of the State government such as Vision 2020, Janmabhoomi, Neeru-Meeru and Self Help Groups have also been available in this site. Various forms of utility can also be downloaded from the website.

Provisions of information by topic has made it simpler and the website is easily navigable. Every single page has also links to relevant sub-topics. For instance, the page on birth registration will be having links to related aspects like on birth and death registrations, registration of birth and death rules and downloaded of various related form. Similar arrangement are made topic-wise and hence the website presents an attractive picture. It could be seen that the volume of services such as online payment through the counters of various banks is increasing continuously since the introduction of the facility in December 2000. The number of banks involved, the number of transactions and the amount remitted in these counters show a steady increase. It is observed that even on Sundays, payments due to the VMC have been made through bank counters, which operate on holidays also. In addition to that the number of visitors to this website also shows an upward trend.

E-Government application by collaborating with various private operators either for accepting online payment, or for designing, hosting and maintaining the website, or laying the optic fibre in all parts of city is a good example of public-private partnership in local public service delivery. In that sense it is a unique experiment in local e-governance in India. Ability to generate reports such as daily report on transactions performed by the civic centres and counters such as birth applications, death applications, buildings applications, tap applications and underground drainage applications in both the categories such as received and disposed, birth and death register details and bank- wise, counter-wise and ward-wise collection reports are some the additional benefits of this website. This would be of help in not only in gauging the performance of the corporation, but also in reducing the workload of the various categories of its employees such as tax collectors. The corporation can effectively redeploy them for carrying out other pressing requirements.

Nevertheless there is enormous scope to improve the existing services by resorting to more transactional services. This can be achieved by increasing the range of transactional services from a few available right now to a maximum possible. Search facilities are available in certain pages only and there is a need to have a comprehensive search facility in the home page itself. There is a necessity to reorient the website in terms of privacy of individuals. For instance, in case of citizen's forum, when irregularities such as violation of building plans are brought to the notice through the website, there is a need to protect the information about the individuals who provided such information. A clear statement about the privacy policy of the corporation is also needed to be incorporated in the website. Though there are a substantial number of visitors to this website, the number of participants in the civic polls are miniscule. If such shortcomings were overcome by incorporating necessary changes in the e-governance policy, VMC would reinforce its position as a model to other city governments.

Conclusion

There have been very few efforts at e-governance by various local governments in different parts of the country ranging from Delhi

Municipal Corporation to smaller sized Village Panchayats. The description of such attempts above is based on the published literature on these experiments and several visits to the websites of some of the local governments. Thus it can be termed that this article just indicates the types of efforts undertaken in India to digitalize the functions of the Local Governments. However it can be concluded that the efforts taken so far in India for adopting e-governance at the Local Government levels are few and far between nevertheless worth appreciation. It must be admitted that these local governments, which have tried to use information technology for the development for their citizens, have just taken a first step towards e-governance and they have to go a long way before realizing the ultimate objective of e-democracy and complete local e-governance. Intermittent efforts by a few Local Government institutions are not sufficient to change the face of the country, which is facing many problems like poverty, inadequate governance, and lack transparency in major functions of the governments at all levels. Unless efforts are made all over the country with the laudable objectives of less corruption, increased transparency, greater convenience, revenue growth and/or cost reductions leading to better public management, such isolated efforts will not yield much result. Concerted efforts are to be made to scale up faster and deliver value to its customers (citizens) by adopting complete e-governance similar to Korea and USA, the Local Government Institutions in India will become a true foundation of democracy.

REFERENCES

Choudhury, S.R., 'Logging on in Belandur', *Frontline,* 19(11), May 25-June 07, 2002, 44-45

Commonwealth Centre for Electronic Governance, 'E-government 2002: A comparative analysis of progress in five countries', London, 2002.

Cook, Meghan *et al.*, 'Making a case for local e-government', Center for Technology in Government, University at Albany, Albany, July 2002.

Haque, M. Shamsul, 'E-governance in India: Its impacts on relations among citizens, politicians and public servants', *International Review of Administrative Sciences*, 68(2), June 2002, 231-250.

Indian Institute of Public Administration (IIPA), *Newsletter*, 46(6), June 2002.

Kraemer, Kenneth L. and John Leslie King, 'The Role of Information Technology in Managing Cities', *Local Government Studies*, 14(2), March/April 1988, 23-47.

Lenihan, Donald G. and Alba Hanna, 'E-Government among Municipalities Experience', Centre for Collaborative Government, Ontario, October 2002.

Moon, Jae M., 'The Evolution of E-Government among Municipalities: Rhetoric or Reality', *Public Administration Review*, 62(4), July-August 2002, 424-433.

Moon, Sing-Young, 'The Utilization of the Internet Technology in the Public Services of Korea', *Asian Review of Public Administration*, 13(1), January-June 2001, 30-45.

Ronaghan, Stephen A., 'Benchmarking E-Government: A Global Perspective, Assessing the Progress of the UN Member States', United Nations Division for Public Economics and Public Administration and American Society for Public Administration, New York, 2002.

Tat-Kei Ho, Alfred, 'Reinventing Local Governments, and the E-Government Initiative', *Public Administration Review*, 62(4), July-August 2002, 434-443.

Venkatakrishnan, V., Local e-governments in India: Review of a few attempts', *Network*, 8(3), July-September 2002, 2-4.

Venkatakrishnan, V., 'E-government at grassroots level in India: Its relevance for developing countries', *The International Global Studies Encyclopedia*, Russian Philosophical Society and Russian Academy of Ecology, Moscow (forthcoming)

Venkatakrishnan, V., 'Digital governance at local level in India: Need for an integrated approach', in S. N. Ratha (ed.), *Panchayati Raj and Rural Development*, Concept, New Delhi (forthcoming).

8

TOWARDS PARTICIPATORY GOVERNANCE AT GRASS ROOTS

Synergization of Rural Communities and Rural Institutions

G. PALANITHURAI

Introduction

This chapter makes an attempt to analyse the importance and implications of the new approach—Participatory Governance—in achieving sustainable development and social justice at the grassroots through the newly created institution—Panchyati Raj. Participatory Governance is a widely recognized concept gaining momentum among the academics at present after witnessing the implications of the participation of people in the development process as stakeholders in many of the nations.[1] In the Indian context, though it is not new, much concientization is needed among all, especially all those involved in development activities at the grass roots, as people have been viewed and oriented as beneficiaries and not as development participants in the last five decades.[2] For the past fifty-four years, gradually, the government has been projected as a giver and the people oriented to perceive that they are the receivers of benefits from the government. As a result government machinery has grown out of proportion, to the extent of eating away 94 per cent of the income of the State for maintenance of the government[3] and it has led to a crisis. Governance at grass roots envisages revival of community organizations and establishment of linkages with the constitutionally created institutions for governance.[4] The possible linkages between community organizations and rural institutions would produce the needed synergized energy for achieving social equity and sustainable development at the grass roots. This kind of linkages are imperatives to cope with the changing paradigm of development. Yet, there are obstacles and impediments in establishing such productive linkages between and among the organizations and institutions. To overcome such barriers a number of steps are to be taken. This chapter will discuss all those issues connected with participatory governance. Before moving further it is necessary to fix the relevance of the new initiative contextually and to locate the problem with its full dimensions.

The Problem and the Context

Even after fifty years of democratic governance through planned activities one cannot state that people are provided with the needed minimum basic facilities to lead a decent human life in the rural areas. Programmes and schemes, both by the Centre and State governments, are many, to the tune of two hundred and fifty-six since independence.[5] To carry out all those schemes and programmes the government has extended its wings, growing beyond expectation to the level of eating away 94 per cent of the total revenue from the State as management cost of development in the form of salary and pension benefits. As a result people have been relegated to the background and government institutions have come to the centre stage. It is portrayed in history that people in pre-British Raj days led their life with self respect by deciding their destiny on their own. Their energy, knowledge and skills found opportunity in the society for utilization. The issues that were affecting their life were well within their framework of actions. One would never find organizations in the rural society in isolation. Varied organizations functioned independent of each other while performing their roles and responsibilities and interdependent while addressing common issues of the communities.[6] It is not a eulogic portrayal of realistic life situation despite several ills in the society while looking at all those issues from the nation-state liberal perspective.

At present an urgent necessity arises to look at governance in terms of its delivery to achieve development and social justice. Government cannot grow beyond the present size and it cannot function as it did in the past. Moreover it cannot make any claim but has to find ways and means to respond to the development challenges. The new challenges to the government cannot be thought of in the conventional sense of the development paradigm.[7] It needs a vibrant solution and it can be tackled only in a new framework. The new framework envisages new partners to achieve development. The new framework redefines the role of government in the development process. Government, in its conventional sense, was portrayed as a provider of service to the people. Now this has been changed. The new role of the government is only that of a facilitator. The withdrawal of government from the centre stage to the periphery in development activities has been visualized both positively and negatively. But the reality remains that government has lost its resilience to achieve development. Officially it was declared in India in 1991 that the concept of government has to be redefined.[8] Thus the concept of decentralization gained currency not in isolation but along with globalization, liberalization and privatization. Globalization of economy has come to stay as a historic force and in the same way decentralization of powers has been thrust on the people. Both Globalization of economy and decentralization of powers are centrally driven initiatives and thereby both meet barriers and resistance.[9] Globalization of economy aims at integration of markets and thereby the elites are competing in the process. Decentralization of powers provides scope for the people to participate in the development process as stakeholders and to decide on the issues which are affecting their life.[10] It is a process by which people are getting power and they have the ability to resist any kind of exploitation by external agencies. The basic question that arises here is as to how the process is perceived and how it is being operationalised in the new context. To answer this question the concept of decentralization of power has to be visualized in a larger context.

Basic Premises and Framework

It is unequivocal that any policy initiative or programme will be successful only if both the initiators and the people who reap the benefits perfectly understand the policy and the programme along with the individuals and organizations involved in the process of implementation. Likewise decentralization of power has to be perceived properly. It is necessary to identify the core value of it. There are two major propositions put forward in this regard. One is that the institutions which are created constitutionally at the grass roots to administer development and social justice are the extension of the government and have all the characteristics of the government.[11] The other proposition is that grass roots institutions are not the extension of the government but the extension of community organizations.[12] Arguments could be projected for both propositions legally and logically. For the first proposition, it is argued that Panchayats are constitutional entities to function as self governing institutions with earmarked roles and responsibilities. There are organizations, groups and intellectuals continuously projecting this kind of proposition. In the existing context the major questions are whether the pronounced objectives are realized and if not, what are the impediments. When this kind of argument is projected, one would be tempted to think that the grass roots institutions would also have the same characteristics as the government. They would not accommodate the people in the governing and development process. Here contextually one has to consider the validity of the proposition and analyse the dimensions, ramifications and implications of all those arguments.

Primarily one has to consider these propositions in the historical context. After independence it was thought that socio-economic reconstruction activities could be carried out only by people's organizations with the involvement of the people and that thereby development should be made participatory.[13] This approach could not gain momentum after some time. After independence we spelt out the ultimate values of democracy: securalism, social justice with rise in productivity, standard of living and socio-economic equalitarianism continuously. What was overlooked was people's participation in nursing the values and achieving the goals. Top down model and trickle down principle were adopted for development and distribution of the fruits of development. It does not mean that India did not have an approach for development of its own.

Gandhiji gave the first exposition of the participatory approach in governance for development when he stated that people are the roots, the state is the fruit; that the classes at the top which are crushing the masses at the bottom must get off their backs; that democracy cannot be worked by twenty men sitting at the top; and, that it has to be worked from below by the people of every village. In this proposition Nehru was in full agreement with Gandhiji and echoed the approach of Gandhiji. While speaking at the Community Projects Conference on 15th December, 1952 he stated, "I think that they will affect our thinking as we affect their thinking. Unless they feel that mental urge, that impact of the creative spirit within them to work". Steps were taken to realize the above propositions. In the First Five Year Plan itself it was unequivocally lamented "Democratic Planning will not succeed unless the sanction of an awakened public opinion operates powerfully and the force of public action in pursuit of constructive ends continuously grows." The ignorance and apathy of the masses have to be overcome. Their (people) own views about their needs and difficulties and the correct solutions must be elicited and given the fullest weight in making the plans in the execution of which they will be called upon to assist. Means have to be devised to bring the people into association both at the stage of formulation of the plans and in their implementation from stage to stage.[14] While seeing the activities of the grass roots organizations in the process of development one would find the slowdown of people's participation in the development activities. Emerging bureaucracy projected a proposition that fast development could be achieved by the development bureaucracy through the centralized planning of programmes and schemes for economic development and social justice; that people involved in activities were slow; and that at every step one has to rely on the people and their leaders; but that bureaucracy has no such barriers and they will act fast and carry out programmes and schemes quickly. Hence political leaders preferred bureaucracy to people to achieve development.[15] Slowly people have been relegated to the background. Steadily the departments and their wings have been expanded by which government assumed the role of a provider and people assumed the role of receivers. But now a situation has arisen where in government cannot discharge its duties and responsibilities without the active participation of the people.[16] Here, to overcome the problems of the bigness of government and non-participation of people in the development process, after a long period of twenty-six years, the concept of grass roots institutions comes in with legal sanctity.[17]

When grass roots institutions are constitutionalized for governance they assume the character of a government. This proposition states that institutions are created for governance at the local level, through the constitution, to achieve development and social justice and that thereby the expansion of the structure continues but decisions are taken at local level. All the formalities of the government have to be adopted. It is normal and natural that the moment the concept government is used it is presumed that it would provide services and facilities and people would receive such benefits. One can expect the same distance between the people and the institutions even in the new dispensation. The present Panchayat system struggles to attract the people towards grass roots governance. Fundamentalists of Panchayati Raj System hold the view that it is a government by itself which should be given powers, functions, functionaries and finance. Most of the State governments hold the view that Panchayats are only implementing agencies and so they are being treated as subordinate institutions which are under the control of the State government.[18] This notion has influenced the local body leaders to perceive that they are mere agents in the hands of the State government and Central government to carry out activities.[19]

This is not the case of India alone. This kind of notions and views are prevalent in many of the nations in the world. To overcome all those problems and obstacles, a new initiative has been taken throughout the world and more specifically in the third world countries which is popularly called "Decentralization of Powers".[20] This envisages the following key principles:

(a) Putting the last (people) first.

(b) Making the government facilitator rather than provider.

(c) Making programmes and schemes which are people's rather than government's.

(d) Not entertaining the concept of beneficiary but of a development participant.

(e) Emphasis has to be given to governance and not to government.

(f) Planning from below.

(g) Direct democracy substitutes representative democracy.

(h) Development localized.

(i) Looking at people as citizens and not as voters.

(j) People's control over government.

(k) Constitutionalization.

(l) Accommodation and Assimilation.

(m) Resources are under the control of the community.

(n) Communication approach.

(o) Conscious of self respect and self esteem.

(p) Enhancing human capability.

Incidentally, to operationalise the new principles, a framework of values was identified in the conference organized in Rio de Janeiro while setting Local Agenda.[21] Among the agreements signed Local Agenda is important and critical if mankind is to do something about the deteriorating environment which will inevitably mean a poorer quality of life in the future. To fulfil effectively the items of Local Agenda, more than one hundred action points have been identified. The identified action plans could be effectively carried out only through grass roots institutions.

On the other hand, this new dispensation has given power to the local communities to decide matters affecting their life and by which they become stakeholders and assert themselves as factors in the development process. Their self respect and self esteem are protected and their capacity is enhanced. They come out from the state of helplessness.

The above mentioned principles have been accommodated in the framework of action which was legally approved in many of the countries. In India in the name of "Power to the People" 73rd and 74th Amendments to the Constitution of India were introduced. Likewise, in the English Parliament, in the name of 'Best Value', an act of Parliament was enacted.[22] The purpose of these acts is more or less the same, namely making the local government more democratic, participatory, gender sensitive, biased towards environmental issues, accountable to the people and providing high quality services to the people to achieve economic development and social justice.

Against the background the position of grass roots organizations, agencies and institutions is to be decided. It is unequivocal that the grass roots institutions are constitutionalised as entities for governance. Hence, there is scope for keeping up the assumption that they are government in strict terms and they will have the character of government. Equally, there are reasons to believe that the grass roots institutions should be made people's institutions to make the people participate in the development process without obstacles as one finds in government. Hence logically it cannot be a government but an institution of the people with more of the characteristics of a community organization than those of a government. Legal sanctity is accorded only to ensure standing and continuity in its performance. It should have more informalities than formalities. It has its own in-built weakness as it brings about community control over the new institutions. Hence it has to be seen as an institution of governance which neither takes the characteristics of a government nor takes the characteristics of a traditional community organization.

Constitutionally created new institutions take position as facilitator to provide more functional opportunities to various grass roots agencies, organizations and institutions for working for economic development and social justice. By doing this people are involved in development activities through their respective functional organizations and they reduce the work load of the government organizations.

Issues Examined

The question as to what extent the framework so developed for development has been realised is the major question not only in India but in the whole world. Contextually the economy of the societies communities and countries has been globalized and it has far reaching implications in the social and political sphere of the society. In order to overcome the problems arising out of globalization and to achieve development, strong and vibrant grass roots institutions are imperative. Grass roots institutions are vibrant and dynamic only when they are participative and accommodative in character.[23]

Normally, institutions and organizations are participatory if they are evolved from the bottom and get a strong support base from the people as these organizations are having the character to reflect the aspirations of the people and to realise the objectives set for these organisations and institutions.[24] The evolved institutions are the creations of the people and not of any external agency. They are more informal and unofficial. They are more flexible in their objectives and operations. In these organizations stakeholders are decision makers and they respect each other through their mutual faith and trust. In these organizations participation begins at the bottom and every one in the organizations gets a chance to participate in the process of decision making wherein allocation of resources is being done.[25]

But the concept "Decentralization of Powers" has come to stay through a centralized process which is always perceived as an imposition of an organization and institution over the people. Most imposed institutions have certain key characteristics, namely:

they are funded by external agencies with a top-down rather than bottom-up approach for development; they believe in trickle down from the above; they are more formal and official; they are driven by the concepts and approaches borrowed from alien culture; and, they are elite oriented.

It is a paradox that to have participatory governance, a centralized drive has been resorted to. As a result the grass roots institutions have been organized but these institutions carry the characteristics of the government rather than informal community organizations. This kind of impositions normally do not attract the people.

It is also true that people in the society at the bottom have their own organizations and associations with a lot of flexibility and informality to cater to their needs and aspirations. The people centred and evolved organizations and the agencies created by the higher level government never integrate themselves in a system to deliver the needed goods to the community. Before the emergence of nation-state and introduction of big government approach, community organizations had their hold over the society. In the last fifty years governments have taken over the responsibilities of the communities totally and people have been made beneficiaries. As a result, even after the introduction of 73rd Amendment to the Constitution of India, people did not take interest in the institutions created by the government. People have seen the fate of many of the institutions and organizations created by the government.[26] Whenever governments were in need of organizations and institutions, they would be created with all fanfare and when they are not needed to the government, they would be relegated to the background. The best example of this is cooperative societies and organizations developed to carry out project works. Modern grass roots level organizations are the creations of the Central and the State governments to carry out certain programmes, duties and responsibilities.

Multiplicity of organizations at the grass roots are not new to the Indian context. Even in the ancient period we had several organizations and groups which specifically carried out certain duties and responsibilities.[27] As in the past even at present we have several organizations functioning simultaneously at the grass roots to carry out specific roles and responsibilities. But there is one difference between the organizations in the past and the present. Present day organizations are specialized, independent, sectoral and vertical in functioning. There is no proper organic linkage among the organizations, because all these associations and organizations have been created for certain projects with specific targets. The moment targets are completed the newly formulated associations and organizations sink into oblivion. But in the past there were different types of organizations which carried out specific responsibilities but they were organically interlinked with each other. Individuals associated with organizations considered themselves stakeholders and actively participated in the activities of the organizations. Those organizations were formed by the people based on their needs and they evolved those organizations from one stage to another stage by making modifications in the organizations relevant to the context. It is obvious that the organizations were in the hands of the people[28]. At present the majority of the organizations are created by the government and all those who participate in the process are onlookers of the events and they never integrate themselves with the organizations as they feel that these organizations are owned by the government.

Today we have self-help groups, cooperative societies, artisan guilds, traders associations, farmers associations, labourers associations, water users associations, temple management committee, Nayaya Panchayat and a number of other groups and organizations which are functioning in the villages. These associations and organizations have independent track for their functioning. They never involve themselves or integrate themselves in a system.[29] They prefer to be independent as they are totally attached to sectoral departments. As long as they function independently, one cannot expect the needed results from those organizations. For the past fifty-four years experience in administering development in the rural areas through the organizations created by the government has proved that they are capable of spending money and carrying out activities but they cannot solve the problems of the people. If these organizations and associations are properly integrated through an independent coordinating agency they would deliver the goods properly and effectively.[30] These associations and organizations are to be effectively and organically linked in a system. It is not so easy to establish linkage among the organizations for effective delivery of services. The very purpose of creating separate organizations for different functions is to have stakeholders in each and every organization. As long as stakeholders are made members, there will be always serious in their participation and hence participation will be effective. They will have self-esteem, self respect and increased capacity. The moment the organizations and institutions are people centered, the approach towards people by the organizations would be positive and participative in nature. Panchayati institution is a nodal institution to coordinate and integrate all the groups and organizations. Panchayat should facilitate these organizations for their effective functioning. Panchayat and its linkages with primary education, health organization, cooperatives, self help groups, labourers organizations, artisan guilds, youth clubs, water user associations could be made effective as they were in the ancient period. Government institutions should have the role of a facilitator and they have to tune their activities to the perspective of the people. People should be made stakeholders and not beneficiaries. They should be made development participants. People's activities are to be supported by the government. People should have power in appropriate fora to decide issues which are affecting their life. In the whole process one has to understand the role of supportive organizations at the higher level. Enabling atmosphere has to be created to scale up the participation. Constantly initiatives are to be taken to make the stakeholders participate in the dynamic process of development

Integrated Analysis

Generally, participation means different things to different individuals. There are different schools of thought on it.

Participation is a process by which people are involving themselves in deciding issues and matters affecting their life. But participation in decision making does not take place on its own. There are impediments, barriers and obstacles. Normally, increased participation would enable the individuals to rise and revolt against the existing order with an aim of establishing themselves as factors to reckon with. This would create conflict among the collectivities as to who would be the beneficiaries. It is proved throughout the world that the increased participation of the poor would be perceived as a threat to those who have traditionally been the dominant decision makers. But, at the same time, there are proofs that organizations, groups and communities which have got enlightened leaders will have new management model by accommodating all social groups as stakeholders in the community activities and thereby a strong social capital is formed. It is also obvious from the experience that, to facilitate participation, institutions involved in the process should have adequate capacity to concientise the people on the issues of development and to overcome the conflict among groups and collectivities.

There are certain factors which are prerequisite for participation. Primarily to bring about a participatory culture among the people, it is imperative that people receive recognition. The existing attitude and belief of the government bureaucracy and the representatives of the people towards people have to be changed. To initiate the whole process of transformation the leaders of the grass roots organizations and institutions should have will, commitment and maturity. Primarily, the leaders could concientise the people on their self and their conditions in terms of their living standard. By doing concientisation work, the leaders have to create a support structure by building up an alliance among organizations and institutions which are working for emanicipation.

In the rural areas in India there had been a number of groups and organizations performing certain earmarked duties and responsibilities. But, while expanding the government, slowly people's organizations were relegated to the background. Now the funding agencies like World Bank, UNDP and other organizations, realizing the potential and implications of social capital, advocate the importance of people's participation in the development activities to achieve the target very effectively. When this proposal is accepted and implemented, people are made assertive. After the introduction of 73rd Amendment to the Constitution of India, space for participation has been created. One Constitutional entity, the Gram Sabha, provides enormous scope for all the people to take part in the deliberations and they have got the power to decide on matters pertinent to their life. Depending on the understanding and perception of the leaders about the importance and implications of the Gram Sabha, it is being operationalised. It is an instrument to achieve social justice and to deliver quality service to the people. People can be mobilized for development task by the Gram Sabha. Hence, all activities of the department of government pertinent to rural development have to be sensitised about the Gram Sabha. A variety of organizations and associations are formed in the rural areas to design and carry out schemes and programmes for development. At present these organizations are not organically linked with organizations and institutions which have been functioning for decades together. The Panchayat has no linkage with traditional organizations and associations formed to carry out projects. To get the real benefits from all the institutions, they are to be integrated informally and organically through the Gram Sabha. They are to be integrated and linked with each other informally because formal integration would create more problems for their independent functioning. Informality would bring more stakeholders into this process. Hence they are to be synergised to get the maximum benefits from these organizations. The space created by the government in withdrawing its activities from various domains has to be filled up by the civil society organizations. Hence the organizations and associations of people have to be linked functionally.

Conclusion

It is unequivocal that there are a variety of organizations, associations and institutions functioning at the grass roots to carry out certain roles and responsibilities. These associations, organisations and institutions are formed by the people themselves, and government departments. All these organizations and associations are independent of each other and there is no linkage among themselves. At individual organizational level they are participative. But the level of participation in the process of activities is not so high. Moreover participation has been viewed in a limited sense. People are made to participate because the funding agencies stipulate so. Traditional organisations have fully involved all the stakeholders in the development process. The 73rd Amendment to the Constitution of India provides ample scope for bringing all those organizations and associations under one umbrella. Panchayats can act as nodal centres to integrate all these associations and organizations. To perform these tasks grass root institutions require capacitated leaders. This kind of initiatives would make all the stakeholders participate in the functioning of the respective organizations and associations and in common fora also. Participation here serves as a means to achieve development. In the process people are empowered and their self respect and self esteem would be protected, passing through conflict to achieve social justice. To achieve this, the Panchayat has to be viewed liberally in terms of synergizing the organizations and associations.

NOTES

1. Hari Mohan Mathur and Palla Helmut (eds.) (1983), *Local Administration and Regional Government*, Berlin: German Foundation for International Development, pp. 197-205.

2. One can get more details about this approach from Chambers Robert, *Rural Development: Putting the Last First,* (1983) Essex: Longman Scientific & Technical.

3. Former Chief Minister J. Jeyalalitha made a statement in the press that Government spends 94 per cent of the revenue of the State in salaries and pension benefits to government employees, *The Hindu*, 25.07.2001.

4. Bhabani Sen Gupta (1996), *India: Problems of Governance,* New Delhi: Konar Publishers Pvt. Ltd.

5. G Palanithurai, (2001), *New Panchayati Raj System (Tamil),* Chennai: South Vision.

6. G Palanithurai, and V. Ragupathy, (2000), *Functional Efficiency of Gram Sabha in Tamil Nadu,* Gandhigram: Rajiv Gandhi Chair for Panchayati Raj Studies, pp. 6-10.

7. Sofi Ali and Anita Rao, (2000), "Reinventing Public Administration for 21st Century," *The Indian Journal of Public Administration,* Vol XLVL: No.2 (April - June), pp. 169-188.

8. In the year 1991 Government of India made it clear through the Budget that the concept of government has to be redefined.

9. UNDP, (2000), *Decentralisation in India: Challenges and Opportunities,* New Delhi: Human Development Resource Centre.

10. Prabhat Datt and Panchali Sen Bhattacharya, "Participatory Rural Governance in India (2000)," *The Indian Journal of Public Administration,* Vol XLVL: (January - March), pp. 38-49.

11. It is a school of thought in India and those who subscribe to this school strongly feel that it is a government by itself. It has its own domains of governance as Central government and State governments. It should have autonomy to decide matters and issues which are earmarked to Local Bodies.

12. There is another school contradictory to the earlier school that in the context of changing role government, the third tier is not a government but institutions to perform certain functions with utmost flexibility. These institutions could enjoy autonomy but they are not government in strict terms of the concept.

13. V.A. Vasudeva Raju (1965), *Indian Community Development Movement,* (Tamil) Pollachi: Valli Publications.

14. *Participation and Governance,* (1998), Vol. 5: No.11 (November).

15. It is major argument whether participation is a means or an end by itself. Initially it was considered as a means, Upendranadh, C. (1997), In Search of Roots Learnings from "Re Visiting Participation," *Participation and Governance,* Vol. 4 : No. 11 (November), p. 19.

16. Appelby Paul, *Report to the Government of India on Administrative Reform,* (1964), New Delhi: Government of India.

17. Both Balwant Rai Mehta Committee and Ashok Mehta Committee Reports emphasized that the participation of people is essential for development of the community and it can be ensured only when they are legalized in the system of Governance. For more details see:Ashok Mehta, (1978), *A Report of the Committee: Panchayati Raj Institutions*, New Delhi: Ministry of Agriculture and Irrigation.
18. For more details see Mathew George, (2000), *Status of Panchayati Raj in the State and Union Territories of India,* New Delhi: Concept Publishing Company.
19. G. Palanithurai, (1999), *New Panchayati Raj System at work: An Evaluation,* New Delhi: Concept Publishing Company.
20. James Manor (1999), *The Political Economy of Democratic Decentralisation,* Washington D.C: The World Bank.
21. Oz Osborne (2000), *Rural Communities and Decision Making: Local Politics in the Twenty First Century,* Tavistock: West Devon Environmental Network.
22. *Ibid.*, pp. 256-257.
23. UNDP, *op.cit.*
24. G Cheema Shaffir and Rondinelli Dennis, A. (eds.) (1983), *Decentralization and Development,* Beverly Hills, Saze, p. 210.
25. Robert Wade (1987), *Village Republics,* Cambridge: Cambridge University Press.
26. R.C. Choudhary and S.P. Jain, (eds.) (1999), *Strengthening Village Democracy*, Hyderabad: National Institute for Rural Development.
27. G Palanithurai, and V. Ragupathy, (2000) *op. cit.*
28. V. Raghupathy, (1999), "Participation in the Management of Natural Resources with special reference to Irrigation Tanks in Panchayats," Ph. D. Unpublished thesis, Gandhigram Rural Institute.
29. G Palanithurai, (2001) "Synergization of Institutional arrangements for Development and Social Justice at the Grass Roots: A Case Analysis," Paper presented in the Foundation Day Seminar of National Institute of Rural Development, Hyderabad from 7th to 8th January.
30. Garry Jacob, N. Asokan, N. Krishna Moorthy, (1989) *Kamadhenu: Prosperity Movement*, Chennai: Radiant Publications.

9

PANCHAYATI RAJ IN PONDICHERRY
A Non-Starter

V.A. Vasudevaraju

The small territory of Pondicherry has gained international reputation in recent history. The French did not capture it either by military force or by other destructive forms of violence. They acquired it as gracious gifts and voluntary donations from the princes to whom it belonged. Thus in Pondicherry no conquerors of conquered were found when it became a French enclave. The French Colony rule was, by and large, generous in the administration and they respected the manners and civilization of the local people.

Gandhiji visited Pondicherry in 1934 followed by Jawaharlal Nehru in 1939. The visits of these architects of Indian Freedom Movement inspired the citizens of Pondicherry and the All French Indian Congress was organized in 1946. When India became independent in 1947 the Indian National Flag was hoisted in all the villages and towns of Pondicherry.

The French enclave of Chandranagore merged with Indian Union by a referendum in 1949 but the same procedure could not be followed in respect of the other four enclaves Pondicherry, Karaikal, Mahe and Yanam. On 13th October 1954 a joint declaration was made by the governments of France and India that the merger of Pondicherry with Indian Union will be left to the elected representatives of Assembly by secret vote held on

18th October 1954 at the border village Kizhur by a majority of 170 out of 178 decided for merger. Thus the *de facto* transfer of power took place on November 1, 1954 followed by *de jure* transfer on August 16, 1962 leading to the celebration of Independence Day both on 15th and 16th August every year.

The elected representatives of local bodies of the territory played a significant role in deciding the Independence of Pondicherry. This kind of role does not appear to have been played by elected representatives of the local bodies in other parts of India in making the final decision on independence.

The local administration set-up in Pondicherry territory differed from what was found in British India. There were no Village Panchayats in Pondicherry. A cluster of 20 to 50 villages including the town areas was organised as a 'commune' patterned after the French system of local administration. Pondicherry region was divided into eight communes. Karaikal region consisted of six communes, Mahe and Yanam regions were each formed as separate communes. Each commune was governed by a separate Municipal Council which were established under the French Decree of 1880.

There were 12 councillors elected by the people directly in each Municipal Council of the communes with the exception of Pondicherry Commune having 15 councillors. The councillors elected one Mayor and two Deputy Mayors for each council with the exception of Pondicherry commune having three Deputy Mayors. Their term of office was for six years. The Mayor of the commune was a powerful executive. Once elected he cannot be removed by no-confidence motion. Hence free from the fear of removal from office he was able to devote his attention to public welfare without fear or favour. The Municipal councils had four sessions in a year and there were extraordinary sessions also. The commune Municipal councils were responsible for providing all basic facilities such as drinking water, roads etc.

To carry out their functions efficiently adequate financial resources were made available to the commune Municipal councils. Own Resources by levying House Tax etc, Assigned Revenue and Statutory Grants, Non-Statutory Grants and other Miscellaneous resources formed part of their income.

Under the French Commune System of Local administration in Pondicherry territory births, deaths and marriages should be registered in the municipal offices within prescribed time limit and no cremation or inhumation can be made without approval of the municipality.

The French system of Commune Municipal Councils continued till 1973 and the last elections to these local bodies were held in 1968. When the rest of India adopted the Three-tier system of Panchayati Raj consisting of Village Panchayat, Block Panchayat Samithi and Zilla Parishad from 1959 onwards Pondicherry did not join the national mainstream till 1973.

The Pondicherry Village and Commune Panchayats Act of 1973 and the Pondicherry Municipalities Act of 1973 were enacted to organise the Local Government set-up on the lines of the Indian system of local administration that emerged after Independence. But it provided for two-tier Panchayati Raj set-up consisting of Village Panchayats and Commune Panchayats. There was no scope for Zilla Parishad as the whole Union territory of Pondicherry consists of only one revenue district. In 1973 Pondicherry and Mudaliarpet municipal councils were merged to form the Pondicherrry. Municipality and in 1994 the Ozhukarai Commune Panchayat was upgraded as a Municipality by a separate act.

The Panchayats and Municipalities Acts of 1973 remained on paper only as no elections were held under these acts for Panchayats and Municipalities so far. After 1973, there were no elected local bodies. The local bodies are under the control of the bureaucrats.

To adhere to the 73rd and 74th amendments of the Constitution of India the Pondicherry Village and Commune Panchayats Act and the Pondicherry Municipalities Act of 1994 were passed and they came into force immediately. These amendments were passed without adequate public debate at the last minute before the deadline of one year prescribed in the constitutional amendment was over. Just a month back the government announced the dates for elections to the Panchayat Raj institutions. But the public doubt if the elections will take place in the present political climate.

The absence of the elected local bodies and the control of the same by bureaucrats have not made things to improve in regard to the basic facilities required by the people both in the urban and rural areas. During the Seventies the administration used to boast that all villages in Pondicherry Territory are provided with good approach roads, potable water and electricity and the visiting dignitaries used to appreciate these achievements. At that time the outlay for the Fourth Plan 1969-74 was only Rs.14.54 crores for the five-year period. Now the Annual Plan outlay for 1955-56 is Rs.175.25 crores. In spite of the phenominal increase in plan outlays and expenditure satisfactory levels in fulfilling the needs of the people of the territory in regard to their basic needs could not be achieved. This is largely due to the absence of elected local bodies in Pondicherry territory during the past twenty-two years.

Increase in Plan allocation and increase in the manpower of the bureaucracy cannot deliver the goods unless there is public participation in identifying the civic needs and development needs of the people, in formulating the plans and in implementing them. To facilitate public participation in the formulation and implementation of plans the Panchayati Raj institutions at the village and Commune levels have to be set up as elected bodies in Pondicherry territory immediately.

In the absence of the elected Panchayati Raj institutions, the MLAs themselves are found to be frustrated since they are not able to satisfy the needs of their constituency. Recently some MLAs have resorted to the novel agitation of 'planting saplings' on rural roads to draw public attention to the pathetic condition of rural roads. The cadres of the CPI and the CPI MLA have started a new style of agitation to highlight the indifference of the officialdom in regard to solving the civic problems faced by the people at Villianur. Since the Villianur Commune Panchayat under the officers did not take any action over a long period inspite of repeated representations, on December 1, 1995 they gathered in front of the Commune Panchayat office and presented petition listing the problems faced by the people to an ass which was specially brought to that place by them. These peculiar styles of agitation show the extent of frustration of the public and they confirm that only elected Panchayat Raj institutions can satisfy public needs immediately.

Pondicherry Administration has to go a long way in setting up and fostering the development of Panchayati Raj institutions. Adequate care should be taken in setting up the village Panchayats in Pondicherry as it would be the first exposure of the people to such an institution. Immediate elections are necessary. Officials and the elected representatives have to be imparted good training in the administrative and planning aspects of Panchayati Raj. The plan schemes have to be classified as village level, and commune level schemes and the staff as well as the outlays for the same have to be transferred to the village and commune Panchayats. Delegation of financial powers and other financial rules need immediate revision, to be in conformity with the decentralization of powers to the Panchayats. Senior officers in the government including the IAS and PCS as well as the Heads of Departments have to be sent on study tour to West Bengal, Karnataka, Gujarat and Maharashtra which are found to be progressive in regard to transferring the funds, powers and staff to the Panchayats during the past two decades and more. Above all political leaders and bureaucrats have to display 'attitudinal changes' that the emergence of strong Panchayats in the villages and communes would be in public interest and the elected local bodies would contribute to more realistic formulation of development programmes and more efficient implementation of the same.

Academic institutions also have an important role to play in the development of Panchayats by undertaking research studies in regard to the administration, management and financial needs of Panchayats.

BIBLIOGRAPHY

Ali, Sofi and Rao, Anita, "Reinventing Public Administration for 21st Century", *The Indian Journal of Public Administration*, Vol. XLVL: No. 2 (April-June, 2000).

Appleby, Paul, *Report to the Government of India on Administrative Reform*, New Delhi: Government of India, 1964.

Bhargava, B.S., and Venkatakrishnan, V., "The Process of Democratic need Drilling in Lakshadweep: The Case of Panchayats", *Madhya Pradesh Journal of Social Sciences*, Vol.1, No. 2, (July-December), 1996.

Bhargava, B.S., and Venkatakrishnan V., "Constitution of Panchayati Raj" in G. Palanithurai (ed), *New Panchayat Raj System: Status and Prospects*, New Delhi: Kanishka, 1996.

Bose, N.K., *Studies in Gandhism*, Ahmedabad: Navjeevan, 1962.

Chambers, Robert, *Rural Development: Putting the Last First*, Essex: Longman Scientific and Technical, 1983.

Choudhary, R.C., and Jain, S.P. (eds), *Strengthening Village Democracy*, Hyderabad: National Institute of Rural Development, 1999.

Choudhary, S.R., "Logging on in Belandur", *Frontline*, 19(11), (May 25 - June 07, 2002).

Common Wealth Centre for Electronic Governance, '*E-Government 2002: A Comparative Analysis of Progress in Five Countries*', London: Common Wealth Centre for Electronic Governance, 2002.

Cook Meghan, E *(et al.)*, "*Making a Case for Local E-government*", Albany: University of Albany, 2002.

Datt, Prabhat and Sen Panchali Bhattacharya, "Participatory Rural Governance in India", *The Indian Journal of Public Administration*, Vol. XLVL, (January-March 2000).

Dr. Mahipal, "Effectiveness of Gram Sabha", *National Herald*, (6th April 2000).

Government of Maharashtra, *The Bombay Village Panchayats Act*, 1958, Mumbai: Government of Maharashtra, 1961.

Government of Maharashtra, *The Maharashtra Zilla Parishads and Panchayat Samitis Act, 1961* Bombay: Government of Maharashtra, 1961.

Gupta, Bhabani Sen, *India: Problems of Governance*, New Delhi: Konar Publishers Pvt. Ltd., 1996.

Haque, M. Shamuel, 'E-Governance in India: Its impacts on relations among citizens, politicians and public servants', *International Review of Administrative Sciences*, 68(2), (June 2002).

Jacobs Garry, Asokan, Krishna Moorthy, N., *Kamadhenu: Prosperity Movement*, Chennai: Radiant Publications, 1989.

Kothari, Rajini, *State Against Democracy: In Search of Human Governance*, Delhi: Ajanta Publications, 1998.

Kvaemen Kenneth, L. and John Leslie King, "The Role of Information Technology in Managing Cities", *Local Government Studies*, 14(3), (March - April 1998).

Mander, Harsh, "Towards Democracy: The Legal Empowerment of Gram Sabha", *Kurukshetra*, Vol. 48, No. 1, October 1999.

Mannadiyar, N.S. (ed), "Administration of Lakshadweep" in the *Gazetteer of India*, Kavarathi, Union Territory of Lakshadweep, 1977.

Manor, James, *The Political Economy of Democratic Decentralization*, Washington DC: The World Bank, 1999.

Mathew, George, *Status of Panchayati Raj in the State and Union Territories of India*, New Delhi: Concept Publishing Company, 2000.

Mathur, Hari Mohan and Palla Helmut (eds), *Local Administration and Regional Government*, Berlin: German Foundation for International Development, 1983.

Meenakshi, Sundaram S.S., *Decentralization in Developing Countries*, New Delhi: Concept Publishing Company, 1994.

Moon Jae, M., "The Evolution of E-Government among Municipalities: Rhetoric or Reality", *Public Administration Review*, 62(4) (July-August, 2002).

Moon, Sing-Young, "The Utilization of the Internet Technology in the Public Services of Korea", *Asian Review of Public Administration*, 13(1) (January - June, 2001).

Osborne, O.Z., *Rural Communities and Decision Making: Local Politics in the Twenty First Century*, Tavistock: West Devon Environmental Network, 2000.

Palanithurai, G. and Ragupathy, V., *Functional Efficiency of Gram Sabha in Tamil Nadu*, Gandhigram: Rajiv Gandhi Chair for Panchayati Raj Studies, 2000.

Palanithurai, G., *New Panchayat Raj System at Work: An Evaluation, New Delhi*: Concept Publishing Company, 1999.

Palanithurai, G., *New Panchayati Raj System (Tamil)*, Chennai: South Vision, 2001.

Patil, P.B., *Report of the Committee on Panchayat Raj Evaluation*, Mumbai: Government of Maharashtra, 1996.

Purohit, B.R., "Panchayat Raj System in Scheduled Areas of Madhya Pradesh" in G. Palanithurai (ed), *Dynamics of New Panchayat Raj System in India, Vol.1*, New Delhi: Concept Publishing Company, 2002.

Rajiv Gandhi Foundation, *Panchayati Raj in India–Status Report*, New Delhi: Rajiv Gandhi Foundation, 1999.

Raju, V.A., Vasudeva, *Indian Community Development Movement* (Tamil) Pollachi: Valli Publications, 1965.

Ramunny, M., *Laccadive, Minicoy and Admindivi Islands*, New Delhi: Ministry of Information and Broadcasting, 1972.

Rao, G.V.K., *Report of the Committee on Administrative Organizations for Rural Development*, New Delhi: Government of India, 1985.

Ronaghan, Stephan, A., *Benchmarking E-Government: A Global Perspective*, New York: United Nations Division for Public Economic and Public Administration and American Society for Public Administration, 2002.

Singh, S.S, Mishra, Suresh and Pratap Sanjay, *Legislative Status of Panchayati Raj in India*, New Delhi: IIPA, 1997.

Sisodia, Yatindra Singh, "Panchayat Raj System in Madhya Pradesh: An Appraisal" in G. Palanithurai (ed), *Dynamics of New Panchayat Raj System in India, Vol.II*, New Delhi: Concept Publishing Company, 2002.

Tat-Kei Ho Alfred, "Reinventing Local Government, and the E-government Initiatives", *Public Administration Review*, 62 (4), (July-August, 2002).

UNDP, *Decentralization in India: Challenges and Opportunities*, New Delhi: Human Development Resource Centre, 2000.

Venkatakrishnan, V., "Digital governance at local level in India: Need for an integrated approach", in Ratha, S.N.(ed), *Panchayati Raj and Rural Development*, New Delhi: Concept Publications (forthcoming).

Venkatakrishnan, V., "Local E-Government in India: Review of a Few Attempts", *Network*, 8(3) (July-September, 2002).

Voluntary Action Network India, *State Panchayati Raj Act—A Critical Review*, New Delhi: Voluntary Action Network India, 1995.

Wade, Robert, *Village Republics*, Cambridge: Cambridge University Press, 1987.

INDEX